Human and Animal Minds

Peter Carruthers is a Distinguished University Professor and Professor of Philosophy at the University of Maryland. He is the author of numerous articles and books in philosophy of mind and cognitive science, and has co-edited seven volumes of interdisciplinary essays in cognitive science. His recent publications include *The Opacity of Mind* (OUP, 2011) and *The Centered Mind* (OUP, 2015). In 2018, he won the annual Romanell Prize awarded by the American Philosophical Association.

Praise for *Human and Animal Minds*

'In this well-argued and engaging book, Peter Carruthers makes a comprehensive case for a first-order global workspace theory of phenomenal consciousness, and then considers the upshot for animals: are they phenomenally conscious, and does it matter morally? Answer: there is no fact of the matter about whether animals are phenomenally conscious, but this doesn't change anything morally, because consciousness is not what matters morally... Conclusion: this is a great book, written with Carruthers' characteristic insight, lucidity, and open-mindedness. Everyone should read it.'

Jonathan Simon, *Notre Dame Philosophical Reviews*

Human and Animal Minds

*The Consciousness Questions
Laid to Rest*

PETER CARRUTHERS

OXFORD
UNIVERSITY PRESS

OXFORD
UNIVERSITY PRESS

Great Clarendon Street, Oxford, OX2 6DP,
United Kingdom

Oxford University Press is a department of the University of Oxford.
It furthers the University's objective of excellence in research, scholarship,
and education by publishing worldwide. Oxford is a registered trade mark of
Oxford University Press in the UK and in certain other countries

First published 2019
First published in paperback 2021

Published in the United States of America by Oxford University Press
198 Madison Avenue, New York, NY 10016, United States of America

British Library Cataloguing in Publication Data
Data available

Library of Congress Cataloging in Publication Data
Data available

ISBN 978–0–19–884370–2 (Hbk.)
ISBN 978–0–19–285932–7 (Pbk.)

for Tony and Liz

—I love you both—

Contents

Preface

There has been a flurry of interest in consciousness in animals lately, including books by Peter Godfrey-Smith (2016) and Michael Tye (2017), as well as the inauguration in 2016 of a new scientific journal, *Animal Sentience*, devoted to the study of the topic.[1] In part this may result from increasing recognition of the strong continuities that exist between human and animal minds. But it is also because many of those who are interested in the morality of our treatment of animals think that the question of consciousness is fundamental. Indeed, there is a long tradition among utilitarians, at any rate (stretching back to Jeremy Bentham, 1789), of treating consciousness as the "magic bullet" that will determine the moral standing of the creatures in question. This is certainly true of Peter Singer (1981, 1993), for example. And even those of a more Kantian persuasion might think that consciousness is critical for the question whether certain treatments of animals are *cruel*, and hence inconsistent with duties of beneficence. As people have become increasingly convinced that animals are capable of genuine mentality, then, it has seemed more and more urgent to address the question of the distribution of consciousness across the animal kingdom—as witnessed by *The Cambridge Declaration on Consciousness* (Low et al. 2012), signed by Stephen Hawking and numerous other leading scientists at the Francis Crick Memorial Conference on July 7, 2012.

I will not be challenging the continuities between human and animal minds in this book. On the contrary, I will be emphasizing them here, as I have done previously (Carruthers 2004a, 2006, 2009a, 2013a, 2013b, 2015a). But the resulting focus on animal consciousness is a mistake. This is not because animals *aren't* conscious, but because there is no fact of the matter. Given our best theory of human consciousness—which is a

[1] I shall refer to nonhuman animals as "animals" throughout—although humans, too, are animals, of course. This is for simplicity only. It is certainly not intended as a commitment to any sort of Cartesian human exceptionalism.

fully reductive form of global-workspace theory, I shall argue—any answer to the question of animal consciousness will involve an important element of stipulation. Even supposing we had full knowledge of the mental states and cognitive organization of an animal, still the further question whether any of those states are conscious ones wouldn't admit of a factual answer, I will suggest. As a result, the question is of no scientific significance. Nor does the issue have the sort of moral importance that many people assume. Sympathy for an animal can be grounded in knowledge of its desires and other mental states, independently of the question of consciousness.

How I propose to get us to that point won't be reviewed here. (Readers interested in looking ahead should note that each chapter begins with a brief abstract and finishes with a concluding summary.) All I will say at this point is that the question of consciousness in animals has been overblown because the so-called "hard problem" of consciousness *in humans* has been overblown. Consciousness in humans only matters because some people have found it deeply puzzling—led especially by philosophers with their thought experiments, of course. Once those puzzles are removed, we can move on to more important matters.

Perhaps I *should* say something here, though, about how I myself arrived at this point, since I have published views on these topics that differ markedly from those defended here. As some readers may know, I previously defended a particular form of higher-order-thought theory of consciousness, known as "dual-content theory" (Carruthers 2000, 2005a). I also argued in those books that it is an implication of higher-order theories generally that most species of animal are *not* phenomenally conscious. At the same time, I argued that we should take the mental states of animals quite seriously, accepting that they have belief-like states, desire-like states, and perceptual states of various sorts (Carruthers 2004a, 2006), while also arguing that the absence of phenomenal consciousness from animals doesn't really matter much (Carruthers 1999, 2004b, 2005b).

Over the decade and more that followed I hardly thought about the consciousness issue at all, and published barely anything on the topic. But at the back of my mind I was becoming increasingly uneasy about the theory I had defended. First, it lacks any form of empirical support that isn't also possessed by first-order global-workspace theories.[2] Second, it requires one to be committed to a particular type of account of the determinants of intentional content (namely, a specific version of the view that the content of a state depends, in part, on what consumer systems for that state are apt to do with it or infer from it). And third, I was gradually coming to feel that the arguments I had used to motivate dual-content theory over first-order theories of a global-workspace sort weren't very powerful. Finally, I took the plunge (Carruthers 2017b), recanted the view, and committed to global-workspace theory instead.

I had always assumed that first-order theories of the sort defended by Bernard Baars (1988), Michael Tye (1995), and others would imply that phenomenal consciousness is *very* widespread in the animal kingdom, being possessed even by invertebrates like ants and bees (Carruthers 2007). But having come to accept a first-order theory for myself, and beginning to think more deeply about its implications, I was not so sure. So I arranged to teach a graduate seminar in Fall 2017 to address the topic. Over the course of that seminar I came to think that global-workspace theorists of the sort that I had become should say, not that most other animals *are* phenomenally conscious (nor that they *aren't*), but that there is no fact of the matter. And that is the view I am defending in this book. One carry-over from my previous views, however, is that the issue doesn't matter much. (Another is the fundamental role played by phenomenal concepts in resolving the puzzles surrounding phenomenal consciousness.) Somewhat ironically, my ultimate goal in the present book is to persuade people that they can—and should—stop thinking about the consciousness question altogether.

I am grateful to a number of people for their help, advice, and criticism. I am especially grateful to the graduate students who suffered through my first attempts to rethink the topic, and who helped me clarify my ideas. They are: Casey Enos, Chris Masciari, Shen Pan, Aida Roige, Julius Schönherr, Moonyoung Song, and Raven Zhang. Moreover, Heather Adair, Chris Masciari, Shen Pan, Aida Roige, Julius Schönherr, and Samuel Warren volunteered to read much of an early draft of the book, providing valuable feedback. In addition, I am grateful to Keith Frankish,

---

[2] Indeed, the chapter newly written for my 2005a (chapter 6) noted that the space between global-workspace-type theories and my own dual-content theory might be quite small.

Luke McGowan, Liz Schechter, and Bénédicte Veillet for comments on earlier versions of some or all of this material, and to the anonymous referees who critiqued it.

Some portions of this book are drawn from a pair of recent papers of mine, and I am grateful to the editors and publishers in question for permission to make use of it. The two papers are:

"Comparative psychology without consciousness," reprinted from *Consciousness and Cognition*, volume 63, Peter Carruthers, "Comparative psychology without consciousness," pp. 47–60, Copyright © 2018, with permission from Elsevier, doi: 10.1016/j.concog.2018.06.012.

"The problem of animal consciousness," Romanell lecture delivered at the 92nd Pacific Division meeting of the American Philosophical Association in San Diego, CA, on March 29, 2018. Reproduced from *Proceedings and Addresses of the American Philosophical Association*, volume 92, Peter Carruthers, "The problem of animal consciousness" (2018 Pacific Division), pp. 179–205, Copyright © 2018.

1

Important preliminaries

This chapter engages in some initial—but important—ground-clearing and foundation-building. It starts by drawing a number of distinctions, more precisely delineating our target, and setting the terms for the debates that follow. It explains some of the different things that people mean by "consciousness," in particular, as well as some of the claims that have been made about the nature of first-personal—or "phenomenal"— consciousness. The chapter also argues in support of a pair of substantive theses on the topic that will be relied upon later. Specifically, it argues that phenomenal consciousness is exclusively nonconceptual in nature, and that it doesn't admit of degrees: it is either categorically present or categorically absent. Finally, the chapter situates the topic of animal consciousness in relation to the traditional problem of other minds.

1.1 Kinds of consciousness

Consciousness research is bedeviled by terminological confusion. In fact, there are a number of different things that people mean by the word "conscious." Failure to distinguish them can lead to important errors, as well as to failure to see what are genuine possibilities.

The kind of consciousness that forms our topic is so-called *phenomenal* consciousness. This is the sort of consciousness that is said to be *like something* to undergo, or that has a distinctive subjective *feel*. Phenomenal consciousness is a species of mental-state consciousness. It is mental states (seeing a sunset, hearing a dog bark, smelling cinnamon) that can be phenomenally conscious. *People* are phenomenally conscious derivatively, by virtue of undergoing phenomenally conscious states. In asking whether animals, too, have phenomenally conscious mental states we are asking whether their experiences are *like something* also.

Human and Animal Minds: The Consciousness Questions Laid to Rest. Peter Carruthers, Oxford University Press (2019). © Peter Carruthers.
DOI: 10.1093/oso/9780198843702.001.0001

It is phenomenal consciousness that is thought to give rise to the "hard problem" of consciousness (Chalmers 1996). For it seems one can conceive of a zombie—a creature that is like oneself in all physical, functional, and representational respects except that it lacks *this* feeling (the distinctive feeling of the smell of cinnamon). Likewise, there seems to be an unbridgeable explanatory gap between all physical, functional, and representational facts and one's current conscious experience. No matter how much one knows about the former, it seems one can always think, "But why should all *that* feel like *this*?" Hence many have been tempted to conclude that phenomenal consciousness involves properties (often called "qualia") that cannot be reduced to any combination of physical, functional, or representational ones. This is qualia realism, to discussion of which we return in Section 1.2.

It should be emphasized that the concept of phenomenal consciousness is a first-person one. The various locutions employed ("like something to undergo," "subjective feel," "qualitative character," and so on) are all intended just to draw one's attention to one's own conscious experiences. Acquaintance with the latter (in some or other sense of that philosophically loaded term) is a necessary condition for grasping the concept, and no definition or third-person explanation could confer understanding of the concept. Indeed, as Block (1995) remarks, adapting a comment about jazz often attributed to Louis Armstrong, "If you gotta ask what it is, you ain't never gonna know." Hence philosophical zombies don't just lack phenomenal consciousness itself; they must also lack the first-person *concept* of phenomenal consciousness (Chalmers 2006). For by hypothesis, there is nothing for them to be first-person acquainted *with*.

I should also emphasize here that although I am, of course, forced to write about phenomenal consciousness and phenomenally conscious properties from an external (third-person and public) perspective, it is really the first-person concept and first-person ways of thinking about one's own experience that are primary. Hence there need be no commitment, in the third-person locutions that I employ, to the real existence of any distinctive set of properties that get picked out when we introspect our own experiences and think things like, "How could any brain state give rise to *this*?" Indeed, what such first-person thoughts really succeed in picking out is a major component of our present inquiry. I will argue in the end that what gets referred to in such thoughts are just the same perceptual contents that can be adequately described and attributed in the third person also. But that is something that needs to be argued for, not assumed.

Phenomenal consciousness is at least conceptually distinct from *access* consciousness (Block 1995, 2007). Both are forms of mental-state consciousness: it is mental states that are thought to have phenomenal properties, and that can be accessible to enter into decision-making, reasoning, and verbal report. As has been stressed, however, *phenomenal* consciousness is a first-person notion. One can only understand what that concept is intended to pick out by directing one's attention to some of one's own phenomenally conscious states. *Access* consciousness, in contrast, is functionally defined, and the concept could be fully understood by a zombie. A mental state is said to be access conscious if it is accessible to a wide range of other systems for further processing, specifically those involved in decision-making, in reasoning, in issuing verbal reports, and in the formation of long-term memories.

It is controversial whether or not there is any real distinction between access consciousness and phenomenal consciousness. Put differently: although the *concepts* are certainly distinct, it is disputed whether the two concepts pick out distinct properties or converge on the same property. There are three separable strands in this debate.

The first is about so-called "cognitive phenomenology" (Bayne & Montague 2011). On the assumption that thoughts and concepts, as well as nonconceptual perceptual contents, can be access conscious, it is debated whether they make irreducible (as opposed to merely causal) contributions to people's phenomenally conscious experiences. Some have argued that they do (Strawson 1994, 2011; Siewert 1998, 2011; Pitt 2004), pointing out, for example, that there seems to be a phenomenal difference between hearing one-and-the-same sentence with and without understanding. Others have argued that concepts make a merely *causal* (rather than a constitutive) difference to the phenomenal properties of the access-conscious states in which they occur—for instance, by directing attention, or by chunking together components of the sound stream (Jackendoff 1987, 2012; Tye 2000; Tye & Wright 2011; Carruthers & Veillet 2011, 2017). Although it is somewhat peripheral to our main topic, I will return to this issue in Section 1.5.

A second strand in debates about the reality of the access/phenomenal distinction is *directly* relevant to our topic. This concerns the alleged richness of phenomenally conscious experience, as opposed to the relative paucity of content that can be made accessible at any one time for reasoning and reporting. Block (1995, 2007, 2011a), in particular, argues that the contents of phenomenal consciousness are richer than the contents of access consciousness. The main evidence provided, is that people claim to see more details in a briefly presented stimulus than they can thereafter report; however, they *can* report any given subset of those details when cued to do so after stimulus offset (Sperling 1960; Landman et al. 2003; Sligte et al. 2008). This suggests that a representation of the full stimulus is present in consciousness while only being available for reporting piecemeal when targeted by attention. As a result, Block thinks that phenomenal consciousness should be identified with the contents of a form of fragile short-term memory that is distinct from both stimulus-bound iconic memory, on the one hand, and working memory, on the other. Access consciousness, in contrast, comprises the contents of working memory. Block's views will be considered in some detail in Chapter 4.

There is yet a third strand in the debate over the reality of the distinction between access consciousness and phenomenal consciousness, however. For even if one thinks that the two concepts are coextensive in normal humans (as does Chalmers 1997), one can claim that there are a special set of properties that are picked out first-personally (so-called "qualia") that aren't reducible to others, and that aren't explicable in third-person terms. These are the properties that a zombie would lack, despite sharing the same access-conscious states as a normal person. This strand of debate will be addressed in Sections 1.2, 1.3, and 1.4. There I will discuss the contrast between qualia realism and qualia irrealism, and will go on to provide a preliminary sketch of how the global-workspace theory that I will be defending in Chapters 5 and 6 can offer a fully reductive account of phenomenal consciousness. Before we embark on that discussion, however, one other pair of distinctions needs to be explained.

Mental-state consciousness (whether access or phenomenal) should be distinguished from *creature* consciousness, which can be either *transitive* or *intransitive* (Rosenthal 2005). Whenever a creature (whether human or animal) is aware of some object or event in its environment or body, it can be said to be (transitively) conscious of that object or event. Put differently, a creature is transitively conscious of an object or event when it *perceives* that object or event. It is debatable whether or not transitive creature consciousness requires mental-state consciousness. For it is debatable whether the perceptual states that enable a creature to be aware of its environment must be conscious ones. At any rate, it is worth noting that there are many kinds of case where one would pre-theoretically ascribe creature consciousness to an agent—since the agent is displaying flexible perceptual sensitivity to the environment—where the states in virtue of which it acts as it does are *not* conscious ones. This point will be discussed in some detail in Chapter 3.

Intransitive creature consciousness, on the other hand, is a matter of being awake rather than asleep, or conscious as opposed to comatose. When the creature in question is a human person, then intransitive creature consciousness would normally implicate some or other form of mental-state consciousness. Whenever one is awake one is normally undergoing some conscious mental state or other. But the reverse need not be true. It seems that dreams are conscious mental states, even though the dreaming subject is asleep, and hence creature *un*conscious.

Note that both forms of creature consciousness admit of degrees. One can be more or less aware of the properties of a stimulus, and one can be more or less awake. Likewise, the concept of access consciousness allows for degrees. A mental state could be available to more, or to fewer, of the systems for reasoning, reporting, remembering, and so on. Phenomenal consciousness, in contrast, is all-or-nothing. It is hard even to conceive of a case of a mental state that is partly *like something* to undergo, partly not. (Remember, one needs to conduct this imagining in the first person, not the third.) Indeed, even if one is only partly awake, some of the states one is in are definitely phenomenally conscious—it is *like something* to be barely awake. And even though one's awareness of an object can be more or less detailed, or more or less rich and vivid, even the most impoverished experience is definitely *like* something. Contrast looking at something in sunlight versus looking at it by starlight when one can barely make it out: nevertheless, it is fully—unequivocally—*like something* to be looking at a dimly lit object, even if one is aware of many fewer properties of it. This point will be developed in more detail in Section 1.6. It is an important premise for some of the arguments of this book.

Our question about nonhuman animals, then, isn't whether animals can be awake, half-awake, or asleep. (Of course they can.) Nor is it about whether animals can be perceptually sensitive to the properties of their environments. (The obvious answer is that they often are.) Our question is whether the *mental states* of animals are ever conscious; specifically, whether they are ever *phenomenally* conscious. And if they are, which ones, in which species of creature? And how would we know?

It is important to keep these different notions of consciousness distinct. Failure to do so can lead to confusion and error. For instance, it might lead one to move from the obviously true claim that a dog is conscious of its owner entering the home (that is: it perceives—or is creature conscious of—the owner doing so, responding with manifest joy at her arrival) to the conclusion that the dog's perceptual state is itself a conscious one. It *may* be that this inference is warranted. That depends on the outcome of our present inquiry in this book. But it certainly isn't warranted merely because the term "conscious" crops up in both premise and conclusion. For those two uses of the term are conceptually quite different, as we have seen.

Asking whether the mental states of animals are phenomenally conscious presupposes that animals have mental states at all, of course. Although this is increasingly widely accepted, it will be worth spending some time defending it, as I do in Chapter 2. For the commonalities and differences between human and animal minds will loom large in the discussion that follows. Moreover, it may be the growing acceptance of animal mentality that has increasingly led people to attribute consciousness to animals. For the distinction between conscious and unconscious mental states is largely invisible from the perspective of common-sense psychology, as are some of the distinctions drawn in the present section. But in fact, as we will see shortly, it is possible to deny phenomenal consciousness to animals altogether while allowing that they have mental lives that are otherwise much like our own. Indeed, no matter how well warranted the latter claim turns out to be, it can't by itself determine an answer to the question of *phenomenal* consciousness in animals.

1.2 Qualia realism

There seems to be an explanatory gap between all physical, functional, and representational facts, on the one hand, and our first-person awareness of our own phenomenally conscious mental states, on the other. There are a number of ways of demonstrating this point. One is simply to reflect that, no matter how much one might know about the brain, the functional organization of the mind, and the contents represented by one's mental states, it would still not explain why one's experience of a red tomato should feel like *this*. Another is to notice that one can conceive of the possibility of a zombie—a being who is like oneself in all physical, functional, and representational respects but who lacks *this* feeling (the feeling of what it is like to be seeing a red tomato). In addition, one can consider color-deprived Mary (Jackson 1982, 1986), who has lived all her life in a black-and-white room but who comes to know everything there is to know about the physiology and functional organization of the visual system, as well as the contents represented via the operations of that system. Still, it seems, Mary would learn something *new* when she leaves her black-and-white room and experiences red for the first time.

Given the existence of the explanatory gap, one can be tempted to conclude that phenomenal consciousness involves properties (qualia) that don't reduce to any combination of physical, functional, or representational ones (Chalmers 1996). These properties are thought to be intrinsic to the states to which they attach, private to the person who has them, directly knowable through introspection, and ineffable (indescribable). In addition to the physical properties that make up the world, then, one might think one is also required to recognize the existence of these *sui generis* properties of conscious mental states. This is qualia realism. But qualia realism comes in two basic varieties: epiphenomenalism, on the one hand, and various forms of Russellian monism, on the other.

First, epiphenomenalism: on this view, as the name suggests, qualia are causally epiphenomenal (Jackson 1982). They supervene on the physical world without having any causal impact on that world. Indeed, most people now assume that the physical world is *causally closed*. That is to say, every event that happens in the physical world—whether it be the movement of the tides, the growth of a tree, or a person uttering a sentence—has a sufficient physical cause. This has been the guiding assumption of scientific inquiry for centuries, and seems amply confirmed by the success of the resulting scientific theories.

If qualia are non-physical properties of our mental states, however, then it follows from the causal closure of the physical world that qualia cannot cause any events in that world. So it isn't strictly the qualia themselves that cause one to believe in the explanatory gap (if one assumes, as most now do, that beliefs are physical properties of one's brain). Nor can it be qualia themselves that cause one to utter the words, "Mary would learn something new when she sees red for the first time." At best, those properties will be *correlated* with what causes one's belief, or one's utterance, perhaps in a fundamentally law-like way. Indeed, if qualia aren't physical properties, but reliably co-occur with certain physical properties, then the laws determining that co-occurrence might be among the basic laws of nature (Chalmers 1996).

Russellian monism, in contrast, tries to avoid making qualia epiphenomenal by placing them at the heart of the physical world itself (Russell 1927; Strawson 2006; Alter & Nagasawa 2012). On this sort of view, either qualia, on the one hand, or proto-qualia-like properties that compose qualia, on the other, provide the categorical grounding for the relational, structural, and dispositional truths of fundamental physics. What makes Russellian monism a form of qualia realism (and not a version of reductive physicalism about qualia) is that fundamental physics tells us about the relational, structural, and dispositional properties of fundamental matter, while being silent about the categorical grounding of those relations and dispositions (here said to be qualia). Reductive physicalism, in contrast, ultimately grounds qualia in the properties physics tells us about.

If it is qualia themselves that provide the categorical basis for fundamental physics, then qualia are ubiquitous in the physical world, and a sort of panpsychism results. For at the center of every subatomic property and process will be a little bit of conscious mentality. On the other hand, qualia might be thought to be composed, somehow, out of intrinsic qualia-like properties that ground all physical processes, but these qualia-like properties aren't themselves mental, and aren't phenomenally conscious. Either way, however, it would seem that Russellian monism faces its own version of the explanatory gap (Carruthers & Schechter 2006;

Goff 2009; Coleman 2012). For how does one get from the fundamental-particle qualia or proto-qualia to Mary's red qualia? And it seems one could know everything about those fundamental properties and still be puzzled as to why one's red experiences should feel like *this*. Moreover, one can likewise conceive of zombies who have all the same low-level qualia as us, but in whom those properties fail to "combine" in the right way to get them the person-level qualia we experience.

There is not the slightest empirical reason to believe that either of these forms of Russellian monism is true, of course, beyond the a priori arguments advanced by philosophers. Somewhat as first-cause arguments for the existence of God are designed to satisfy the intuition that every event must have a cause (without really doing so), so Russellian monism is intended to satisfy the intuition that dispositional and relational properties should be grounded in categorical ones. But the hypothesis that qualia or qualia-like intrinsic properties underlie the structural and dispositional facts of basic physics doesn't do any real explanatory work. It doesn't add anything to the physics we already have—no new predictions or empirical results are forthcoming. And it can't explain the dispositional properties in question either, such as whether a given elementary particle is spin-up or spin-down. Nor can it even explain the difference between the circumstances in which a physical disposition becomes actualized and those in which it doesn't. This is in marked contrast with cases where categorical properties actually succeed in explaining something (at least in outline)—such as explaining the brittleness of a glass (its disposition to break when struck with a certain force), or explaining why the glass did actually break, in terms of its molecular structure.

What implications would qualia realism have for the distribution of phenomenal consciousness across the animal kingdom, however? The answer depends on the kind of qualia realism in question. For those who are epiphenomenalists, the answer will depend on the exact nature of the laws correlating qualia with physical properties. Since we can only seek evidence of these in ourselves, and since the evidence that we can gather in the first person only concerns qualia we are aware of having, not any that we might be *un*aware of, the question becomes intractable. Even if one thinks, for example, that qualia co-occur with access-conscious nonconceptual contents in ourselves, there is no way to discover which of the many physical and functional properties involved should actually figure in the laws of correlation. Perhaps, for example, qualia only get attached to access-conscious events in minds that are capable of verbally reporting them. How could we get evidence either for or against this hypothesis? Moreover, there is no way to rule out the hypothesis that qualia attach to many other events that *aren't* access conscious, that subjects themselves aren't aware of and cannot report.

For qualia realists who are Russellian monists, in contrast, everything will depend on whether qualia are at the heart of every single physical process (in which case panpsychism is true), or whether they are some-how composed out of qualia-like but non-mental intrinsic properties that ground all physical processes. The former view at least provides a determinate answer to the question of which things are phenomenally conscious. The answer is: everything. If qualia are composed of non-qualia properties, in contrast, then the question is likely unanswerable. For no one has the slightest idea how the compositional process is supposed to work, nor how this could be discovered empirically.

In consequence, qualia realism leaves the distribution of phenomenal consciousness entirely open. It might be that only adult human beings are phenomenally conscious.[1] Or it might be that every living creature—including bacteria—has phenomenally conscious states. Indeed, it is even left open that every single physical particle in the universe might come with qualia-properties attached, which is what panpsychists maintain (e.g. Strawson 2006). Nevertheless, since qualia are real, there is a real fact of the matter. It is just that such facts are likely unknowable by us, except on quite tenuous grounds.

That qualia realism makes it hard to know which creatures are phe-nomenally conscious and which aren't isn't itself a reason for rejecting it. For similar difficulties are likely to arise whatever one's view of the nature of consciousness. This is because the concept of phenomenal conscious-ness is a first-person one, as we noted at the outset, grounded in one's acquaintance with one's own experiential states. Since one's induction base is so small (essentially, just oneself and other humans who can

---

[1] Notice that we would then be claiming that although dogs, for example, are aware of the world around them—they are transitively creature conscious—they lack phenomenally con-scious mental states. This is one way in which creature consciousness and phenomenal consciousness might come apart.

describe their experiences to us), it becomes quite difficult to know how far phenomenal consciousness projects beyond that narrow base. But qualia realism has this problem, and then some. Since qualia realism places phenomenal consciousness outside the causal order of the world (if epiphenomenalism is true), or embedded within that causal order in a way that makes no causal difference (if Russellian monism is), it becomes especially hard to know what sorts of evidence might constrain one's hypotheses about its distribution.

1.3 Tacit dualism

Many of us recognize the real existence of properties above the level of basic physics, of course. One can believe in the reality of properties such as photosynthesis and neurotransmitter uptake without thinking that such properties can be reduced, type-for-type, to properties recognized by physics. And one can likewise think that such higher-level properties play a causal and explanatory role in the natural world. Properties picked out by the special sciences are real, and such sciences cannot be replaced by the science of physics. Nevertheless, anyone who is a physicalist needs to accept that events involving such properties must admit, in principle, of reductive explanation in physical terms, at least on a token-by-token basis. Put differently, once all the facts expressed in the language of physics are fixed, then so too are the facts described by the special sciences. Qualia realists, in contrast, think that all physical facts can be fixed, and yet facts about qualia can vary or be absent altogether. Indeed, this is implicit in the very idea of a zombie.

The consequences of qualia realism should be hard for scientifically minded people to accept. For in addition to the laws, generalizations, properties, and physical mechanisms discovered and discoverable by science, one would be postulating an additional set of laws and/or nonphysical properties, supported only by a combination of ordinary introspective awareness together with philosophical argument. These additional properties would do no additional scientific work, and they aren't needed to explain any facts or events in the world. Indeed, they don't even explain the tempting thought experiments that have led philosophers to believe in them. This is because it isn't qualia that cause philosophers to have those thoughts and beliefs, and to say the things that they do, but rather the physical correlates of qualia or the physical processes grounded in qualia. In consequence, the burden of proof required for one to accept qualia realism should be quite high.

Why, then, do so many scientists seem to take qualia realism seriously? The answer probably derives, in part, from an intuitive, unreflective, Cartesian dualism about the mind in general. This leads people to have at least a tacit expectation that minds are separate from brains, while interacting causally with them. This sort of ontological dualism is arguably an innately channeled feature of our common-sense psychology, continuing to operate tacitly even when explicitly rejected (Bloom 2004). Certainly it has been a central aspect of intuitive folk belief across all pre-scientific cultures and historical eras (Boyer 2001; Cohen et al. 2011; Roazzi et al. 2013). Moreover, we know that intuitive beliefs in general can continue to exist alongside scientific ones, rather than being replaced by the latter, and while continuing to exert their influence on people's thoughts and behavior (Shtulman & Valcarcel 2012); and the same is also true of mind–body dualism (Forstmann & Burgmer 2015). I submit that in the absence of intuitive dualism, scientists would pay just as little attention to philosophers' views on this topic as they do to other sorts of metaphysical claim made on the basis of purely philosophical argument, such as Wittgenstein's (1922) thesis that the world is composed of simple, changeless, necessarily existing objects.

I should emphasize that it is people's intuitive dualism about the mind that makes qualia realism seem more plausible than it is, rather than the other way around. It surely isn't the case that people the world over have felt the force of the "explanatory gap" between physical facts and phenomenal consciousness, and for that reason have embraced an ontological dualism of mind versus body. Rather, what seems to be the case is that dualist beliefs are innate or innately channeled aspects of folk psychology, thereby making people more receptive of qualia realism than they otherwise would be. There are a number of reasons for thinking this. One is the sheer implausibility of claiming that hunter-gatherers, subsistence farmers, and young children across cultures should have been influenced by consideration of an explanatory gap. Another is that even seven-month-old infants seem to think that minded agents aren't subject to ordinary physical laws (Kuhlmeier et al. 2004).

Moreover, the explicit dualistic beliefs of children in Western cultures get *less* strong with age (Bering 2006). This suggests that dualism is the default setting of the folk-psychological system, which gets weakened by cultural input in scientific cultures—at least at the level of explicit verbal expression—rather than depending on such input (Riekki et al. 2013; Willard & Norenzayan 2013; Forstmann & Burgmer 2015). Indeed, dualist intuitions are prevalent in both children and adults, even in cultures whose norms discourage overt attention to mental states, albeit becoming weaker as a function of exposure to Western education (Chudek et al. 2018).

In addition, both children and adults are more ready to think that non-sensory mental states like beliefs might survive the death of a biological agent than they are to think that phenomenal experiences could continue (Bering & Bjorklund 2004). And the same thing is found in medieval Christian theology, where the afterlife prior to the resurrection of the body is thought to consist in continuation of the individual's beliefs and values, rather than in sensory experience (Geach 1957). Since beliefs are by no means paradigmatic phenomenally conscious states, this suggests that it is intuitive dualism about the mental as such that is more basic, perhaps produced by the deep disconnect between an innately channeled "core knowledge" of folk-physics and the core assumptions of our early-emerging theory of mind (Bloom 2004). Indeed, since the evolutionary and developmental foundations of our folk psychology are third-personal rather than first-personal (Carruthers 2011a), we can conclude that folk dualism, too, is basically third-personal. So it is dualism that operates in the background, providing tacit support for qualia realism, rather than the other way round.

1.4 Qualia irrealism

Contrasting with qualia realism is qualia *irrealism*. The latter comes in a number of different forms, some of which will be explored in due course. But all seek to *identify* phenomenal consciousness with some natural (physical or physically realized) property. On the view I will ultimately defend, phenomenal consciousness is said to be nothing other than access-conscious nonconceptual content. In addition, the view will come paired with an account of how the explanatory gap arises, consistent with phenomenal consciousness actually being, itself, a representational-cum-functional property. This will be explained in terms of a special class of acquaintance-based indexical concepts that we can activate in the presence of such properties, where the concepts themselves have no descriptive content, nor any conceptual connections with physical, functional, or representational concepts. All this will happen in Chapters 4 through 6. We will then explore the consequences of such a view for the question of consciousness in nonhuman animals (as well as human infants and dementia patients) in Chapters 7 and 8.

It is worth noting that qualia irrealism is a close relative of what Frankish (2016) calls "illusionism" about consciousness. Both are defined by their outright rejection of qualia-properties. I prefer the term "qualia irrealism," however, because illusions generally arise spontaneously, and don't depend on reflective forms of thinking or reasoning. For instance, perceptual illusions are mostly universal among humans, and occur whenever the stimuli are correctly constructed and presented to people. Likewise, cognitive illusions of the sort investigated by Tversky & Kahneman (1983), Stanovich (2009), and others occur as soon as the question is asked: one has a strong (but incorrect) intuition as to the correct answer. The temptation to believe in qualia, however, is quite different. It depends on distinctive forms of reflective thinking, and on carefully constructed philosophical examples. Indeed, one generally has to do quite a bit of *work* to get people to see the problem of consciousness (even given the head-start provided by most people's tacit Cartesian dualism). Belief in qualia doesn't result from an illusion, but from philosophical argument.

It might be claimed, nevertheless, that the role of the arguments in question is just to bring out the presuppositions implicit in our concept of phenomenal consciousness. Perhaps what the "hard problem" thought experiments show is that we naively take our conscious experiences to possess nonphysical qualia properties. Hence the illusion might be thought to be embedded in the way ordinary people *conceptualize* their conscious experiences. As we will see in Chapter 6, however, this claim is false. Phenomenal concepts of the sort that give rise to "hard problem" thought experiments are just acquaintance-based indexicals referring to one's current access-conscious perceptual or perception-like states, and make no commitments regarding the nature of the referred-to states. For it is one thing to say that those concepts *lack* conceptual connections with physical or functional concepts (as we will see), and it is quite another thing to say that they *imply the absence* of such connections, and so commit their users to the nonphysical nature of their instances.

In denying illusionism, however, am I committed to thinking that phenomenal consciousness is in some way *real*? And what could that reality consist in if not the existence of qualia or qualia-like properties? For isn't our concept of phenomenal consciousness that of a state that has qualitative, intrinsic, directly known attributes? It may well be that many people (mostly philosophers) sometimes think of phenomenal consciousness this way. But to reiterate what was said in Section 1.1: phenomenal consciousness is *basically* a first-person notion. Indeed, Balog (2009) draws a useful distinction between *basic* and *non-basic* phenomenal concepts to mark just this contrast.

Public talk of "subjective feels" and "what it is like" are just invitations to pay attention to and think about the mental states we are aware of in ourselves, in fact. So the best interpretation I can give of the question, "Do you think phenomenal consciousness is real?" is to transpose it into the question: "When Mary leaves her black-and-white room, sees a ripe tomato for the first time, and thinks, 'So *this* is what it is like to see red', does she think something *true*?" I take it to be obvious that she does. In that case, since some phenomenal thoughts are true, what those thoughts are about must be real. It is another question, however, *what* those thoughts are about (whether they are about intrinsic and/or nonphysical properties, and so forth). That is where the philosophical debates should begin.

Before concluding this section, it is worth stressing again the extraordinary *hubris* that it takes to believe in nonphysical qualia on the basis of philosophical argument. Relying just on ordinary introspection combined with a few thought experiments (that one can conceive of zombies and so forth), one claims to know something about the fundamental structure of reality: namely, that it contains nonphysical properties that are either linked by some set of causal laws to physical properties or that somehow provide the intrinsic grounding for physical laws. Any scientist should ask: why should I believe that the structure of my thoughts and concepts enables me to discover, on their own, aspects of the basic ontology of the universe? How could the human mind itself have acquired such miraculous powers?

In what follows, then, I shall be assuming that qualia irrealism should be the default view. But that doesn't absolve us, of course, from providing good explanations of the contrast between conscious and unconscious states, while also explaining why people should be tempted to believe in qualia when they reflect on the matter. These are tasks to be taken up in Chapters 4 through 6.

1.5 Phenomenal consciousness is nonconceptual

It is common for philosophers to draw a distinction between conceptual and nonconceptual content, or conceptual and nonconceptual forms of mental representation. The present section will argue that phenomenal consciousness is exclusively nonconceptual in nature. Not a lot will turn on this point for our purposes, however. The discussion is included here to explain why I shall be framing theories of consciousness in nonconceptual terms throughout, as well as to outline the framework I shall be using to talk about the contents of access-conscious states.

I take the basic contrast in question to be between representations that involve categorical boundaries of some sort (that are "chunked") and those that are fine-grained and continuous (or "analog") in nature. This way of drawing the distinction between conceptual and nonconceptual content is pretty standard in the philosophical literature (Tye 2000; Bermúdez 2015; Beck 2019) and has been familiar since at least Peacocke (1992). Thus thinking that ripe tomatoes are red is a purely conceptual judgment, composed of the concepts RIPE, TOMATO, and RED.[2] In contrast, perceiving a roundish-shaped object whose surface is covered with some specific range of shades of red (but without conceptualizing the object *as* a red tomato) is a purely nonconceptual state.[3]

---

[2] I adopt the standard practice of using small capitals to designate concepts or mental representations, reserving italic for the *contents* of those representations (as well as using italic, as I have just done, for emphasis).

[3] Those who deny the existence of nonconceptual content, like McDowell (1994), could recast everything I say in terms of course-grained versus fine-grained indexical judgments.

Typically, perceptual and imagistic states contain both conceptual and nonconceptual content. While initial processing of a stimulus is non-conceptual, the emerging structures rapidly begin to interact with stored knowledge and concepts. By the time the resulting content is made access-conscious, it will generally comprise an object-file or event-file into which both conceptual and nonconceptual representations have been bound. A perception of a ripe tomato on the kitchen surface will represent the fine-grained shape, texture, and shade of color of the tomato, as well as embedding the concepts RED and TOMATO, such that one sees it *as* a red tomato.

Something similar happens in connection with speech. When someone says something in a language one understands, the impact of the sound-stream on one's eardrums will initially be processed for low-level auditory features, but will soon begin to interact with linguistic knowledge. By the time the utterance becomes access-conscious, the result is an event-file containing details of pitch, timbre, and accent, but also with word boundaries, syntactic structure, and meaning imposed on it. Indeed, mental-state information, too, can be bound into the auditory stream, so that one hears the person *as* speaking ironically, for example— that is, as intending to communicate the opposite of what is literally said.

Much more could be said on this topic, of course. (Those interested might like to look at Carruthers 2015a, 2015b, 2018a.) But this will do for our purposes here. Given that an access-conscious state such as hearing someone say, "You are welcome in my home" comprises both low-level nonconceptual representations of sound and high-level conceptual and semantic information, and given that the state is phenomenally conscious (as it plainly is), we can ask whether both the nonconceptual and the conceptual components make constitutive contributions to the mental state's phenomenal properties.[4]

Everyone in this debate allows that the meaning component makes at least a *causal* difference to the phenomenology of the event. For instance, a non-English-speaker hearing that sentence won't parse the sound

---

[4] Remember, there need to be no commitment here to the real and separate existence of such properties. A theory-neutral way to frame the question is to say that it is about whether both sorts of components (conceptual and nonconceptual) can be picked out by the distinctive first-person concepts that are employed in "hard"-problem thought experiments. See the discussion that follows.

stream into distinct words in the way that an English-speaker will, thereby causing a difference in the nonconceptual content of the resulting state (and hence making a difference to what it is like to be in that state). The real question is whether the conceptual contents of the state contribute phenomenal properties in their own right.

In work done with Bénédicte Veillet (Carruthers & Veillet 2011, 2017) I have argued that the way to make progress on this issue is to consider whether the two sorts of components each give rise to "hard problem" thought experiments (zombies, partial zombies, and the rest). For what would be the point of describing something as *phenomenally* conscious (as opposed to just access-conscious) if those thought experiments couldn't gain any purchase? Now, it is obvious that nonconceptual content gives rise to those problems. When experiencing the shade of red of the tomato, for example, one can think that there could be a creature exactly like oneself in all respects except that its percept of the tomato isn't *like that*. But we suggest that conceptual content doesn't allow for such thoughts. When looking at a duck in the park, for example, and seeing it *as* a duck (deploying in one's experience the concept DUCK), one cannot coherently think, "*This* experience [the seeing-as-a-duck one] might not have represented duckhood, and could have been reliably caused by some other property instead."

Others have accepted that phenomenally conscious states can be characterized as those that give rise to zombie-type thought experiments, but have used this to draw the opposite conclusion (Horgan 2011; McClelland 2016). However, they misapply the method, we claim. Horgan (2011), for example, constructs a partial-zombie scenario to argue that the meaning-component of speech perception is phenomenally conscious. He asks one to imagine someone who is a complete functional duplicate of oneself, who is physically, functionally, and representationally identical, and who also shares the same nonconceptual phenomenal experiences. But this person is meaning-blind. Although he talks as normal, and responds to other people's utterances as normal, he experiences speech and writing (both his own and other people's) *as meaningless*. We are invited to conclude that what is missing from his life is *what-it-is-like to comprehend meaning*.

Horgan's (2011) mistake, in our view, is that he fails to appreciate the relevance to his thought experiment of the distinction between access consciousness and phenomenal consciousness. That there is at least a conceptual distinction between the two isn't in dispute, as we noted above. To say that a mental state is access conscious is to say that it is available to a wide range of cognitive systems—for forming memories, for reporting in speech, for action-planning, for use in executive decision-making, and to systems that create full-blown emotional responses, among others. Phenomenal consciousness, in contrast, can be operationalized in terms of its aptness to give rise to "hard problem" thought experiments (or so we suggest). Now notice that access consciousness is implicit in the very idea of a zombie: a zombie is supposed to be a creature that is physically and functionally indistinguishable from a normal person. That means that it, too, must have content-bearing states that are available to inform just the same range of functions and cognitive processes as a normal person.

Horgan, however, doesn't seem to recognize that the partial zombie's state of understanding—the state of grasping the meaning of a sentence—would have to be access conscious in order for him to qualify as a partial *zombie*. After all, the meaning of the sentence is access conscious for a regular ordinary hearer. So the meaning of the heard sentence would have to be available to the partial zombie's systems for memory, for planning, for verbal report, and so on, thereby having a direct impact on those systems of just the sort that happens in a normal person. So the partial zombie will immediately know what has just been said to him, and can immediately formulate a reply, recognizing it *as* a reply when hearing himself speak. In consequence, the partial-zombie would be *aware* of the meaning in a purely functional, access-conscious sense of "aware." Given the identity in sensory experience between the partial zombie and his normal counterpart, and given that both are immediately aware (in the access-conscious sense) of the same meaning, what else could the partial zombie possibly lack?

Of course, there is more that could be said here, and other examples could be considered (Carruthers & Veillet 2017). But on these sorts of grounds we think it is reasonable to claim that the conceptual content of perceptual and imagistic states *doesn't* make a constitutive contribution to the phenomenal properties of those states, but at most a causal one. Indeed, Carruthers & Veillet (2017) go on to suggest that *all and only* access-conscious nonconceptual content is intrinsically phenomenally conscious, including not just nonconceptual sensory content but also the valence component of affective states like pain and the time-representing components of sequential experiences and episodic memories.

Notice that this conclusion implies that there is a real (and not just a conceptual) distinction between access consciousness and phenomenal consciousness, at least when applied to the component contents of mental states, as opposed to those states considered as wholes. Since the conceptual components of normal sensory experience are access conscious without being intrinsically phenomenally conscious, it follows that there are some properties of our mental states (namely, their conceptual contents) that are often access conscious without being phenomenally conscious. Consistent with this one can claim, of course, that all and only access-conscious *states* are phenomenally conscious. One could also claim that all and only access-conscious nonconceptual contents are phenomenally conscious. Just such a view will be defended in due course.

In what follows, therefore, I shall be assuming that only nonconceptual contents are intrinsically phenomenally conscious. But as I remarked at the outset of the section, not a great deal turns on this assumption. If one thinks that conceptual contents, too, can be phenomenally conscious, much the same questions concerning phenomenal consciousness in animals will arise, and for the most part they will have the same range of possible answers. More substantively, however, I shall also be assuming that phenomenally conscious *states* characteristically comprise both conceptual and nonconceptual components.

1.6 Phenomenal consciousness is all-or-nothing

Recall that the concept of phenomenal consciousness is a first-person one. Phenomenally conscious states are ones that humans, at least, can be introspectively aware of, and which, when one is aware of them, are apt to give rise to "hard problem" thought experiments. In general, such awareness is definitely present or definitely absent. Indeed, it is hard to imagine what it would be like for a mental state to be partially present to one's awareness. Items and events in the world, of course, can be objects of merely partial awareness. Someone who witnesses a mugging on a train platform might say, for example, "It all happened so fast I was only partly aware of what was going on." But this is about how *much* of the event one is conscious of, or how rich an interpretation one arrives at for the event. The experience in question is nevertheless determinately present, available to introspective awareness, and subject to "hard problem" thought experiments. One can think, for example, "There could be someone like me in all physical, functional, and representational respects, who nevertheless lacked *that sort* of inchoate impression of the unfolding events."

Despite this, a number of recent studies of conscious experience have employed a graded "perceptual awareness scale," and have used it to suggest that consciousness might admit of degrees (Ramsoy & Overgaard 2004; Overgaard et al. 2006; Andersen et al. 2016; Tagliabue et al. 2016). But the scale in question arguably measures degrees of detail and clarity in perceptual *content*, rather than degrees of mental-state consciousness. It is used in conjunction with reports of the content of experience (e.g. "square" or "diamond"), and comprises the four options (1) not seen at all: merely guessing; (2) merely glimpsed: a feeling there was something there; (3) almost clear experience: partial content seen; and (4) clear experience: unambiguous content. But there is still something that it is (unequivocally) *like* to have a mere glimpse of something, even if the content of the glimpse is left wholly ambiguous (beyond a mere impression of shape of *some* sort, perhaps). Degrees of content are one thing (and are undeniably real), whereas degrees of phenomenal consciousness are quite another (and arguably are *not* real).

The *contents* of consciousness can be more or less rich and determinate, then. In consequence, it certainly makes sense to say that one is more or less aware of a set of stimuli, or of the world around one. But this is about degrees of transitive creature consciousness, not degrees of phenomenal consciousness. Even if one is wrapped up in one's own thoughts and barely attending to the screen in front of one, having only the vaguest impression of some sort of forest scene, still it seems it is definitely *like something* to have a vague visual impression of a forest scene. Similarly, if one is struggling to make out a shape in the dark as one walks home, still it seems, nevertheless, to be determinately— unequivocally—*like something* to have a visual experience of an indeterminate shape.

Consciousness can fade, of course. But in this case it is *in*transitive creature consciousness that fades. As one slips into sleep, or is slowly rendered unconscious by administration of an anesthetic, one will be subject to *fewer* conscious mental states and/or will have states with increasingly impoverished contents. But so long as one retains some degree of intransitive creature consciousness one will have *some* phenomenally conscious mental states. And no matter how impoverished their contents, it will be determinately *like something* to be in them. Even if all that remains is an indistinct impression of flickering light, or a vague impression of people talking in the distance, the experience of a faint flickering light, or of indeterminate voices, seems to be unequivocally phenomenally conscious.

It is worth noting, too, that many of the stimuli used by experimental psychologists who study consciousness are at the very borders of discriminability, as we will see in more detail in Chapter 3. A faint shape might be flashed on a screen for a few milliseconds, for example, before being replaced by another (generally called a "masking stimulus"). If the timing and intensity parameters are set correctly, people may only detect the faint shape on about 50 percent of the trials. Still, when the subject reports "seen," it is assumed that the perceptual state is definitely phenomenally conscious; and when the subject reports "unseen," phenomenal consciousness of the stimulus is absent.

It is true that participants in such experiments will often express greater or lesser degrees of confidence in having seen the stimulus. Someone might report, for example, "I *think* I saw a shape that was oriented to the left, but I'm not sure—I might have imagined it." Now this particular kind of case causes no problem for our thesis, since visual images as well as visual percepts are phenomenally conscious. Even if someone is unsure whether what they experienced was a visual percept or a visual image, still what they experienced was phenomenally conscious. More challenging would be cases where someone reports, "I *think* I saw a shape, but I'm not sure—I might have experienced nothing." Two points are worth noticing here, however. One is that it seems to be definitely *like something* to be unsure whether or not one saw a shape. The other is that what one is actually unsure of, here, is whether one saw a shape *or a blank screen*. Hence either way one has a phenomenally conscious experience. It is *like something* to see a faint shape. And it is likewise *like something* to see a blank screen.

Rosenthal (2018) argues that in addition to degrees of detail and vividness in the *content* of a perceptual state, there can be degrees of *awareness of* the occurrence of that perceptual state. As we have just noted, for example, one might be unsure whether one saw anything on a given trial in a backward-masking experiment. If a higher-order theory of consciousness were correct, then degrees of awareness of a state might amount to degrees of conscious status for that state, just as Rosenthal (2018) claims. But I will ultimately be defending a first-order account, according to which phenomenal consciousness can be equated with a certain sort of (first-order) access consciousness. If there is no perceptual state of the kind in question, of course, then *that* state cannot be phenomenally conscious. But it is nevertheless determinately *like something* to be unsure whether or not one saw anything on the screen at that moment.[5]

I conclude that we can't make sense of degrees of phenomenal consciousness. The concept of phenomenal consciousness is given to us through our introspective first-person awareness of our own mental states. And it seems, then, that anything we are introspectively aware of (provided it has fine-grained nonconceptual content) is a definite instance of the concept. This is a claim that will prove important when we turn to consider phenomenal consciousness in other species. For a number of the theories that have been put forward to explain consciousness in the human case are framed in terms that will only be instantiated in other species *to some or other degree*.

1.7 Other minds and others' consciousness

Finally, in this chapter, we should situate our topic in relation to the traditional philosophical problem of other minds. The problem is generally expressed like this: how do I know that other people (let alone

---

[5] In any case, even if we agreed that a fleeting indeterminate visual experience was to some lesser degree phenomenally conscious, this wouldn't help us to make sense of degrees of consciousness across species. For in the latter case we may be dealing with fully detailed, temporally extended perceptual states, but ones that are only partly comparable to human phenomenally conscious perceptual states—because they are available to fewer or less sophisticated consuming systems for the access-conscious information, for example. This point will prove important in Ch. 7.

other animals) have minds like my own? For all I ever see are their circumstances and behavior. But if the question is about minds and mental states in general, as opposed to phenomenally-conscious experiences more narrowly, then it makes a false presupposition. In effect, it takes for granted that knowledge of my own mind is prior to, and more basic than, my knowledge of the minds of others. Elsewhere I have argued that this gets things completely back-to-front (Carruthers 2011a). Our knowledge of mental states depends on the operation of an innately channeled "mind-reading" or "theory of mind" faculty, which is present in nascent form in infancy, and which is designed in the first instance for attributing mental states to other people. Knowledge of one's own mental states results from turning that same mental faculty on oneself, relying not just on external behavioral and contextual cues but also on the perceptual and imagistic contents that are made available to it as input (including one's own visual imagery and inner speech).

While our knowledge of mental states begins with an innately channeled mind-reading faculty, it can thereafter be supplemented and corrected by science, of course. Thus the folk notion of *belief* is known to fragment into at least four distinct types of information storage: episodic memory, semantic memory, rote memory (as in "seven sevens are forty-nine"), and what Frankish (2004) calls "commitments," which are really intentions to behave and reason as if a certain proposition were true. We can rely on both sets of resources when attributing mental states to others, with greater or lesser degrees of confidence. And of course similar resources can be used to interpret the behavior of nonhuman animals as well. Chapter 2 will outline some of what is known on that front, temporarily setting the consciousness question to one side.

Embedded within the question of other *minds*, however, is a narrower issue, which one might call the problem of others' *consciousness*. I have introspective awareness of my own phenomenally-conscious experiences, of course, since perceptual and imagistic contents that attract attention are "globally broadcast" (as we will see in Chapter 5), and made available as input to a range of different systems for reporting and decision making, including one's mind-reading faculty. Indeed, as we stressed at the outset, the very notion of *phenomenal* consciousness is grounded in first-person acquaintance with one's own experiential states. I can wonder, therefore, how I can know that other people undergo states *like this*. And I can wonder how I can know that everyone else isn't a zombie.

The solution to the problem of others' consciousness relies on an inference to the best explanation. This is at its strongest when dealing with other adult humans. Such people belong to the same species as me, with the same sense organs and with similar brains that are organized (to the best of my belief) in the same way that mine is. Moreover, they behave and respond to the world in ways similar to myself, crying out when injured, navigating around obstacles in the light but not in the dark; and so on. Similar sorts of evidence can be available for other animals, of course, but in a graded manner. The brains, sense organs, and behavior of chimpanzees are more similar to mine than are the brains, sense organs, and behavior of mice; which are in turn more similar to mine than are the brains, sense organs, and behavior of chickens; and so on. A natural first thought, then, is that an inference to the best explanation when attributing phenomenal consciousness to other creatures besides oneself can be made with lesser and lesser *confidence* as one moves from other humans, through other great apes, to monkeys, to mice, to birds, to reptiles, and then to invertebrates like bees and spiders.[6]

Given this background of similarities, however, the most important fact about other humans (and only other humans) is they can talk to me about their own experiences, telling me that the nature of those experiences seems ineffable; and I can get them to puzzle over the "explanatory gap" and the question whether everyone but themselves might be a zombie. These latter facts, in particular, provide powerful evidence that other people's experiences are presented to them in the same sort of first-person way that mine are presented to me, and are likewise *like something* for them to undergo. In short, they provide powerful evidence that other people, too, are phenomenally conscious (but without providing

---

[6] Notice that the inferential principle at work here seems to be something like this: creatures that are alike in one set of respects (brains, behavior, descent) are probably alike in other respects, too—specifically, in being phenomenally conscious. It is unclear how reliable this sort of inductive principle is in predicting unobvious properties of organisms, however. Indeed, that might depend on how detailed an understanding one has of the nature and role of the property being projected. (If one lacks any understanding of what the appendix does in human physiology, for example, then one lacks a basis for predicting its presence in other creatures, whether closely or distantly related.) In fact, the main moral of Ch. 3 will be that one cannot hope to project capacities for phenomenal consciousness across creatures in the absence of a good *theory* of consciousness.

complete certainty, of course, since it remains *conceivable* to me that everyone else is a zombie).

Recall from Section 1.5, moreover, that one good theory-neutral way of characterizing phenomenal consciousness is to say that it comprises whatever properties of mental states give rise to typical "hard problem" thought experiments. Whether one believes in qualia or not, everyone can agree that phenomenal consciousness is distinctive in giving rise to a special set of puzzles (at least in creatures capable of such puzzlement). The strongest grounds one can have for attributing such consciousness to others, then, is that some of their mental states *do* give rise to such puzzles *for them*. At least, this is true given a background of other commonalities in evolutionary descent, brain organization, mentality, and behavior. For of course we would have quite low confidence in the phenomenally-conscious status of a laptop computer that had been programmed to express such puzzlement, no matter how convincingly it did so.

As a result, and despite the fact that phenomenal consciousness is a first-person notion, we can reasonably claim to *know* that other humans undergo mental states that are phenomenally conscious (or at least *most* other humans—difficult cases will be discussed in Chapter 8). This is enough to enable a science of phenomenal consciousness to proceed, despite the first-person character of the subject matter. But it means that special priority must be given, in such a science, to evidence collected from normal adult humans.

Only a subset of the evidence described above is available in the case of nonhuman animals (as well as human infants), of course. They can't talk to us, and so cannot provide the same sort of direct evidence that one can get of a first-person perspective on their experiences that one can obtain for other adult humans. But they can be more or less similar to us in biological descent, in brain structure and organization, and in nonverbal behavior. In advance of further inquiry, these similarities provide *some* reason to think that the creatures in question are phenomenally conscious, with a degree of confidence graded by the degree of similarity between us. Chapter 3 will consider how strong this evidence is on its face (when considered in the absence of any scientific theory of consciousness), concluding that it isn't very powerful. Then Chapters 4 and 5 will embark on the search for such a theory.

The main point to stress here, however, is just that a theory of phenomenal consciousness needs to take its start from, and prioritize, evidence provided by adult human beings. This is because it is here that evidence for the sort of first-person acquaintance with phenomenal properties that we each find in ourselves is at its strongest, and it is this that provides the most direct evidence that we have of the existence of phenomenal consciousness in others.

1.8 Conclusion

This chapter has advanced two definite theses, one of which is more central to the project than the other. The important claim—which will be relied on in what follows—is that phenomenal consciousness is all-or-nothing. Either a mental state is *like something* for its subject to undergo, or it is not. There is no half-way house. More peripherally, I have also claimed that only nonconceptual contents make a constitutive contribution to the phenomenal properties of the mental states in which they occur (as opposed to a causal one).

In addition, a number of important conceptual distinctions have been drawn. One is between mental-state consciousness and creature consciousness. Within the former, we distinguished between access-conscious mental states and phenomenally-conscious mental states, where the latter notion is distinctively first-personal in nature; and within creature consciousness, we distinguished between transitive and intransitive varieties. The extent to which these concepts pick out distinct properties or converge on the same property will be discussed in what follows.

This chapter has also introduced the debate between qualia realism and qualia irrealism. The latter should be the default view for anyone who takes science seriously. We should believe in qualia only as a last resort—and perhaps not even then, even if it were to turn out that we can't provide a successful reductive explanation of phenomenal consciousness. Indeed, it might be more reasonable to conclude that consciousness is a scientific mystery (as does McGinn 1991), rather than accept an ontology driven by philosophical intuition.

Finally, we noted that one has, in advance of further inquiry, varying *degrees* of evidence for the presence of first-personal phenomenal consciousness in other creatures—among which by far the strongest evidence exists for other adult humans. This is because such people can talk to one, can reflect on and describe the nature of their experiences, and can (especially) display puzzlement about the place of those experiences in the natural order, just as one does oneself.

2

Animal minds

The state of the art

If animals lack mental states altogether, then of course they can't be capable of phenomenal consciousness, either. And even assuming that they have mental states, it would be natural to think that much might turn on just how sophisticated the minds of various species of animal are, and on the extent of the discontinuities between human and animal minds. The present chapter argues against strong discontinuity views. It also considers evidence of working memory, planning, self-control, metacognition, and language in animals—attributes that are especially relevant to later discussions.

2.1 Discontinuity views

Everyone allows that there is *some* sort of significant discontinuity between human and animal minds. Only humans contemplate the origins of the universe, the possibility of life after death, and the nature of right and wrong. Only humans build complex multipart tools, make kayaks, and hunt with weapons. And of course only humans perform exact mathematical calculations, conduct scientific experiments, and evaluate the strength of an argument for a conclusion. These and other differences have enabled us ultimately to travel to the moon, to construct skyscrapers and the internet, and (unfortunately) to alter the climate of the planet itself.

It is tempting to think that a behavioral discontinuity of this magnitude is best explained by some equally radical *mental* discontinuity. Humans must have a different *kind* of mind from the minds of other animals, one might think. The most extreme form of discontinuity-view

Human and Animal Minds: The Consciousness Questions Laid to Rest. Peter Carruthers, Oxford University Press (2019). © Peter Carruthers.
DOI: 10.1093/oso/9780198843702.001.0001

is to deny that animals have minds at all, as René Descartes famously did. If this were correct, then it would settle our question about phenomenal consciousness in animals quite straightforwardly. If animals lack mental states altogether, then plainly they can't possess phenomenally conscious mental states.

While no one accepts the Cartesian view any longer, there are still plenty of defenders of mental discontinuity. I shall consider two such proposals in the course of this chapter. One is to deny that animals are capable of genuine *thought*, while allowing that they enjoy mental states of other kinds. The other is to claim that the human mind comprises *two systems* for thinking, reasoning, and decision-making, only one of which is shared with other animals. I shall suggest that neither view is defensible. The upshot is that the human mind is strongly continuous with the minds of nonhuman animals. But, as we will see in due course, this by no means settles the question of phenomenal consciousness in animals.

On the view that I favor, humans and other animals share minds of the same general sort with the same overall architecture (Carruthers 2006, 2015a). But humans have a number of distinctive adaptations. Some of these have to do with sources of motivation (especially of a prosocial sort), while others facilitate learning in particular domains (notably language and other forms of social cognition). The result is that humans collaborate and learn from others while living together in large groups of unrelated individuals, and with successful innovations in culture, technology, and thought being retained and transmitted across the generations, gradually "ratcheting up" overall human capacities. I won't say much in elaboration or defense of this kind of continuity account here, but will focus on critiquing claims of *dis*continuity.[1]

In addition to considering claims of discontinuity grounded in the vast gap in cumulative cognitive achievement between humans and other animals, I will also consider evidence of a number of other capacities in animals that will be relevant to discussions in later chapters. These include capacities for attention and working memory, for reasoning and reflective decision-making, for executive function and inhibitory

---

[1] For a brilliant and highly readable recent discussion of the coevolution of human cognition and human culture, see Henrich (2016), who draws heavily on archeological, historical, and anthropological data to make his case.

control, for mind-reading and metacognition, and for language and communication.

2.2 Concepts and thoughts

One sort of radical discontinuity view is that animals are incapable of genuine thought, because they lack real concepts. (Since concepts are the building blocks of thought, the former are required for the latter.) Now, one might wonder about the relevance of this view for the question of animal consciousness, especially given the claim defended briefly in Chapter 1, that phenomenal consciousness is exclusively nonconceptual in nature. As we will see in later chapters, however, some theories of consciousness presuppose that conscious creatures are capable of thought (even if those thoughts themselves aren't conscious). This is true of so-called "higher-order" theories, for example, which claim that conscious states are those that one is conceptually aware of. It is also true of any account that links phenomenal consciousness to access consciousness, since the "access" in question is to systems that enable thinking, reasoning, and decision-making. On either of these views, then, if animals are incapable of thought they will likewise be incapable of phenomenal consciousness.

Following Evans (1982), many philosophers have endorsed a constraint on what it takes to possess concepts and genuine thoughts (Bermúdez 2003; Camp 2004). This is the so-called "Generality Constraint." The idea is that in order to have concepts at all, you must be capable of thinking the thoughts that result from combining any one of your concepts with any other. If you have the concepts LION, GAZELLE, and EATS, then you must be capable of thinking, *The gazelle is eating the lion* as well as, *The lion is eating the gazelle*. Roughly, the constraint is one of unlimitedly flexible concept-recombination. More precisely, the constraint is that concept possession requires capacities for flexible recombination that are constrained only by the "logical form" of the concepts involved. (One cannot think, *eats lion*. A relational concept like EATS requires two *relata*.) While human conceptual capacities satisfy the Generality Constraint, it is said that other animals fall short. In particular, a gazelle might be incapable of thinking of a gazelle eating a lion. So while humans have concepts and think thoughts, nonhuman animals have, at best, *proto*-concepts and think *proto*-thoughts, resulting from their limited powers of conceptual combination.

The Generality Constraint is poorly motivated, however (Carruthers 2009a). It conflates a capacity for *creative* thought with capacities for thought as such. Granted, humans can combine together concepts in novel and surprising ways, as people do in jokes, fantasy, and metaphor. When Romeo thinks, *Juliette is the sun*, he thinks something Juliette's dog probably never could (even though it might have each of the concepts—strictly, on this view, proto-concepts—JULIETTE and SUN). But why should we insist that genuine thinkers must be capable of thinking in metaphors or engaging in fantasy? Such thoughts can be fun, and can turn out to be illuminating. But what thoughts are fundamentally *for* is learning, reasoning, and problem-solving. Each of these things animals can do (at least to a limited extent), as we will see shortly. In effect, the Generality Constraint exalts a particular kind of *use* of thought (creative thought) over all others.

If we grant that humans are unique in the extent to which they can generate thoughts creatively, we can then ask whether we need to postulate a completely different mental architecture, or a whole other kind of mind, in order to explain it. The answer is that we don't. Creativity requires enhancements in executive-function abilities that we share with other animals, enabling us to suppress the obvious and to select from among unobvious possibilities. And it might also be supported by capacities for language, which although uniquely human do not confer on us a completely different kind of mind. For language gives us the capacity to combine together words in any syntactically permissible order, thereby enabling us to entertain the corresponding thoughts. Simply by virtue of being able to *say*, "The gazelle is eating the lion," we can thereby entertain the thought expressed. Adding such capacities to minds that are capable of mundane thought (where those thoughts are nevertheless constructed out of recombinable components) might be sufficient to explain our capacity for indefinitely flexible creative thinking.

If animals are to be capable of thought of any kind, of course, then they must be capable of learning. And what they learn must be structured out of components, thus permitting inferences that are sensitive to those structures. But even bees have such capacities. A bee can learn that there is a tall tree 100 meters north of the hive whereas there is a lake 50 meters east, and it can use that information to figure out where it is in relation to the hive when it observes the same tree or the same lake from a different perspective.[2] In fact, bees have map-like knowledge of the various landmarks in the vicinity, which they can use in a flexible way to compute novel traveling routes in pursuit of a variety of goods, such as nectar, pollen, water, and tree sap (Menzel et al. 2005, 2011; Cheeseman et al. 2014).

In addition, bees are known to be capable of encoding quite abstract categories, generalizing in terms of those categories across sensory modalities and properties of stimuli. They can employ the abstract categories of *same* and *different,* for example (Giurfa et al. 2001). Trained to turn right at the second gate in a maze if the doorway is marked with the same color as the first, bees will spontaneously generalize to turn right during test trials if the second doorway is marked with the same *odor* as the first. More recent studies have shown that bees can categorize in terms of relational concepts like ABOVE and BELOW, LEFT and RIGHT, and BIGGER and SMALLER, as well as in terms of conjunctions of such concepts, such as ABOVE AND BIGGER (Avarguès-Weber et al. 2012, 2014). Moreover, in an especially remarkable recent result, bees trained to categorize varied stimuli by *number* spontaneously treated a stimulus containing zero items as smaller than stimuli containing some other number of items (Howard et al. 2018).

Even invertebrates are capable of thought, in my view. Or if one prefers, and wants to insist on employing a concept of thought that anchors it in the human case, they have states that are thought-*like.* What differs is that humans and other mammals have many *more* thoughts, about a greater range of subject-matters. But the basic status *thinker* is quite widely shared.

---

[2] Of course bees don't possess the concept METER, nor the exact numerical concept of 100. But they have representations of distance and numerical magnitude that approximate to these. Despite what some philosophers have claimed (Davidson 1975), the fact that their concepts lack exact human counterparts aren't good grounds for saying that bees lack concepts altogether.

2.3 Working memory and attention

Working memory has been heavily studied, in both humans and other animals. Indeed, much of what we know about working memory and its properties is derived from animal models (Goldman-Rakic et al. 1990; Goldman-Rakic 1995; Luck et al. 1997; Baluch & Itti 2011). Working memory is thought to provide a central "workspace" in the mind, in which representations can be sustained and manipulated. For example, a rat participating in a match-to-sample task will need to keep in mind the properties of a previous stimulus for a short interval in order to compare it to the upcoming sample. And among humans, working memory is employed when one repeats a phone number to oneself while searching for a notepad to write it down, or when engaging in mental arithmetic. Entry into working memory is thought to depend on the direction of attention, and its contents are always conscious (at least in the access-conscious sense).[3]

It seems that major components of the endogenous attention networks that control entry into working memory are strongly conserved across species, and are at least partially homologous in birds and mammals—as is working memory itself (Winkowski & Knudsen 2007, 2008; Mysore & Knudsen 2013). It may be that this set of networks performs a key organizing role in many animal minds. Attention selects, from among the multitude of stimuli that are present, those that are most relevant to current needs or ongoing concerns, and then sustains representations of those stimuli for short periods of time in such a way that multiple systems can draw inferences from them, respond affectively to them, and take decisions on the basis of them. The systems that consume and respond to the contents of working memory will vary widely across species, of course. But the basic "centering" function of working memory seems to be highly conserved (Carruthers 2015a).

Notice the close match between the properties of working memory, as studied by psychologists and comparative psychologists, and the concept of access consciousness as introduced by philosophers. Indeed, for a mental state to be access conscious likely reduces to the fact that it is

---

[3] For a review of much of this literature and discussion of its implications for the nature of conscious thought, see Carruthers (2015a).

sustained in working memory, given that, among humans, the systems that consume and respond to the contents of working memory include the ones that figure in the definition of access consciousness (namely, capacities for higher-order thought about one's own mental states, as well as capacities for reasoning, decision-making, and verbal reporting). If working memory has a claim to be considered a natural psychological kind, then—being partly homologous and performing the same "centering" function across multiple species—the same should likely be said about access consciousness. Many creatures, too, will have access-conscious mental states, although the systems that access those states may vary quite widely. It might be thought, then, that a theory equating phenomenal consciousness with access-conscious nonconceptual content would imply that phenomenal consciousness is just as widespread across the animal kingdom as is working memory. That is what I myself once thought (Carruthers 2000). But as we will see in due course, things are not so simple.

While there is robust evidence of covert attention and working memory across multiple species, the extent of the similarities in the psychometric properties and underlying networks involved is far less clear. In the human case, for example, it required a good deal of careful experimentation—designed to exclude both strategies of mental rehearsal and chunking together of stimuli—to establish that the working-memory limit in simple retention tasks is around just four items (Cowan 2001). And although there were some suggestive similar findings with monkeys (Hauser et al. 2000; Botvinick et al. 2009) and horses (Uller & Lewis 2009), until recently the kind of careful comparative work needed to establish similar (or lesser) capacity limits across species had not been done (Carruthers 2013a). However, Buschman et al. (2011) employed exactly the sorts of working-memory tasks with monkeys that have been employed with humans, finding the same working-memory limit of four items.[4]

Moreover, it is as yet unclear whether some of the studies claiming to find evidence of working memory in invertebrates—specifically honey

---

[4] One might be puzzled that basic working-memory limits are the same across humans and monkeys, despite the fact that humans are so much *smarter*. But simple working-memory retention capacities are poorly correlated with general intelligence (Engle 2010), which has much more to do with flexible *use* of the networks involved.

bees—are really investigating the same phenomenon at all (Zhang et al. 2005; Gross et al. 2009). On the positive side, these experiments find memory abilities manifested over short periods of time, as well as the smooth temporal decay function characteristic of human studies of working memory. But in the human case we know that the latter is an artifact produced by averaging over multiple trials. In fact, in humans, working-memory retention is all-or-nothing. Either the memory-item remains as a focus of attention, in which case it is fully retained; or attentional focus is lost, in which case that memory is lost (Zhang & Luck 2009; Souza & Oberauer 2015). The smooth decay function produced from averaging over trials simply reflects the fact that, with the passage of time, there are more opportunities for attention to be distracted. What we don't know is whether the same is true of honey bees; nor, indeed, do we even know whether the same is true of other animals generally.

In short, while there is evidence of working memory, or something resembling working memory, across a great many animal species, there is also an immense amount of difficult, careful, experimental work yet to be done by comparative psychologists to chart the exact contours of the commonalities and differences.

2.4 Reasoning and reflection

Any process that extracts new information from old can be described as a form of reasoning. By that token, reasoning abilities of various sorts are extremely widespread in the animal kingdom. For instance, a honey bee that has been captured, transported, and released at a novel site, and needs to compute a new trajectory back to the hive following its recognition of some nearby landmarks, can be said to reason its way to a representation of that new flight-path (Menzel et al. 2011). My focus here, though, will concern the sorts of reasoning that generally take place consciously in humans (utilizing the resources of working memory). For it is these that are most relevant to the question of consciousness in animals, as we will see in due course.

Much human reasoning is verbally mediated, of course. We think things through linguistically, either in silent inner speech, aloud, or on paper; and we often do so in discussion with other people. Indeed,

Mercier & Sperber (2017) argue that there is a distinct adaptation for verbally mediated reasoning that becomes activated whenever humans argue and discuss with one another. This faculty of reasoning emerged out of an evolutionary arms race when systems of human communication were evolving, resulting from the conflicting interests of senders and receivers of information. This sort of verbally mediated reasoning will, of course, be uniquely human.

In addition, however, humans engage in a form of reasoning and decision-making that has come to be known as *prospection* (Wilson & Gilbert 2005; Gilbert & Wilson 2007). This involves imagining future scenarios, and entertaining representations of those scenarios in working memory, thereby enabling them to interact with the various inferential, affective, and decision-making systems that consume the contents of working memory, which inferentially elaborate them, respond affectively to them, and ultimately decide between them. Prospection can sometimes involve imagination of the outcomes of action (e.g. living in Chicago, if what is to be decided is whether to accept a job offer in Chicago). But it can also involve images created by mental rehearsal of the actions under consideration. In addition, it is thought that prospection is both supported and elaborated by knowledge stored in episodic memory. For the same brain networks are involved in each, and people suffering from amnesia are also deficient in future-oriented imagining and decision-making (Schacter et al. 2007; Buckner 2010; Seligman et al. 2013; De Brigard 2014).

There is now significant behavioral evidence of episodic memory in a number of avian and mammalian species. Or at least (since some are doubtful whether these states have the full first-person qualities said to be possessed by human episodic memory), there is evidence that these creatures can remember *what* happened, *when* it happened, and *where* it happened (Clayton et al. 2001, 2003; Roberts et al. 2008; Eacott & Easton 2010). Moreover, the brain networks underlying these capacities (specifically the hippocampus and its connections to frontal decision-making regions of the brain) appear to be highly conserved across birds and mammals at least, and are at least partially homologous in these two groups (Allen & Fortin 2013). So there is good reason to think that some of the mechanisms that underlie prospective reasoning are in place in multiple species.

It is hard to get *direct* evidence of prospective reasoning in animals, of course. But there is now good behavioral evidence of capacities that, in humans, would be enabled by prospection. Most of this work has been done with corvids (rooks, crows, jays, and the like) and with great apes. For instance, animals from both groups can solve the "floating peanut" problem, seemingly by insight rather than trial-and-error (Mendes et al. 2007; Bird & Emery 2009; Hanus et al. 2011). This is the problem of how to reach a food-item that is too far down in a fixed Perspex tube to be reached by hand or beak. The solution is to spit water into the tube (in the case of the chimps), or to drop stones into the tube that already contains some water (in the case of the rooks), so as to float the item far enough up to be reached. The same problem is solved by most 8-year-old human children, but by hardly any 4-year-olds. Introspectively, it seems that one solves this problem by imagining various things one might do with the available materials until one hits on the correct solution. We don't know that the animals in question achieve their insights in the same way, of course; but the simplest hypothesis is that they do.

Other evidence of future planning in apes derives from a careful set of observations of the behavior of an alpha-male chimpanzee in an open-plan zoo (Osvath 2009; Osvath & Karvonen 2011). This male collected and stored stones at times when the zoo was closed, in order to throw them at zoo visitors later in the day as part of an aggressive threat display. Indeed, he proved quite adept at concealing his stashes of stones from the zoo keepers, and at manufacturing new projectiles (by breaking off pieces of concrete from the walls of the enclosure) when the keepers managed to remove all his stashes. This sort of behavior in a human would likely be caused by imagining—in advance, and while in a state of low emotional arousal—attacks on the zoo visitors, resulting in feelings of anticipatory satisfaction that motivate collection of the required materials.

There is also *experimental* evidence of future planning in apes (Mulcahy & Call 2004; Osvath & Osvath 2008; Völter & Call 2014). For example, one finding is that chimpanzees will select and carry with them to their overnight sleeping quarters a tool that will be needed to access a desired reward next day, remembering also to return with it in the morning. Indeed, when presented with a number of unfamiliar objects in advance (but without being permitted to handle them), they select and carry with them the one best suited to open the apparatus to achieve the reward. Humans would solve a task of this sort by mentally rehearsing actions involving the various tools in order to predict which of them would be most likely to prove successful.

Especially striking data of this sort derives from work done with New Caledonian crows, suggesting capacities for planning (Taylor et al. 2010; von Bayern et al. 2018). These animals are naturally adept at using tools (held in their beaks), but each of these experiments presented them with a novel problem. In the experiment conducted by Taylor et al. (2010), for example, there was some meat visible deep inside a Perspex container, so far inside that it would require the use of a long stick to reach it. Nearby there was a sufficiently long stick behind the bars of a cage, but so far behind the bars that it would require the use of a short stick to reach it. And then finally, there was a short stick hanging from a string on a perch. In order to solve this problem, the birds would first have to pull up the string to get the short stick; then use the short stick to get the long stick; and then use the long stick to extract the meat from the container.

In familiarization trials, the birds had previously been given experience of: (1) using a long stick to get meat from the Perspex container; (2) getting the long stick with their beaks when reachable behind bars; (3) using a short stick to try to get meat from the container, but failing; and (4) pulling up a string with meat attached. In contrast, they had never: (5) used a short stick to get a long one from behind the bars; nor (6) had they ever pulled up a string to get a stick or any other tool.

All four birds solved this problem by the second trial; two of them solved it on the first trial. How these two birds did so is especially suggestive. One examined the set-up for a full 110 seconds before seamlessly executing the entire sequence. The other examined the set-up for 43 seconds before starting to pull up the string. Then (seemingly having doubts) it dropped the string again, and examined the set-up for a further 40 seconds before completing the entire three-step sequence. What were these two birds doing during those intervals of time? We don't know. But humans would be mentally rehearsing some of the actions suggested by the affordances of the situation, foreseeing the consequences, and then combining and recombining various combinations of simulated action until hitting on the correct solution. Although this isn't direct evidence of prospective reasoning in birds, it is certainly suggestive.

2.5 Executive function and inhibition

Executive function encompasses a broad set of abilities. Indeed, working memory itself, as well as the control of attention on which it depends, are generally thought to require executive-function abilities. The same is true of the sorts of controlled uses of working memory that enable prospective reasoning and decision-making. In fact, what we refer to collectively as "executive function" is really a set of different capacities that are at least partly independent of one another (Miyake et al. 2000; Diamond 2013). In addition to the control of attention and mental rehearsal of action, these include: selecting from among competing action schemata, inhibiting prepotent or habitual actions, forming intentions for the future, implementing intentions, switching from one task goal to another, searching memory, and modulating emotion.

It is generally agreed that executive function abilities are uniquely developed among humans, partly as a result of our especially large brains, but partly also resulting from the relative expansion of prefrontal cortex that took place in the primate—and especially in the hominin— lineage (Donahue at al. 2018). Indeed, one can informally deduce as much from the fact that humans routinely form and implement intentions across intervals of days, weeks, and even years. Comparative data, even for individual executive-function tasks, are not generally available, however.

One exception is the "A not B" test of inhibition, which has been widely used with human infants, and has now been employed in a large comparative study of 36 species of mammals and birds, including 21 species of nonhuman primate (MacLean et al. 2014).[5] In this test, participants are first repeatedly shown a reward placed in one of three locations (location A), and are allowed to select it. Then in the test trial, the reward is initially placed in the familiar location A, before being moved to an alternative hiding place B in full view of the subject.

---

[5] MacLean et al. (2014) also used a motor-inhibition "cylinder" task with similar results. However, Kabadayi et al. (2016) find that when a greater range of avian species are tested, corvids (rooks, crows, etc.) perform at the same level as apes in this task, despite having much smaller brains (but with success rates nevertheless correlating with brain size among birds themselves). To the best of my knowledge the cylinder task has not been employed with human children, however.

Participants commit the A-not-B error when they perseverate and select location A. Human infants will generally pass this test by around the end of the first year of life (Wellman et al. 1986; Marcovitch & Zelazo 1999). Passing rates across adult members of other species are quite varied, ranging from 100 percent down to 10 percent among primates, and from around 50 percent down to 10 percent among birds. The best predictor of success across species is overall brain size (excluding elephants, who astonishingly have a success rate in this task of 0 percent).[6]

One other test of executive function often used with human pre-school children has now been employed across multiple other primate species. This is a version of the famous "marshmallow test," which requires participants to choose between an immediate smaller reward or a later larger one (Mischel & Mischel 1983). A version of this test conducted with members of 21 different primate species found average wait-times for a double-sized reward ranging from five seconds to about two minutes (Stevens 2014). As with the A-not-B study discussed above, wait times across species correlated with absolute brain size (which also correlates with body size and lifespan). Note that the human brain is about three times larger than that of our nearest primate relative, the chimpanzee.[7]

Recent findings suggest, however, that when used with human children the marshmallow test doesn't so much measure their underlying executive *capacity* to inhibit an immediate response as measure the child's estimate of the likelihood that the future reward will be achieved. For when given previous evidence of the reliability or unreliability of the experimenter in fulfilling her promises, children's wait times were, respectively, either 12 minutes on average (with many waiting the full 15 minutes allowed by the experimenter) or two-and-a-half minutes on average (Kidd et al. 2013). Moreover, it turns out that much of the

---

[6] Interestingly, perseverative errors among human infants turn out to depend, in part, on the presence of ostensive-learning cues inadvertently provided by experimenters during the normal experimental procedure (Topál et al. 2008). It seems that infants infer that they are being taught something by the adult experimenter during the initial A-location trials, and so later ignore the correct B-location in order to demonstrate what they have learned. If ostensive signals are removed, perseverative errors are significantly reduced, even among 10-month-olds.

[7] As Stevens (2014) also notes, however, one might expect to find large domain-specific differences among species, dependent on differences in lifestyle. Predators like cats and lions, for example, can display considerable patience when stalking prey, resisting the impulse for an immediate attack.

longitudinal predictive value of the marshmallow test really derives from factors such as social class and maternal background (Watts et al. 2018), which are likely proxies for the extent to which the child's circumstances are stable and predictable. It seems increasingly likely that all human children have the ability to defer gratification for extended periods of time, provided they have sufficient confidence in the outcome.

2.6 Mind-reading and metacognition

Comparative psychologists have paid quite a bit of attention over the last 40 years to the question whether animals are capable of representing mental states of various sorts, either in other agents (mind-reading) or in themselves (metacognition). In part these investigations have been informed and fueled by familiar disputes between proponents and opponents of Cartesian approaches to epistemology. On the Cartesian view, all knowledge—and specifically knowledge of the mental states of other agents—is grounded in first-person knowledge of one's own mind. In order to read another agent's mind one has to adopt their perspective, reason within that perspective, and then attribute the introspected results of that reasoning to the other person (Goldman 2006). The contrasting approach maintains that capacities for mental-state representation evolved in the first instance for social purposes, either competitive, cooperative, or both (Byrne & Whiten 1988; Hrdy 2009). Awareness of one's own mind is achieved through the use of that same mind-reading system, in part because one's own perceptual states are available as input to that system, and otherwise (as in the case of beliefs) via self-directed interpretation (Carruthers 2011a).

Elsewhere I have argued at length for the primacy of mind-reading over metacognition, in both evolution and infant development (Carruthers 2009b, 2011a; Carruthers et al. 2012). Here I will confine myself to brief consideration of the distribution of each of these capacities across the animal kingdom.

Initial investigations of mind-reading capacities in other primates produced negative results (Povinelli 1999). But it turns out that the experiments in question (conducted with chimpanzees) weren't ecologically valid. Specifically, they tested the animals in conditions where they needed to seek help to achieve a food reward, whereas chimps are intensely competitive about food. In contrast, when chimpanzees are tested in a competitive situation, the results are positive, suggesting that they can track at least the perceptual access, perceptual and inferential knowledge, and intentions of other agents (Call & Tomasello 2008; Kaminski et al. 2008). More recently, experiments using implicit measures of the sort previously employed with human infants have turned up positive results for false-belief representation in great apes as well. One of these used anticipatory looking toward an expected outcome dependent on an agent's belief (Krupenye et al. 2016); the other used low-cost helping, where what counts as "help" depends on the target agent's true or false belief (Buttelmann et al. 2017). Experiments with monkeys suggest that they, too, are capable of tracking perceptual access, goals, and knowledge states, but have as yet failed to find evidence of reasoning about false beliefs (Marticorena et al. 2011; Drayton & Santos 2016).

At this point in time there is little evidence of mind-reading abilities outside of the primate line. There is some evidence that dogs may be capable of reading human perceptual access and intentions (Maginnity & Grace 2014). And one might expect that some limited mind-reading capacities, at least, might be found in other highly social creatures such as dolphins and elephants. Moreover, there is evidence that corvids can interpret the line of sight of another (Dally et al. 2006). For they will rebury their food stashes when alone if the original hiding event took place in view of another bird, but only if they themselves have previously had experience of pilfering other birds' caches.

Evidence of metacognition in animals has mostly come from work done with monkeys (Templer & Hampton 2012; Smith et al. 2014), although some have claimed to find evidence of metacognition in rats (Templer et al. 2017), and even bees (Perry & Barron 2013). On the other hand, it has been argued that metacognition is absent in pigeons (Sutton & Shettleworth 2008). I myself have been a persistent critic of the positive findings (Carruthers 2008, 2011a, 2017a; Carruthers & Ritchie 2012). But this is not because I think the studies were poorly conducted, but rather because the data admit of simpler first-order explanations.

While many of those critiquing the animal metacognition findings have offered associative-learning explanations instead (Jozefowiez et al. 2009; Le Pelley 2012), that has not been my own approach. Rather, I have offered explanations modeled on what I take to be the best explanation of similar behavior in humans. Consider, for example, the so-called "uncertainty monitoring" paradigm. In such experiments an animal might need to make a discrimination of some sort, with two primary response options. Correct responses are generally rewarded, whereas incorrect responses result in a time-out before the next trial (a mild penalty). But the animals are also offered an "opt-out" response, which simply moves them on to the next trial without a time-out. The basic finding is that animals opt out more often when the primary discrimination task gets harder. This is said to reflect their metacognitive awareness of their own uncertainty about the correct choice.

A better explanation of these findings, in my view, is grounded in the human literature on prospection and prospective reasoning. When faced with a difficult choice, one will experience anxiety at the thought of taking either option. An opportunity to avoid having to make that choice, in contrast (by opting out), will be appraised in positive terms by comparison, making it seem like a better choice in the circumstances. Here one chooses, not on the basis of metacognitive knowledge of one's own uncertainty, but rather because the primary response options *seem less good*, resulting from one's appraisal of them as unlikely to succeed. Likewise, then, in the case of other animals.

This explanation seems quite natural in light of what we know about human decision-making, and receives direct support from studies of the latter conducted with both autistic and neurotypical individuals (Nicholson et al. 2019). The experimenters set out to test the implications of mind-reading-based and first-person-based accounts of the relations between mind-reading and self-awareness in general, finding robust evidence for the former. But they also tested whether uncertainty-monitoring tasks of the sort employed with animals are genuinely metacognitive. They were able to do this using human subjects (rather than nonhuman animals), because of the implication that implicit (nonverbal) tests of uncertainty monitoring the sort employed with animals *should share resources with* explicit (verbal) metacognition, provided that the former is genuinely higher-order in nature. Explicit (verbal) judgments of confidence will of course draw on mental-state conceptual resources (together with the abilities needed for linguistic expression of one's higher-order awareness). And those should be the same conceptual resources that are involved in so-called "uncertainty monitoring." In fact, however, Nicholson and colleagues found that human performance in matched versions of the two kinds of test were virtually uncorrelated (opting out of difficult trials in one condition, and making verbal reports of their confidence in another). Moreover, they found that rates of success in the one sort of task predicted hardly any variance in performance at the other. These findings are deeply problematic for the claim that nonverbal uncertainty-monitoring is genuinely metacognitive, and lends support to a purely first-order account of the decision-making processes involved.

Another important consideration supporting the same conclusion is that uncertainty-monitoring behavior of the sort investigated in monkeys has also been found in honey bees (Perry & Barron 2013). Bees, too, will opt out of a task more often (hence avoiding a time-out) when the difficulty of the discrimination increases. But how likely is it that bees have any sort of model of their own minds, and can represent their own states of knowledge and uncertainty? In contrast, it seems quite plausible that bees can learn and represent the basic structure of the experiment, and can experience something resembling anticipatory anxiety when considering the prospect of either of the two primary response options. It is much more likely that the bees are engaging in first-order risk-based decision-making, since we already know that they can weigh up the costs and benefits of the options open to them, and choose accordingly (Menzel & Giurfa 2001; Ravi et al. 2016).

Uncertainty monitoring is not the only paradigm that has been used to test for metacognitive awareness in animals, of course. Other researchers have claimed to find evidence of memory monitoring in animals, again using an opt-out paradigm (Hampton 2001, 2005). Monkeys in a match-to-sample task are more likely to opt out of the memory test with increasing lapses of time following stimulus presentation, suggesting that they are aware of the presence or lack of memory (since memory fades with time). And others have argued that some animals are aware of their own ignorance, since they will look selectively in trials and in locations where they have been denied perceptual access to the hiding of a reward (Beran et al. 2013; Rosati & Santos 2016).

I have criticized each of these paradigms, too, arguing that the data are better explained in terms of first-order cognitive processes. For example,

I have argued that so-called "memory monitoring" just requires that the animals in question *have* memories, and can make appropriate use of the presence or absence of memory. It doesn't require them to have any *conception* of memory, or awareness of their own memories as such (Carruthers 2017a). Likewise, I have argued against the look-and-see paradigm that successful performance doesn't require awareness of one's own ignorance, but just first-order affective states of questioning or curiosity, which are *caused by* one's ignorance without representing it (Carruthers 2017a, 2018b).

My own view, then, is that there is very little direct evidence of self-awareness of mental states in nonhuman animals, and that we should expect such awareness to be possible only in highly social creatures capable of third-person mind-reading. The precise extension of the set of species capable of thoughts about their own perceptual states is, of course, unknown at this point. But it seems likely that the class of such creatures is quite small.

2.7 Language and communication

A great many creatures employ communicative signals of one sort or another (Hauser 1997). These are mostly auditory, but also include bodily movements and other forms of physical display. For the most part such signaling is expressive rather than referential, serving to attract mates, deter competitors, or signal aggression, and is rarely under flexible intentional control. One of the few examples of referential signaling, however, comes from studies of vervet monkeys, who famously employ three distinct kinds of alarm call—one for eagles, one for panthers, and one for large snakes (Seyfarth et al. 1980). But while vocal signals in these monkeys (and in primates generally) can be inhibited in a top-down manner, they aren't strategically selected.

Another example of referential behavior is provided by honey bees, who use their figure-of-eight dances to signal the distance and direction of a food source (Gould & Gould 1988)—with distance being coded by the number of "waggles" through the center of the figure-of-eight, and direction being represented by the orientation of the dance on the vertical wall of the hive. Indeed, honey-bee dances are generated by a productive system, in which novel messages can be encoded that have never previously been perceived. Moreover, their dances seem to be under something at least resembling intentional control, since whether or not a foraging bee will dance on returning to the hive reflects not just the quality of the foraging patch it has visited, but also local conditions in the hive itself, such as an urgent need for nectar or water (Seeley 1995).

Aside from these two examples, referential uses of signals among animals are rare. But there have been numerous attempts to teach animals to use something like a human language, most famously by teaching parrots to speak (Pepperberg 1999), and by training chimpanzees or bonobos to use specially created lexigrams (Savage-Rumbaugh & Lewin 1994; Rumbaugh et al. 2003). In many ways the results have been impressive. Vocabularies of a few hundred words have been acquired, and the animals can answer questions, follow simple commands, and make requests. But (in stark contrast with human children) none understand more than a simple word-order "grammar," and none of the languages acquired include more than a few of the sorts of grammatical function markers (prepositions, tenses, and so on) that constitute a large proportion of human speech. Moreover (and again in contrast with human children), apes rarely use their symbol systems to comment on the world around them, or to offer information to others spontaneously (as opposed to when responding to a request).

In addition, the simple languages taught to animals have required extensive training. Human children, in contrast, learn language of their own accord, with at least approximate meanings of many common words already encoded by the age of 6 months (Bergelson & Swingley 2012), and with the full grammar of the language encoded within a few years (Tomasello 2008). During the first year of life infants already start to use language and gesture to draw caregivers' attention to things, rather than to secure their own goals. And even more impressively, deaf children brought up in hearing communities, who are thus deprived of any language model, will *invent* their own gestural languages, called "homesign." These sign systems have many of the properties of a natural language, and can be used to communicate about things displaced in both time and space, to communicate hypotheticals, to tell stories, and to comment metalinguistically on the signs of oneself and others, among other functions (Goldin-Meadow 2003; Coppola & Newport 2005; Franklin et al. 2011; Brentari & Goldin-Meadow 2017).

While the vocal productions of apes aren't intentionally produced, apes do make frequent use of gestures to communicate with others, and do so in flexible ways. But these gestures are almost entirely imperative in nature, with meanings such as, *give that to me*, or *groom me*. Apes don't comment on the world around them in the way that human children do from an early age. And surprisingly, it seems that ape gestural systems are largely innate, since many of their gestures are used in common across all primate species, but without being obviously iconic (Byrne et al. 2017). Immature apes will generally employ a multitude of different gestures on any given occasion that have the same meaning, gradually settling on those that are most effective in the local population.

Importantly for our purposes, while the simple language-like systems that have been acquired by parrots and apes can tell us a lot about their cognition, they provide little evidence that these animals can take a first-person perspective on their own mental states. While they can use symbols to express their own desires and emotions, they cannot use symbols to comment on the way those states feel to them. This doesn't show that they *aren't* phenomenally conscious, of course. But it does mean that we can't hope to get the sort of direct evidence of phenomenally conscious experience obtainable from other humans, who can tell us about their experiences and get puzzled by the "hard problem" thought experiments and the explanatory gap.

2.8 Two systems, two minds?

Having discussed evidence of working memory, reasoning, inhibitory capacities, metarepresentation, and communication in animals, let me now turn to the other main argument for a discontinuity view. This one is much better grounded empirically than the one discussed in Section 2.2 (the Generality Constraint), but turns out to be equally flawed.

Starting with the work of Kahneman and Tversky on heuristics and biases (Kahneman et al. 1982; Kahneman 2011), psychologists who study human reasoning and decision-making have mostly converged on some form of two-systems view. System 1 is supposed to be fast, parallel, unconscious in operation, and associative in nature. Call this "the intuitive system." System 2, in contrast, is supposed to be slow, serial, and conscious, and many have thought that it operates in accordance with rational rules. Call this "the reflective system." Many in the field have claimed that the intuitive system is shared with other animals, whereas the reflective system is uniquely human. In the view of such theorists, capacities for rational reflection confer on us, in effect, a whole other kind of mind (Dennett 1996; Frankish 2004, 2009; Evans 2010)—albeit, in Frankish's case, a sort of *virtual* mind, constituted by practices of mental rehearsal and mental commitment.

There is nothing intrinsically rational about reflective thinking, however. Suppose you live in a culture where people believe that the right way to make an important decision is to consult the entrails of a dead chicken. When faced with such a decision, you might have an intuitive "gut reaction" about the choice you should make. But if you stop and reflect, you will recall that you should be sacrificing a chicken, and will likely use that method instead. In this case intuitive responding might be a great deal better than reflective thinking. Indeed, there are many circumstances where this has been demonstrated experimentally. In fact, if one is trying to estimate the personal value of a number of complex outcomes, one is better off reviewing what one knows about each and then "going with one's gut" than one is when reasoning reflectively about the properties of those outcomes (Wilson & Schooler 1991; Wilson et al. 1993).

Increasingly, psychologists who work in the field have come to recognize that the only thing truly characteristic of reflective thinking is that it makes constitutive use of the resources of working memory (Evans & Stanovich 2013). But working memory isn't uniquely human, as we have already seen; and nor, it seems, is the capacity to manipulate representations in working memory using mental rehearsal, as we saw in Section 2.4. In fact, variations in human performance on reasoning tasks are explained by a combination of three factors (Stanovich 2009). One is fluid intelligence (IQ), which correlates quite strongly with working-memory abilities (Conway et al. 2003; Broadway & Engle 2010; Redick et al. 2012). A second is what psychologists refer to as "need for cognition," which roughly amounts to how inclined one is to stop and reflect before making up one's mind about anything. And the third is what Stanovich (2009) calls "mindware." This comprises one's explicit knowledge of norms and principles of reasoning. There is nothing here to suggest the existence of a novel kind of mind—just minds with either more or fewer culturally acquired cognitive resources, combined with a feature of character (reflectiveness), and greater or lesser working-memory capacities.

On the account I propose, reflective (System 2) reasoning is not uniquely human. Both humans and (some) other animals can make use of working memory to entertain and evaluate possibilities, and to rehearse potential actions. What seems different about humans is that they make *chronic* use of working memory in these ways. Whenever one isn't engaged in a task (and sometimes when one is, when one mind-wanders), one will be rehearsing things one might say, things one might do, things one could have done better, and so on. Our minds are continuously ranging over the landscape of possibilities, visiting and revisiting the options. (Indeed, this sort of unfocused mind-wandering may be one of the sources of our greater creativity.) We don't know whether any nonhuman animals spend their "down-time" in this manner. But if they did, one might expect that they would be rather more creative and innovative than they actually are. So one thing distinctive of humans may just be that they make greater *use* of reflective thinking than other animals do.

Humans can also learn cultural rules for how they should make use of their working memories, of course—they can acquire mindware. We learn multiplication tables that enable us to transform exact numerical information "in our heads," much as we can do on paper. We learn rules of logic, probability, and scientific method. When tackling a reasoning problem reflectively, then, one can—if one has acquired the right cultural knowledge—approach that problem in accordance with the norms one has learned. If those norms are good ones, then one will reason rationally, whereas if they aren't, then one won't. (Recall the norm about consulting the entrails of a chicken.) There is nothing intrinsically rational or irrational about the reflective reasoning system. That will vary with cultural input. But in creatures capable of cultural learning, such as ourselves, it can be a powerful adaptive force.

2.9 Conclusion

The human mind is fully continuous with the minds of nonhuman animals, I suggest. Most other animals are capable of compositionally structured thought, and have minds organized around a central work-space (working memory). In the course of our evolution we surely acquired some additional mental capacities, such as language. And we greatly extended the sophistication and scope of others (such as executive function). But one major source of the vast behavioral differences we noted at the outset is cultural. It is our status as cultural beings, not our possession of a radically distinct kind of mind, that explains why our achievements far surpass those of other animals (Henrich 2016). None of this entails that animals are capable of having phenomenally conscious mental states, however. Cognitive organization is one thing; phenomenally conscious qualities may be quite another.

3

The need for a theory

The present chapter argues that the problem of animal consciousness can't be tackled directly, without commitment to any particular theory of consciousness. In the course of doing so, it discusses evidence of unconscious perceptual states, as well as one recent effort to put the emergence of consciousness into phylogenetic context. Finally, it outlines the constraints that a successful theory of phenomenal consciousness should meet.

3.1 Newton's Principle

We noted in Chapter 1 that an extension of the argument that warrants us in believing in phenomenal consciousness in other adult human beings might also apply to animals, at least to some degree. Specifically, to the extent that other animals share recent evolutionary ancestry with us, have similarly organized brains, and display similar behavior, then that might provide a reason for believing in animal consciousness with a degree of confidence that tracks the extent of the similarities.

Tye (2017) develops a strategy of this sort in detail. Provided one accepts that conscious states play a causal role in the production of behavior, one can apply Newton's Principle, he thinks: similar effects have similar causes. So when one sees an animal exhibiting behavior similar to that displayed by human beings—and specifically, when one sees an animal showing flexible, perceptually grounded sensitivity to properties of its environment or its own body—then one can conclude that it enjoys conscious experience. I will argue, in contrast, that one needs a theory of consciousness (or at least a theory of the functional and/or neural correlates of consciousness) if one is to address the question of phenomenal consciousness in animals. One needs to know what consciousness *is* before one can ask about its distribution across the animal kingdom.

Human and Animal Minds: The Consciousness Questions Laid to Rest. Peter Carruthers, Oxford University Press (2019). © Peter Carruthers.
DOI: 10.1093/oso/9780198843702.001.0001

The basic idea behind Newton's Principle turns on considerations of simplicity of explanation, or Occam's razor: don't multiply explanatory factors beyond necessity. Suppose conscious experience explains some behavior B in humans, and that one observes instances of B in other animals. If one hypothesizes that the animals in question *don't* have conscious experiences, then one will have to postulate two distinct kinds of cause: the conscious states that cause B in humans, and the unconscious states that cause B in animals. It is simpler—and hence more reasonable—to accept the existence of just a single cause, thereby also unifying a wider range of data within a single causal-explanatory framework. In fact, Tye thinks, attributions of consciousness to animals can be justified on the basis of an inference to the best causal explanation, independent of background theories of consciousness as such.

Applications of Newton's Principle can be defeated by additional evidence, of course. In particular, this will be so whenever one has independent evidence of differing causal factors underlying the two sorts of behavior in question. In consequence, much of Tye's (2017) book is occupied with discussion of possible defeaters for attributions of consciousness to animals, including the question whether absence of a cerebral cortex is a defeater for conscious experience. If consciousness is realized in cortical activity of some sort in humans, and is the cause of a given behavior, but some other creatures lack a cortex altogether while exhibiting the same behavior, does that defeat the inference to consciousness as a cause? Tye argues not, on a variety of grounds—some of which we will consider in due course.

Although not espousing any particular theory of consciousness, it is plain that Tye (2017) is nevertheless a physicalist. Indeed, if he weren't, then he couldn't deploy Newton's Principle—at least, provided he accepts, as most people do, that all causes are on some level physical ones. So Tye's strategy for tackling the question of animal consciousness isn't available to a qualia realist. It is worth asking, however, whether a similar principle might apply. If some behavior B in humans is caused by brain events that have nonphysical qualia attached—perhaps attached as a matter of basic scientific law—and one observes behavior B in animals, can one conclude that the brain events that cause B in animals will likewise come with qualia attached?

Plainly this argument won't go through, however, unless one knows precisely which properties of the brain events in ourselves mandate the attachment of qualia. For there will inevitably be many differences between the brains of humans and other animals. In effect, one would need to know which properties figure in the basic laws in question. It seems plain, then, that qualia realists can't hope to co-opt a variant of Tye's theory-free strategy. On the contrary, they will need the backing of a psycho-physical theory in order to tackle the question of the distribution of qualia across the animal kingdom.

Crucial for Tye's application of Newton's Principle is what he calls the "simple view" of consciousness: phenomenal consciousness just *is* experience. This isn't intended as a merely definitional move.[1] Rather, the simple view reflects Tye's commitment to the claim that all forms of perception are conscious. Although he allows a use for the phrase "unconscious vision," for example, he insists that this just refers to conscious visual states *of which* one isn't conscious (that is, states one lacks transitive creature consciousness of). So unconscious perceptual states, for Tye, are just states that we lack higher-order awareness of; but all such states are nevertheless phenomenally-conscious ones. For instance, he explains the famous case of absent-minded driving (Armstrong 1968), by saying that the driver has phenomenally-conscious visual perceptions throughout, but lacks higher-order awareness of what he is seeing until something unexpected happens, thereby restoring that awareness.

This account of the absent-minded driver case is quite implausible, on both intuitive grounds and in light of the evidence of unconscious sensorimotor visual guidance to be discussed in Section 3.2. Granted, the driver is unable to report what he has been seeing, which suggests lack of higher-order awareness. But equally, he is unable to report details of what transpired on the road, which requires only first-order perception. Indeed, it is characteristic of such cases that one lacks any memory of the period of travel during which one was absent-minded; and there is no reason whatever to think that memory formation depends on higher-order awareness. Moreover, there is likewise no reason to think that what

---

[1] It is quite common for people to insist on restricting the use of the term "experience" to cases of perception that are phenomenally conscious. Although I don't share this intuition, talk of "unconscious experience" strikes many people as anomalous or somehow contradictory. I myself use the terms "experience" and "perception" interchangeably in this book, without commitment to the phenomenally-conscious status of the states involved.

accounts for one "coming to" from such driving—for example, when a child is seen playing in the road up ahead—is that one becomes meta-aware of one's visual experience as such. It isn't higher-order awareness that explains one's subsequent avoidance behavior, but just awareness. When one returns attention to the road, the relevant content that motivates applying the brakes is surely, *a child is in the road*, not, *I'm seeing a child in the road.*

Given his commitment to the simple view, Tye (2017) thinks that behavioral evidence of seeing (or any other form of sensory perception) is automatically evidence of consciousness, warranting an application of Newton's Principle in the absence of an effective defeater. But the case of the absent-minded driver suggests that the simple view is false. And in Section 3.2 this conclusion will be strengthened and corroborated. Flexible forms of behavior can be—and often are—guided by forms of perception that are wholly unconscious. And that is sufficient to block any straightforward application of Newton's Principle. It will require a theory of the difference between conscious and unconscious perception, and their respective roles in influencing behavior, before we can even begin to draw inferences about conscious experience in animals.

Section 3.2 will consider evidence of environmentally sensitive behavior in humans that is actually caused by perceptual states that are deeply unconscious; and Section 3.3 will then continue with discussion of states that are more contingently unconscious. These two sections will provide some of the data that a good theory of consciousness needs to explain, as will be elaborated in Section 3.6. But what about actions of the sort that are definitely caused by conscious experience in humans? Would it be possible to apply Newton's Principle if we could find the same or similar behavior in animals? Not in the absence of a good theory of consciousness, I will suggest. This topic will be taken up in Section 3.4, following our discussion of the varieties of unconscious forms of perception.

3.2 Deeply unconscious perception

Tye's (2017) reliance on Newton's Principle is flawed. And the simple view that equates all forms of perception with consciousness is mistaken. For it neglects a wide range of environmentally sensitive forms of behavior in humans that are at least to some degree flexible, but are caused by *un*conscious perceptual states. Consider, for example, a baseball batter facing a fastball traveling at 96 miles per hour. The distance between the pitching plate and the batting plate is 60 feet, hence there are about 55 feet from the point at which the pitcher releases the ball to the point of contact for the batter. The fastball will travel that distance in around 400 milliseconds. In that 400-millisecond interval the batter has to estimate the trajectory of the ball (will it pass through the strike-zone or not?), initiate a swing, and then plan and execute the motor instructions for a specific type of swing, aimed at the expected location of the ball.

Our best estimate of the time that elapses between presentation of a stimulus (in this case, light hitting the retina from the ball as it exits the pitcher's hand) and conscious experience is somewhere around 350 milliseconds, however (Dehaene 2014). It is likely, then, that the swing is initiated *before* the batter's perception of the trajectory of the ball becomes conscious, and that the execution of the swing is likewise guided by unconscious perceptual states throughout. It seems that while the batter's swing is *accompanied* by conscious experience, it isn't caused by it. So Newton's Principle cannot apply. This means that when one observes an animal responding to its environment in this sort of swift online manner, one can't use Newton's Principle to infer that it enjoys conscious experience.

Admittedly, the timing estimate for conscious experience mentioned above is drawn from work done within the global-workspace framework. Other theories of consciousness might predict a swifter onset for conscious experience. This is likely to be true of Block's (2011a) fragile-short-term-memory account, for example, since contents are held in this sort of memory as a result of an initial forward sweep of processing through the visual system, and are only broadcast subsequently following the impact of attention. But this just emphasizes my central point: one cannot know which perceptual states are conscious and which of them cause any given type of behavior in the absence of a good theory of consciousness. It should be noted, however, that the contents of fragile-short-term-memory are unlikely to cause swift online responses, either, since they belong to the ventral visual stream, whereas it is contents in the dorsal stream that guide online action, as we will see next.

The existence of unconscious forms of perception is vindicated, and the data above are explained, by the discovery of two visual systems in humans (Milner & Goodale 1995; for recent reviews, see Goodale 2014 and Goodale & Milner 2018). As is now familiar to many people, visual processing proceeds in two distinct cortical streams.[2] The ventral stream runs forward from the visual cortex at the back of the brain through the lower portions of the temporal lobes along the side, whereas the dorsal stream runs upward through the parietal lobes toward the somatosensory and motor regions that stretch in two bands across the top of the brain on either side of the central sulcus.

Processing within the ventral stream results in object recognition, with the relative positions of objects represented in allocentric space. Processing in the dorsal stream, in contrast, is coded in limb-centered and body-centered spatial coordinates, and is specialized for online guidance of action. Moreover, the two streams utilize different cellular pathways that remain distinct from one another all the way back to the retina. The ventral steam is a continuation of the parvocellular pathway, whereas the dorsal stream is a continuation of the magnocellular pathway. Notably, given the points about speed made in the previous paragraphs, transmission of signals through the magnocellular (dorsal) pathway is significantly faster than through the parvocellular one.

Multiple lines of evidence suggest that, while the two visual streams interact with one another in their early stages, their outputs are distinct. These include data from neurotypical people as well as from those who have suffered neurological damage (Goodale 2014). For example, damage to the dorsal stream can result in optic ataxia, in which visually guided reaching and grasping becomes halting and inaccurate while conscious experience is fully intact. In contrast, damage to the ventral stream can result in agnosia (an inability to consciously identify objects and shapes), while leaving visually guided motor control intact. Indeed, it seems that while the outputs of the ventral stream *can* be unconscious (see Section 3.3 for discussion), the outputs of the dorsal stream are deeply inaccessible to consciousness.

---

[2] Similar distinctions can be drawn with respect to other sensory systems. For the case of audition, see Rauschecker & Tian (2000), Hickok & Poeppel (2004), and Rauschecker (2018). For the case of body-sense, see Dijkerman & de Haan (2007).

Consider, in particular, D.F., a patient with bilateral temporal-lobe damage who has been extensively studied (Milner & Goodale 1995). D.F. suffers from complete visual-form agnosia. While she can still experience colors and textures (and hence might be able to guess at the identity of a banana from its distinctive yellow color and mottled texture), she can no longer experience the shapes or orientations of objects. For example, she cannot recognize a banana from a line drawing of one, she is at chance when judging the orientation of a pencil (whether upright or horizontal), and she is at chance when judging whether a block of wood is square or oblong. But her reaching-and-grasping behavior is indistinguishable from normal. She will orient her hand appropriately when grasping a horizontally or vertically held pencil, using a normal finger grip (but without being able to report the pencil's shape or orientation in advance). And she is just as accurate as neurotypical people when posting a letter through a letter-box arranged at various angles (while remaining at chance when consciously judging those angles).

It is also thought to be the dorsal visual stream that underlies the well-known phenomenon of *blindsight*, in which people with damage to the primary visual cortex become blind (that is to say: incapable of conscious experience) in a portion of their visual field, while being well above chance in identifying simple shapes and patterns of movement presented in their blind field (Weiskrantz 1986; Persaud et al. 2011). For there are projections from the retina to the parietal cortex via a subcortical region known as the superior colliculus (bypassing primary visual cortex), whereas there are no such subcortical projections direct to the temporal cortex. Moreover, we know that the monkey Helen, who had the whole of the primary visual cortex surgically removed, could nevertheless move around and pick up objects normally, while being unable to identify objects except by touch or taste (Humphrey 1974).[3]

---

[3] It could well be that blindsighted people don't generally act as the monkey did because they *believe* themselves to be blind, and hence inhibit spontaneous use of the sensorimotor visual system. It should be noted, however, that what initially suggested to investigators that blindsight in humans might be a possibility was the observation that a blindsight patient could walk across a cluttered room much more easily than one might have expected; see Weiskrantz (1986). The same behavior has since been demonstrated in someone with complete bilateral damage to the primary visual cortex who lacks conscious visual experience altogether (De Gelder et al. 2008).

It appears to be the dorsal stream, too, that underlies habitual sensorimotor action. There is good reason to think that habitual behavior can occur without being initiated or guided by conscious experience (Lisman & Sternberg 2013; Wood & Rünger 2015). Moreover, we know that the ventral stream projects to a subcortical structure known as the ventral striatum, which is heavily involved in goal formation and value-based decision-making; whereas the dorsal visual stream projects to dorsolateral striatum, which is the locus of sensorimotor control in habitual responding (Saint-Cyr et al. 1990). Indeed, as control of behavior shifts during learning from goal-oriented to habitual responding, one can trace a corresponding shift in the networks involved from those centered on the ventral striatum to those involving the dorsolateral striatum (Redgrave et al. 2010; Burton et al. 2015). This comports well with one's everyday experience. One can engage in routine activities (like driving a car along a well-known route) without conscious awareness of the stimuli involved in the activity, and while one's conscious mind is wholly engaged with other matters.

It seems likely that sleepwalking implicates a similar dorsal route. While there are a number of different kinds of motor-involving sleep disorder, sleepwalking is the sort that takes place during the two deepest forms of sleep, in the absence of any of the rapid eye-movements (REMs) that would normally indicate the presence of dreaming. (That said, sleepwalkers do sometimes report dream-like experiences after waking from a sleepwalking episode; Oudiette et al. 2009.) Indeed, sleepwalking (and in some documented instances, even sleep *driving*) takes place with the prefrontal cortex and most other regions of the cortex fully suppressed (as in non-REM sleep generally). Yet the eyes are open and there is local activation of sensory cortices, the amygdala, and motor regions of the cingulate cortex (Terzaghi et al. 2012; Januszko et al. 2016).[4]

Finally, in this catalog of environmentally sensitive actions that can take place in the absence of conscious experience, one should include the behavioral components of emotional states such as fear and anger. Although such emotions generally give rise to distinctive forms of

---

[4] The amygdala is a subcortical structure heavily implicated in emotion-processing; the cingulate cortex lies deep in the fold between the two cerebral hemispheres, wrapping around over the top of the corpus callosum, which is the big bundle of nerve fibers that links together the two hemispheres.

conscious experience (at least in humans), the behaviors in question are initiated directly and swiftly—and independently of conscious experience—by subcortical circuits that include especially the amygdala (LeDoux 1996, 2017; Panksepp 1998; Childress et al. 2008; Olofsson et al. 2008; Tamietto et al. 2009). It is these circuits that are responsible for the fight-or-flight response, setting in train a variety of physiological changes (increased heart-rate and breathing-rate, release of the stress-related hormone cortisol into the bloodstream, and so on), activating emotion-expressive facial expressions (the fear-face, the anger-face, the disgust-face), and initiating adaptive forms of behavior guided by affordances of the environment (fleeing, freezing, fighting, and more). Such emotion-expressive actions will automatically run through to completion unless inhibited by executive signals from the prefrontal cortex.

Emotionally arousing stimuli will attract one's attention, of course; hence one will soon undergo conscious experiences of the relevant events. No doubt such experiences play a role in sustaining and/or modulating one's ongoing emotions. But they aren't necessary (indeed, they aren't present) at the outset. Emotion-expressive behavior is initially caused by perceptual contents that are *unconscious*. We can thus explain Tye's (2017) example of someone visiting the reptile exhibit in a zoo who jumps back in alarm when a snake strikes at the glass. It is, as Tye points out, *like something* to leap back in fear. One's experiences of fear and of movement are conscious ones. But those experiences aren't the ones that initiate fear in the first place; nor are they the ones that cause one to leap back. But they *do* play a role in causing one's fear to subside, perhaps as soon as one notices the solid glass of the cage-front that is positioned between the snake and oneself.

Given that there are multiple instances of unconscious perception, Tye's (2017) simple view is false: we cannot equate perception as such with phenomenal consciousness. Notice, moreover, that all of the cases of unconscious perception discussed in this section might be described as *deeply unconscious*. For they are the output of sensorimotor networks specialized for fine-grained control and/or initiation of behavior, and as such they are incapable of being conscious. In cases of regular attentive action, indeed, there will be two sets of perceptual states constructed in parallel (albeit on different temporal time-scales). One is the output of ventral-stream processing and can be conscious, whereas the other is produced more swiftly by the dorsal stream, and can't be conscious. In Section 3.3, in contrast, we will consider evidence of unconscious perceptual states produced by the ventral stream that are only contingently unconscious. Both of these kinds of conscious/unconscious distinction will need to be explained by any adequate theory of conscious experience.

3.3 Contingent unconsciousness

In addition to deeply unconscious perceptual states produced by the dorsal—sensorimotor—visual system, there are also contingently unconscious states produced by the ventral system. These unconscious percepts can nevertheless influence—or "prime"—behavior in various ways. The extent to which they are inaccessible to consciousness comes in degrees. At one extreme there are perceptual contents that Kouider & Dehaene (2007) refer to as "subliminal." These are percepts produced by stimuli that are especially faint and fleeting, realized in neural activity that is too weak and short-lived to be boosted over the threshold for consciousness by attention. So subliminal percepts are ones that can't be conscious, no matter how hard subjects try to make them so. Nevertheless, they occur within a visual subsystem whose outputs *can* be conscious; and it can be true that, had the stimuli been a little more vivid or long-lasting, then the content in question *could* have been conscious. (In contrast, there is nothing that can make contents produced by the dorsal visual system become conscious.)

Kouider & Dehaene (2007) contrast subliminal percepts with those they describe as "preconscious," which only require targeting by attention to become conscious. Such contents remain unconscious, in effect, as a result of a sort of inattentional blindness. Many famous demonstrations of the general phenomenon are readily available on the internet, including the video of a man in a gorilla suit who interrupts a basketball game. He stands fully visible in the middle of the court and beats his chest, but remains invisible to most experimental participants who have been given an attentionally demanding task, such as counting the number of times the ball is touched by players in white T-shirts.

In carefully controlled conditions, the same phenomenon can be exploited experimentally using a technique known as the "attentional blink" (Raymond et al. 1992; Marti et al. 2012). In this paradigm, participants are shown a rapid sequence of stimuli with the task of identifying one of the stimuli later in the sequence. On surprise probe trials, however, they can be asked whether they saw one of the stimuli earlier in the sequence. Although the earlier stimulus is easily visible in the absence of a task, when attention is directed toward the later stimulus consciousness of the earlier one can be lost. One nice feature of this technique is that the timing and vividness of the stimulus parameters can be titrated for each individual participant in such a way that the "blinked" stimulus is visible on around 50 percent of the trials. This enables experimenters to vary and compare conscious and unconscious conditions while keeping the stimuli exactly the same between them.

In addition to the attentional blink, a number of other techniques have commonly been employed to investigate the nature and extent of unconscious priming effects. One is *backward masking*, where a very brief stimulus (often presented for around only 20 milliseconds) is followed swiftly by a series of other stimuli, which "drown out" the neural activity produced by the masked stimulus before it can reach the threshold for consciousness (Breitmeyer & Ogmen 2000). Another experimental technique is *continuous flash suppression*. This builds on the phenomenon of binocular rivalry, in which distinct images are presented to the two eyes. These compete with one another in the visual system, with the result that only one of them is conscious at any one time (Tong et al. 1998). In continuous flash suppression, an image (of a face, say) is shown continuously to one eye while the other eye is presented with a flashing Mondrian-type stimulus (Wilke et al. 2003; Tsuchiya & Koch 2005). The latter dominates initially, while the former stimulus emerges into consciousness later from the noise. During that interval one can investigate the effects of the suppressed (unconscious) image on behavior.

In general, priming effects are investigated via facilitatory or inhibitory effects on subsequent goal-driven action. For example, if the task is to press one key if an image or name of a living thing is presented, but another key if an image or name of an artefact is shown, then unconscious presentation of a congruent word or image will speed reaction times, whereas presentation of an incongruous one will slow them. (Note that the actions here aren't habitual ones, and don't simply depend on the resources of the sensorimotor system.) Such experiments have shown that unconscious perceptions can be quite abstract. For instance, it can be the *meaning* of an unconsciously presented word (not the word itself) that primes subsequent action (Dehaene et al. 1998; Kouider & Dehaene 2009).[5]

Indeed, unconscious priming can even depend on extraction of concepts as abstract as SAME and DIFFERENT (Lin & Murray 2014). More remarkable still, it can depend on unconscious *combinations* of concepts (van Gaal et al. 2014). Suppose two words are presented in succession to form phrases with positive or negative meanings, such as "not happy" or "very happy," but are masked below the threshold for consciousness. These unconsciously presented phrases will completely change people's responses to consciously presented follow-up terms such as "love" or "war," by producing congruous or incongruous three-word phrases (e.g. "very happy love" versus "not happy love"). In fact, some researchers have even claimed that unconscious presentations of simple arithmetic problems such as "9-3" will prime or inhibit responses to potential solutions, suggesting that the answer has been computed unconsciously (Sklar et al. 2012).

There should be no doubt, then, that contingently unconscious percepts produced by the ventral visual system can have an influence on behavior, in addition to the deeply unconscious products of the dorsal sensorimotor system. These findings are among those that any good theory of consciousness will need to account for, also.

3.4 Where consciousness seems necessary

Sections 3.2 and 3.3 have demonstrated the falsity of the "simple view" espoused by Tye (2017), which equates consciousness with perception. Numerous forms of behavior are caused by unconscious perceptual states. At the same time, those sections have introduced a body of data that any acceptable theory of phenomenal consciousness will need to

---

[5] At the same time such experiments have decisively refuted a view that was once widely accepted, that "binding" of shape, color, and other properties into a single percept depends on attention and consciousness (Kahneman & Triesman 1984). For there is no way that the meaning of a word can be extracted unless the shapes of the individual letters are recognized and bound together into a single spatial unit.

accommodate. This point will be elaborated and developed in Section 3.6. The present section takes up the challenge left over from Section 3.1: even if we can't apply Newton's Principle in connection with *all* forms of perceptually guided behavior, surely it can be applied to behavior that *is* caused by conscious experience in humans? If there are types of behavior displayed by humans for which phenomenally-conscious experience is necessary, and we find similar behavior in animals, can't we *then* conclude that the animals in question have conscious experiences?

Various proposals of this sort have been made in the literature. For instance, Varner (2012) suggests that both flexible reversal-learning and systematic probability-matching behavior in animals can demonstrate the presence of phenomenally-conscious experience, since such learning seems to require consciousness in ourselves.[6] And Bronfman et al. (2016a, 2016b) argue that flexible evaluative learning, including both operant conditioning and second-order conditioning, is a reliable indicator of phenomenal consciousness in animals—again because it seemingly requires conscious experience in ourselves. The details of these proposals needn't concern us, since any such suggestion faces a decisive objection, grounded in something that has been accepted since Nisbett & Wilson (1977), at least. This is that causality isn't an introspectable property of our mental lives. Even if it were true that mental states of all sorts can be introspected (which I deny: Carruthers 2011a), the causal relationships among them, and between them and subsequent behavior, can't be.

Suppose we find in our own case that some behavior B is always preceded by a type of phenomenally-conscious state P. That much can be discovered on the basis of introspection and memory. But how do we know that the phenomenal status of P plays a *causal* role in the production of B? For one alternative possibility could be that both P and B are products of an underlying common cause, which exists outside of our awareness. And then it might be that in animals the common cause in question results in B *without* producing the accompanying phenomenal state P.

---

[6] Varner (2012) also argues at length that evidence of pain-perception in animals is evidence of phenomenal consciousness, seemingly assuming that pains are necessarily conscious. This is false. But the case of pain will be considered separately in Ch. 8.

Now, this challenge as it stands can perhaps be answered in the absence of a theory of phenomenal consciousness. For our best theory of the cognitive processes involved in the production of behavior B might implicate the phenomenal-state P, and might treat the latter as necessary for B to be produced. But a deeper problem remains. This is that it might not be the phenomenally-conscious status of P, as such, that is involved in the causation of B. The state P might possess two distinct sets of properties, those in virtue of which it causes behavior B, and those in virtue of which it is phenomenally conscious. We can't know (or even reasonably believe) that this isn't the case in the absence of a theory of phenomenal consciousness, I suggest. And note that this objection is fully consistent with Newton's Principle. For it can be the very same properties of the state that causes B in humans that also causes B in animals, in which case we aren't required to postulate two distinct types of cause. It is just that in humans the state in question has some *additional* properties that render it phenomenally conscious. Moreover, these might be properties (like language or metacognition) that we are required to believe in anyway, so there would be no violation of Occam's razor.

To illustrate the point, reflect on a specific example. Consider an act such as the deliberate choice of one alternative over another, which is reliably preceded by conscious experience in ourselves. Specifically, consider prospection-based decision-making, of the sort humans engage in when they reach decisions reflectively but nondiscursively. The visual and other images one entertains when one engages in prospection are phenomenally conscious. And we saw in Chapter 2 that there is reason to think that some animals, too, engage in such reasoning. So can we conclude that they, too, are subjects of phenomenally-conscious imagery?

Of course, we would first have to know whether prospection in humans can take place unconsciously as well as consciously. And in any case it is difficult be confident, on the basis of current evidence, that animals are solving planning problems of the sort we considered in the same way as a human would. But as we also saw in Chapter 2, there is evidence in other animals of some of the systems that enable prospection in humans—specifically, attention and working memory. So let us assume that the New Caledonian crows in Taylor et al.'s (2010) experiment solved the problem by mentally rehearsing the actions open to them, sustaining the resulting images in working memory, and evaluating likely success on that basis. Still, how are we to know (in the absence of a good theory of consciousness) whether the underlying factors that make these images phenomenally-conscious in the human case are among those that cause the choice? It might be that only a subset of the factors that render imagery conscious are actually involved in causing the choice; and it might be that only the latter subset is involved in reflective choosing in other animals. Indeed, it might be the case that consciousness is epiphenomenal, not in general, but in respect of the type of behavior in question.

To make the point more concrete, suppose that phenomenal-consciousness depends on some threshold being crossed for the extent of informational integration of the states in question with others. (Integrated-information theories of consciousness will be considered in Chapter 4.) It would then be possible that the images deployed by the New Caledonian crows fall below that threshold, whereas human imagery is generally above it. Or suppose that phenomenal-consciousness depends on the presence of higher-order awareness of the states in question. (Higher-order theories of consciousness will also be discussed in Chapter 4.) Then it might be just the images themselves, interacting via working memory with evaluative systems, that explains choice, not the accompanying—consciousness-determining—higher-order thoughts. Until we know what the relevant factors are underlying phenomenally-conscious experience, it is impossible to know. And that means we need a theory of consciousness.

3.5 The origins of subjectivity

We have considered Tye's (2017) solution to the problem of animal consciousness, and found it wanting. A recent suggestion by Godfrey-Smith (2016) is also worth considering. This is that we might begin to understand the emergence of consciousness in evolution by breaking consciousness down into its components.[7] Specifically, he thinks that

---

[7] Godfrey-Smith actually uses the term "subjectivity," in this context, suggesting that it is simpler than full-blown consciousness of the sort humans enjoy. But subjectivity is still supposed to be the way things are *like* for the organism. In my own use of the term "consciousness" I too intend—like Godfrey-Smith—to refer to the subjective feel of experience.

sensory subjectivity and *affective* subjectivity might have evolved separately, and each might be present individually in distinct lineages. Tentatively, he suggests that wasps might possess sensory subjectivity without affective subjectivity. Their lives may be organized by abstract fixed-action plans (for mating, nest-building, and so on) in the absence of any capacity for evaluative learning or decision-making, but nevertheless guided in sophisticated ways by sensory and cognitive information. Slugs, in contrast, might have affective subjectivity without sensory subjectivity. For they are capable of instrumental learning, but have only the most rudimentary forms of sensory access to the world, and seemingly lack anything resembling a "world model."

While these ideas are interesting—and indeed promising, in their way—I think they conflate different notions of subjectivity. All forms of perception are "subjective" in the sense that they represent only those aspects and properties of the world that can be detected by an organism's sensory transducers. Hence all perception is subjective in the sense of being *partial*. Moreover, once organisms reach a stage of cognitive complexity where they start to encode some sort of model of the surrounding world through their sensory contact with it, then the result is subjective in an even deeper sense. For what is represented will only comprise those aspects of the world that potentially *matter* to the organism (whether this is explicitly represented in the organism's values, or implicit in the lifestyle that has been selected for it by evolution).

Likewise, all affect, and all valuation, is subjective, in the sense of coding objects and events as good or bad *for the organism*. Even if there are such things as mind-independent values, as some philosophers maintain, unless one of those values is simply *being adaptive*, the affective systems of organisms won't track them. Rather, they will track objects, properties, and events engagement with which, or avoidance of which, have increased the inclusive fitness of that organism's ancestors.

None of this has anything much to do with the sense of "subjective" that characterizes phenomenal consciousness, however. Recall that the concept of phenomenal consciousness is first-personal. The most direct way to characterize it is to attend to some experience or feeling that one has and think, "Consciousness comprises states like *this*." It may turn out that having an internal model of the world is sufficient for having a (perceptual) state like *this*. But to suggest so is to put forward a substantive theory of consciousness. And in any case, such a theory seems incapable of explaining even the basic distinction between conscious and unconscious perception in ourselves. For human cognitive systems and sensory processes involve multiple mental models that don't figure in consciousness. Similarly, it might turn out that a capacity for instrumental learning is what makes an affective state of any sort feel like *this*. But again this to advance a substantive theory of what makes affective valence conscious. And there is nothing in our first-person conception of our own affective states that requires us to accept such a theory.

Moreover, we have already seen in Section 3.2 that sophisticated, flexible, sensorimotor behavior in humans can be guided by perceptions that are *un*conscious. So the fact that wasps, for example, implement their motor routines in ways that are guided, in detail, by the perceptual affordances of their environment does nothing to show that their perceptual states have *feel* or are *like something* to undergo. The same is true in the domain of emotion and affect. We know that there are multiple forms of evaluation, and multiple affective states, that remain unconscious in humans (Winkielman & Berridge 2004; Barrett & Bar 2009; Pessoa 2013; Smith & Lane 2016). So the fact that slugs are capable of evaluative learning does nothing to show that their affective states are phenomenally-conscious ones.

In light of our discussion both here and in Section 3.2, however, someone might nevertheless want to say that the wasp is *transitively creature conscious* of aspects of its environment (and also that the slug is *aware of* the goodness of the substances it ingests). Might this be what Godfrey-Smith has in mind? Supposing that our sketch of the wasp's mental life is correct, can we describe her as *conscious of* the mud she collects for her nest, or as *aware of* the tree she uses as a landmark to guide her route home? These descriptions seem plausible and natural enough, even if we are clear that the wasp is incapable of evaluative learning and engages in nothing resembling value-based decision-making. This suggests that sensorimotor forms of perception might be sufficient for creature consciousness.

On the other hand, however, we would surely resist saying that the blindsight subject tested by De Gelder et al. (2008) is conscious of the obstacles he successfully navigates around, since he will tell us at the same time that he is completely blind and can't see them. This would suggest, in contrast, that transitive creature consciousness needs to be grounded in perceptual states that are to some degree access-conscious, at least. In fact, given the distinction developed in Section 3.2 between unconscious kinds of sensorimotor perception, on the one hand, and the perceptual states that can inform planning and decision making, on the other, we need to decide what should be done with the language of transitive creature consciousness. For I doubt that ordinary intuition can settle the matter.

One option would be to allow that there are different *kinds* of transitive creature consciousness, much as we allow that there are different kinds of belief (as noted in Chapter 1). We could say that the wasp has one sort of creature consciousness, while saying that what the blind-sighted person lacks is a different kind of creature consciousness. Another option would be to restrict creature consciousness to cases where the perceptual states that guide behavior are available to a set of central decision-making processes (and are thus to some degree access conscious). This would mean *denying* that the wasp is conscious of the mud she collects. And yet another possibility would restrict creature consciousness to cases where the underlying perceptual states are *phenomenally* conscious, thus narrowing its extension quite drastically if the arguments of Chapter 7 are sound.

I don't have (nor need to have) a horse in this race. But given that some theorists in the field are apt to muddle together creature consciousness with phenomenal consciousness (as we will see in Chapter 4, and as may also have happened here), it might be better for scientific purposes to drop the former language altogether. We should confine ourselves to stating what a creature *perceives*, while being explicit about the role or roles that its perceptual states play in its overall mental economy. And we can then inquire separately whether its perceptual states are phenomenally conscious or not.

3.6 Constraints on a theory

It is plain that Varner (2012), Godfrey-Smith (2016), Tye (2017), and others are mistaken. We can't hope for insight into, let alone a resolution of, the distribution of phenomenal consciousness across the animal kingdom without first settling on a *theory* of consciousness. And since our concept of phenomenal consciousness is a first-person one, that theory will need to be constructed primarily from evidence collected in our own case (the human case). The only truly direct evidence one has of phenomenal consciousness is one's own, of course. But other people can provide us with evidence that comes close. Not only do they respond to the world (and to events happening to their bodies) in similar ways to oneself while sharing a nervous system and brain that closely resembles one's own, but they can describe their experiences to us in the sorts of first-person ways that make it reasonable to believe that they, too, have experiences *like this*.[8]

What should a successful theory of phenomenal consciousness look like? It may be helpful to think of the task as falling into two distinct parts: one empirical and one philosophical. Empirical data and theorizing are necessary for us to discover the functional and/or neural correlates of phenomenal consciousness. Which brain networks, playing what roles, are minimally necessary and jointly sufficient for phenomenal consciousness to occur? Philosophical argument is then needed to establish whether, and if so how, the resulting account can provide a successful reductive explanation of phenomenal consciousness. I will say something briefly about each of these tasks in turn.

One thing that a good theory of consciousness needs to do is explain the difference between conscious and unconscious forms of perception. It needs to tell us about the brain networks and their respective functional roles that underlie both conscious and deeply unconscious (sensorimotor) perception. Likewise, a good theory needs to explain the difference between conscious experience, on the one hand, and subliminal and preconscious perceptual states, on the other. For this we need carefully controlled experiments together with data collected using various forms of brain-imaging (fMRI, EEG, MEG, and so on), as well as

---

[8] This conclusion isn't strictly forced on us, of course. Remember the conceivability of zombies. It is at least conceptually possible that although other people behave and talk just like me, their experiences aren't really *like anything* on the inside. It is conceivable that everyone but myself is a zombie. But it isn't reasonable to believe so. An inference to the best explanation warrants concluding that other humans, at least, have states that are *like something*, as we saw in Ch. 1.

from direct neural recordings where available, and also from instances of neurological damage.

In what follows I propose to set aside theories that are incapable of explaining even these basic distinctions. These include panpsychism (Strawson 2006) as well as those that draw on subatomic quantum indeterminacies (Hameroff & Penrose 1996), which are surely incapable of doing so. (If every particle in the universe has a little bit of phenomenal consciousness attached, then there *is no* conscious/unconscious distinction, for example.) We will focus on the set of theories that might have the resources to account for the distinction between conscious and unconscious mental states.

There are five such theories that are taken seriously (at least by some people) in the current literature. One is integrated-information theory, proposed initially by Tononi (Tononi 2008; Tononi & Koch 2015). Another identifies consciousness with states of the upper brain-stem, which integrates perceptual, evaluative, and motor information (Merker 2007). A third equates phenomenally-conscious experience with the contents of a fragile form of short-term memory (distinct from working memory), realized in mid-level sensory processing regions, proposed by Block (2011a). A fourth is higher-order thought theory, defended (in different forms) by Rosenthal (2005) and the present author (Carruthers 2000). Finally, there is global-workspace theory, which has been proposed and elaborated in slightly different forms by Baars (1988, 1997, 2002), Tye (1995, 2000), Prinz (2012), Dehaene (2014), and others. Chapter 4 will consider and evaluate the first four of these five kinds of account in turn, critiquing them while noting their implications for the question of animal consciousness. Chapter 5 will then present and defend the global-workspace account.

In addition to providing us with the functional and/or neural correlates of consciousness, a good theory of consciousness should explain why consciousness is so puzzling—why it should seem to give rise to the so-called "hard problem" (Chalmers 1996, 2018). This part of the task is philosophical, not empirical.[9] Since I am rejecting any appeal to qualia,

---

[9] I don't mean to suggest here that there is a sharp distinction between the two. Indeed, most theories of consciousness integrate and interweave both empirical and conceptual considerations in ways that can be hard to separate. The distinction I am drawing here is more rhetorical than substantive.

we need a theory that successfully explains away the appearance of an explanatory gap, explains why zombies should be conceivable although they aren't really possible, and so on. Indeed, we need to explain why people should be so tempted to believe in qualia, thinking that their experiences have intrinsic properties that aren't physical ones. Likewise, we should be able to explain why conscious experiences should seem ineffable (indescribable) and private to their possessors. These tasks will occupy us in Chapter 6. Then, armed with the resulting best overall theory, the remainder of the book will tackle the question of the implications of that theory for the distribution of phenomenal consciousness among animals, as well as the practical implications (if any) of our conclusions.

3.7 Conclusion

This chapter has argued that one cannot address the problem of animal consciousness without commitment to any particular theory of consciousness. Since we now know that humans routinely undergo unconscious perceptual states, all forms of which can influence our behavior, we cannot simply conclude from the fact that an animal is displaying perceptual sensitivity to its environment or its own body that the perceptual states in question are conscious ones. We first need a theory of the distinction between conscious and unconscious forms of perception. Indeed, even in the case of human actions that are caused by conscious experience, we cannot know in advance of a theory whether the consciousness-determining properties are themselves among the causal factors that produce the action. So even if we can identify similar actions in animals, we cannot use Newton's Principle to infer the presence of consciousness as a cause.

This chapter has also suggested that selection among candidate theories of consciousness should respect two rather different sorts of constraint. One is that it should explain the precise contours of the conscious/unconscious distinction that has emerged from decades of experimental inquiry. The other is that it should explain people's temptation to believe in qualia, eliminating (or at least explaining away) the explanatory gap.

4

Some initial possibilities

The present chapter surveys and critiques the leading competitors lined up against the global-workspace theory of consciousness, which will be presented and defended in Chapter 5. These are: integrated-information theory (Tononi 2008); a theory that identifies phenomenal consciousness with information represented in the upper brain-stem (Merker 2007); a theory that identifies it with the contents of a fragile form of short-term memory, distinct from working memory (Block 2011a); higher-order thought theory (Rosenthal 2005); and dual-content theory, which is also higher-order in nature (Carruthers 2000). The implications of these theories for the distribution of consciousness across the animal kingdom are also considered.

4.1 Integrated-information theory

According to integrated-information theory, consciousness can be measured by the extent to which information is integrated in the brain via complex reverberating feedback loops and functional connections (Tononi 2008; Tononi & Koch 2015). One immediate problem with the theory is that integrated information is a matter of degree, whereas (as we noted in Chapter 1), phenomenal consciousness is either categorically present or categorically absent. This suggests that the theory might better serve as an account of creature consciousness (whether transitive, intransitive, or both), which likewise admits of degrees. And indeed, Tononi & Koch (2015) themselves tout the benefits of integrated-information theory in accounting for partially conscious states of light anesthesia, and in accounting for specific experiences (such as perceptions of red as opposed to blue), which will correspond to distinct packages of integrated information.

Human and Animal Minds: The Consciousness Questions Laid to Rest. Peter Carruthers, Oxford University Press (2019). © Peter Carruthers.
DOI: 10.1093/oso/9780198843702.001.0001

Moreover, since information integration is a graded notion, and is present in many aspects of cognition, the theory implies a limited form of panpsychism, as Tononi & Koch (2015) themselves note.[1] For even paradigmatically unconscious blindsight-like states will contain some degree of informational integration, as will states of subsystems within the cerebellum and spinal cord. Indeed, even a single neuron will be to some degree phenomenally conscious, on this view, since it serves to integrate the information received via its dendrites. Moreover, Tononi & Koch themselves note that even a photosensitive diode with a memory component will be to some small degree conscious, as will people during the deepest phases of sleep. But these claims are wholly unmotivated. Why would anyone want to claim that mental states during deep sleep are a little bit phenomenally conscious, except when dictated by a theory? For there are no first-person facts here that we know of that need to be explained.

Notice, however, that it isn't actually mandatory for an integrated-information theory to claim that phenomenal consciousness is a matter of degree, even though it is developed out of materials that admit of degrees. Tononi could have—and arguably should have—proceeded differently. He could have started from first-person facts about phenomenal consciousness in humans, characterizing the degree of informational integration that is present in even the most fleeting and fragmentary conscious experience. That would provide a sufficient condition for phenomenal consciousness. He could then have looked at paradigmatic cases of unconscious mental states in humans, whether in blindsight, deep sleep, or binocular suppression (say), characterizing the degree of informational integration present in those (which would presumably be non-zero). That would set up two poles of a categorical explanatory framework. It would specify a degree of integrated information that is definitely sufficient for phenomenal consciousness at one end, and a degree of integrated information that is definitely *in*sufficient, at the other. (What should be said about the space remaining between these poles, if any, is something we will return to in a moment.)

---

[1] It is a limited kind of panpsychism because not all information-processing systems and subsystems contain any degree of integration (and hence consciousness), on this account. Specifically, purely feed-forward processing is said not to issue in consciousness.

Even if Tononi were to aim at constructing a categorical concept of integrated information in order to match the all-or-nothing character of phenomenal consciousness, however, there is no guarantee that things would turn out as I described in the previous paragraph. What might emerge is that the degree of information integration present when someone is dreaming, say, or barely aware of a backward-masked stimulus in a psychophysical experiment, is actually *lower* than the degree of information integration that is present in the dorsal visual system that guides skilled sensorimotor action, or that is present in someone who is sleepwalking. That would amount to a decisive refutation of integrated-information theory, in my view. And this is not merely a conceptual possibility. For we know that the motor system is highly integrated, with forward models created from one's motor plans at many different levels of abstraction in constant interaction with afferent feedback as the action unfolds, interacting also with one's more abstract goals (Wolpert & Kawato 1998; Wolpert & Ghahramani 2000; Jeannerod 2006). Yet all of this processing takes place unconsciously—or so it seems, to anyone not in the grip of a theory.

Although Tononi & Koch (2015) make a big show of starting from first-person facts, those facts aren't carefully tailored towards *phenomenal* consciousness. (Had they been so, they would arguably have included the fact that phenomenal consciousness seems to be either categorically present or categorically absent in the human mind.) They point out that distinct experiences generally have distinct contents, for example. But explaining the *differences* among distinct phenomenally conscious experiences is one project, explaining phenomenal consciousness itself (one might think) is quite another. Moreover, when they stress that conscious states are integrated, what they seem to have in mind is that the different components are bound together into a structured whole. In effect, they are talking about *binding*, as when the color of a book is bound to representations of its shape and position (an example they themselves use). But we know that binding can take place within unconscious states, too (Dehaene 2014). So it is far from clear that an account of phenomenal consciousness needs to explain binding. Indeed, it seems obvious that it doesn't. And in any case it is possible for people to have phenomenally conscious experiences (of color, say) that *aren't* bound together with others, as is the case with Milner & Goodale's (1995) patient, D.F.

In addition, nowhere in the development and defense of integrated-information theory is any attempt made to explain why phenomenal consciousness should strike people as so puzzling. Nor is it clear how the theory could begin to do this, except by embracing qualia realism, and hence accepting that phenomenal consciousness is an anomalous and unexplained aspect of an otherwise physical world. It is hard to see how the theory could make any use of the phenomenal-concept strategy, for example (which will be developed in Chapter 6), except by combining it with central elements of global-workspace theory.

By way of summary, I once heard a speaker at a conference remark that although he was sure that integrated-information theory was a theory of *something*, he wasn't sure *what* it was a theory of; yet he was quite sure that it wasn't a successful theory of phenomenal consciousness. I concur with that assessment. Nevertheless, it is worth briefly considering the implications of the approach for the distribution of consciousness across the animal kingdom.

Consider first the form of integrated-information theory that is actually developed by Tononi and colleagues, where consciousness is said to be a matter of degree. A clear implication of this account is that phenomenal consciousness will be quite widespread. Indeed, *all* creatures will be to some degree phenomenally conscious (as will many of their parts), including not only insects like ants and bees, but also bacteria. This may match some people's pre-theoretical intuitions. But notice that the claim is not just that all creatures have a *few* phenomenally conscious states, or are phenomenally conscious infrequently. Rather, it is that the states that exist in a bee when it detects the scent of nectar, for example, are *to some small degree* phenomenally conscious, and are *like something* for the bee to undergo *to some small extent*. Such claims are hard to make sense of. For as we noted Chapter 1, our first-person concept of phenomenal consciousness is all-or-nothing. One wants to insist: granted, the bee's discriminatory capacities may be crude, and its representation of the world highly fragmentary and indeterminate, but either the mental states of the bee when detecting nectar have *feel* and are *like something*, or they aren't. They surely can't be *like something* for the bee *to some small degree*.

Notice that it makes perfectly good sense to say that a bee's perception of the world (or its transitive creature consciousness of the world, if we continue to use that language) is a matter of degree, and is quite limited. It is surely correct that a bee is aware of much less of the world around it than we are. Indeed, our perception of the world is orders of magnitude richer. But as we noted in Chapter 1, even the most fragmentary and indeterminate of conscious perceptual states (such as a vague impression of light or sound) would nonetheless be described as determinately phenomenally conscious. So the fact that transitive creature consciousness plausibly varies by degrees across species does nothing to support a parallel claim about degrees of phenomenal consciousness.

Suppose, instead, one opted for an ungraded, categorical notion of integrated information. Then we would be left with a problem not unlike the one that will confront global-workspace theory, as we will see in Chapter 7. Starting from the first-person (human) case, one could specify a degree of information integration that is sufficient for phenomenal consciousness; likewise, from experimental investigation of the human case, one can set a lower bound of information integration where consciousness is determinately absent. But what are we to say if the states of most creatures fall between those two poles? We could insist that a creature will be phenomenally conscious if its states are *closer* to the human case that we have first-person knowledge of, in terms of degree of integrated information, than it is to any of the forms of unconscious perception that we know of. But it is quite unclear what could warrant such a claim. Nor is it clear how we could set about finding out the answer empirically. Indeed, it may be that anything we chose to say, here, would be a matter of stipulation, not discovery.

4.2 Integration in the brain-stem

Merker (2007) identifies phenomenal consciousness with a set of serial, limited-capacity representations in the upper brain-stem, where motivational and sensory information are integrated in the final common pathway for the online control of behavior. One strand of evidence said to support the view is apparently-purposive behavior displayed by surgically decorticated animals. Another is the emotional responsiveness of children born without a neocortex, who smile at caregivers, giggle when tickled, fuss and cry when upset, and so on. This suggestion can be dealt with quite briskly. But it needs at least to be addressed, because people in the animal-consciousness literature often cite it in support of their views.

We have already seen in Chapter 3 that online visual control of action in humans takes place independently of consciousness; so it is unclear why sensorimotor action in decorticated animals should count as evidence of consciousness. Indeed, it is surely clear that it shouldn't. For we have direct evidence from the human case, not only that sensorimotor activity doesn't depend on consciousness, but also that a functioning neocortex is *necessary* for consciousness. Thus people who have had primary visual cortex destroyed become blind; those who have lost auditory cortex become deaf, and so on. It seems Merker must claim that phenomenal consciousness persists in such cases (supported by representations in the brain-stem) but in a way that is inaccessible to the people themselves.

Similar problems attach to Merker's (2007) claims of consciousness in hydrocephalic children, who possess little or no cortex. For as we also noted in Chapter 3, emotion-expressive behavior of the sort exhibited by these children is directly caused by subcortical affective systems independently of consciousness. Although it might be compelling to observers of the children's behavior that they are experiencing conscious emotions in response to stimuli (especially when those observers are the children's caregivers, as was for the case for the survey data collected by Aleman & Merker 2014), we know that behavior of just this sort can be caused unconsciously. Indeed, cases of pathological laughter or crying in humans generally result from lesions to the higher-level cortical systems that would normally inhibit such behavior, thereby releasing the subcortical behavioral network in question (Lauterbach et al. 2013).

Note the methodological oddity of developing a theory of consciousness in the way that Merker (2007) does—at least, if his target is phenomenal consciousness, and not just sensorimotor sensitivity to the environment. For, as we stressed in Chapter 1, phenomenal consciousness is a first-person notion. But instead of starting from the first-person, and from cases where we can gather direct and indirect first-person evidence (i.e. adult humans), Merker chooses to build a theory grounded in neurophysiological knowledge of the integrative capacities of the upper brain-stem, together with third-person observation of the sensori-motor properties of that system in beings who lack a cortex. But we already know that information can be integrated unconsciously, and that sensorimotor behavior, too, can be unconsciously caused.

Moreover (and just as we saw to be true of integrated-information theory in Section 4.1), Merker makes no attempt to show how the theory can explain the puzzling character of phenomenal consciousness, or why the latter should seemingly give rise to an explanatory gap. Nor is any attempt made to explain the distinction between conscious and unconscious forms of perception, manifested in a wide range of experimental conditions, including backward masking, inattentional blindness, and more.

Despite its lack of plausibility, we can ask about the implications of the brain-stem theory for the distribution of consciousness across the animal kingdom. The theory presumably implies that consciousness is present in all vertebrates, at least, since all seem to share a similar sort of brain-stem coordination network. And indeed, Merker's work is cited approv-ingly by Tye (2017) as demonstrating that since cortical activity is unnecessary for consciousness, the absence of a cortex in creatures like birds and fish shouldn't count as a defeater for applying Newton's Principle, and thus for granting them consciousness.[2] Furthermore, the integrative-brain-stem account is taken as a model by Barron & Klein (2016), who argue that the central complex in the insect brain plays a similar integrative function to the mid-brain of vertebrates, suggesting that insects, too, are capable of conscious experience.

In summary, the data cited by Merker (2007) are readily explicable by known properties of the human brain without requiring any appeal to consciousness. In addition, the theory itself makes no attempt at explain-ing the puzzling properties of phenomenal consciousness or known facts

---

[2] Note that this seems to be a clear case of circular reasoning. Tye uses the brain-stem account to justify extending Newton's Principle to creatures who lack a cortex. But Merker's claims must themselves depend on Newton's Principle (or something quite similar). We cannot, of course, gather first-person evidence of consciousness from a decorticated cat or a hydro-cephalic child. So the argument must be that the behaviors exhibited are nevertheless similar enough to those that result from conscious experience in ourselves to warrant belief in the same kind of cause.

about consciousness in humans. So the brain-stem account has little to be said for it.

4.3 Fragile short-term memory

Block (2007, 2011a) identifies phenomenal consciousness with the contents of a form of fragile visual short-term memory (as well as with the contents of equivalent mid-level sensory memory buffers in nonvisual modalities). It is fragile because its contents decay over the course of just a few seconds in the absence of attention, whereas working-memory contents can be sustained for much longer periods. Critically, these short-term memory contents are said to be richer than those accessible via working memory for planning or reporting. Indeed, the main evidence offered in support of the short-term-memory view is that people claim to see more details in a briefly presented stimulus than they can thereafter report; but when probed on specific items with a cue after stimulus-offset, they display awareness of much more than the limited number of items that can be sustained in working memory, seemingly bearing out their subjective reports (Sperling 1960; Landman et al. 2003; Sligte et al. 2008). As a result, Block thinks that phenomenal consciousness should be identified with the contents of fragile short-term memory, whereas access consciousness and reportability comprise the contents of working memory.[3]

Critics have replied that people's intuition that they see the stimulus in rich detail can be explained away, in part by appealing to background scene statistics that are known to be swiftly computed by the visual system (Cohen & Dennett 2011; Cohen et al. 2016). What is consciously experienced, on this view, isn't the complete detailed display of letters in

---

[3] Fragile visual short-term memory is also thought to be distinct from *iconic* memory, which depends on after-images remaining on the retina. Note that global-workspace theorists, too, can accept the existence of these forms of memory; they just deny that the contents of fragile short-term and iconic memory are conscious prior to the impact of attention and global broadcasting. Note, too, that global-workspace theorists should allow that the comparatively rich contents of fragile short-term memory will continue to exist for a period following stimulus offset, while gradually decaying, needing only to be targeted by attention to become conscious. Nothing resembling imagery *construction* is required. So it is no argument against the view that people who are poor at visual-image construction perform as normal in these retro-cuing tasks (*contra* D'Aloisio-Montilla 2017).

the stimulus. Rather, it comprises a few detailed letters, perhaps, together with a statistical distillation of the scene with a content somewhat along the lines of "a bunch of letter-like shapes arranged in a grid" and/or some *imprecise* representations of the locations or identities of some other specific letters (Wu & Wolfe 2018). Detailed representations of the remaining letters only *become* conscious when people are provided with a local post-stimulus cue, enabling attentional signals to broadcast those items from among the rich contents of fragile short-term memory. In support of such a view, we know that the statistical properties of background scenes in change-blindness experiments require very little in the way of attentional resources to be consciously experienced, in contrast with focal objects. (But they are, nevertheless, still attention-dependent; Cohen et al. 2011.)

An additional problem facing the fragile-short-term-memory view is that it seems incapable of explaining the all-or-nothing character of phenomenal consciousness. (Higher-order theories and global-workspace theory *can* explain this, as we will see in due course.) This is because the neural networks that realize this sort of short-term memory will surely admit of a spectrum of levels of activation, and it is quite implausible that literally *any* degree of activation of a content in short-term memory is sufficient for it to become conscious. Indeed, there is evidence that it isn't. Stimuli that are too brief and/or faint to be reported can nevertheless cause some degree of activity in higher regions of the visual system, which are thought to realize fragile visual short-term memory (Dehaene & Changeux 2011). One could insist, of course, that these contents *are* conscious (precisely because they have entered fragile short-term memory). But this would be a stipulation, not anything for which we (or subjects themselves) have evidence.

The closest the view can come to explaining the all-or-nothing nature of phenomenal consciousness is this. Suppose that there is some threshold of neural activity in short-term memory below which attentional signals are incapable of causing that activity to be globally broadcast (and suppose that global broadcasting, in turn, is an all-or-nothing matter, as we will see later that it is). Then contents that fall below that threshold can be said to be unconscious, whereas those that are above it can be said to be conscious. The trouble here, however, is that attentional signals can themselves vary in strength. So we have replaced one spectrum with another. And if one formulates the view in terms of the level of activity below which even the most focused and intense attentional signals can't initiate global broadcasting, then this will have unpalatable consequences. It will result in us having to say of someone who reports that she *doesn't* have a conscious experience that really she does, provided her degree of attention to it falls below the maximum possible, and that the maximum *would have* resulted in a positive report. It will thus emerge (more or less by stipulation, without direct evidence) that people are systematically mistaken about undergoing conscious experiences, often thinking that they aren't when really they are.

Despite such criticisms, Haun et al. (2017) present a number of arguments in support of the view that the contents of conscious experience are rich (much richer than can enter the global workspace appealed to in global-workspace models).[4] One is the finding by Wallis et al. (2016) that people can discriminate changes in the periphery of the visual field surprisingly well. Haun and colleagues take this to show that we generally experience a richly detailed periphery (albeit not as detailed as focal vision), rather than a mere statistical summary. But this is a blatant non sequitur. The fact that the periphery of the visual field can be rich, *when attended* (as in Wallis and colleagues' experiments), shows nothing whatever about the *unattended* or *barely attended* periphery (which may be restricted to summary scene statistics). The central claim made by global-workspace theory is that conscious contents are those that are "globally broadcast" to a range of different systems for reasoning and reporting, not that conscious contents (when visual) depend on foveal vision; and most theorists think that such broadcasting is attention-dependent. Moreover, global-workspace theory will of course allow that *attended* objects or regions can be richly represented.[5,6]

---

[4] Note that the other three authors of this paper—Giulio Tononi, Christof Koch, and Naotsugu Tsuchiya—are among the main critics of global-workspace theory. Hence it is reasonable to take this paper to be their "best shot" at defending a rich-contents alternative.

[5] Note that the limited contents of working memory—said to level off at around four items—comprise those items *together with fine-grained properties of shape, color, and so on* that are bound into the object-files or event-files in question (Luck & Vogel 1997; Zhang & Luck 2009; Ecker et al. 2013; Fougnie et al. 2013). People in working-memory tasks can identify minor changes in such properties across significant intervals of time, for example. There is a sense, then, in which representation of those four items is "rich." Thus the sparsity of everyday conscious experience should not be exaggerated.

[6] It is also worth noting that it took carefully controlled experimental studies to show that the working-memory limit is around only four items (Cowan 2001). If the stimuli are such that

Haun et al. (2017) also cite the finding by Kaunitz et al. (2016) that people have impressively good memories for non-target faces in crowds, which is said to be far better than might be expected if incidental visual experience were sparse, as global-workspace theorists generally claim. But again, this is a complete non sequitur. The sense of "incidental" that figures in global-workspace accounts concerns stimuli that are unattended or only barely attended, not stimuli that are goal-irrelevant. In the study by Kaunitz and colleagues, people were searching for a specific face in a crowd of faces, which meant that they had to engage in serial search. But they were later tested on non-target faces *on which they had foveated* (and to which they had presumably fully attended, albeit momentarily). Perception of each of those faces would thus have been fully conscious, on any account; and there is no reason to think that these goal-irrelevant experiences would need to be sustained in working memory in order for later recognition to occur. So the "impressively good memory" for these non-target faces reflects the properties of long-term recognition memory, and hence shows us nothing about the bandwidth of consciousness.

Finally, Haun et al. (2017) cite Vandenbroucke et al. (2014), who show, using measures of metacognitive accuracy, that attention-limited working memory and pre-attentive fragile short-term memory are equally accessible to introspection, while displaying the familiar richness advantage for the latter. Haun and colleagues claim that this debunks the claim that fragile short-term memory "is unconscious or illusory." But no one claims that fragile short-term memory is illusory. What is said by global-workspace theorists to be illusory is the sense of richness that attends conscious *working* memory. Nor does anyone claim that the contents of fragile short-term memory are unconscious

---

people can "chunk" some of the presented items into groups or categories—in the way that most natural scenes will allow—then they can recover much more than that. Even 14-month-old infants can greatly extend their working-memory capacities if stimuli are presented in spatially aligned groups, or are grouped under distinctive categories (Feigenson & Halberda 2008). And among adults, more items can be identified in working-memory tasks when familiar real-world items are used (Brady et al. 2016). Chunking, however, seems to involve a mechanism distinct from *binding*. While the latter really does extend the amount of information that can be held actively online (and hence consciously), the former seems to depend on an interaction between online "labels" for familiar items and long-term memory. For one recent finding is that reporting information from chunked as opposed to unchunked items comes with reaction-time costs, suggesting that the information isn't immediately available online but needs to be unpacked from memory (Huang & Awh 2018).

when attended to. On the contrary, the standard explanation given by sparse-consciousness opponents of such results is that any given item remaining in fragile-short-term memory can *become* conscious when retro-cued and hence attended to. And this was precisely the paradigm employed by Vandenbrouke and colleagues.

Vandenbroucke et al. (2014) themselves make a somewhat different claim. They first describe their finding that people's metacognitive knowledge of the contents of fragile short-term memory is equal to or greater than their metacognitive accuracy about the contents of working memory. And then they say that this shows that the former is not based on implicit (hence unconscious) information, but rather reflects explicit (and hence conscious) processing. But this is to play fast and loose with the different meanings of "implicit." Sometimes people use the term as a stand-in for "unconscious," with "explicit" meaning "conscious." But it can also be used to refer to information that isn't directly encoded or represented. (The information, "light shines from above" is in this sense probably implicit in the operations of the visual system, for example, rather than stored as a structured proposition-like representation.) Sparse-consciousness theorists will of course allow that the contents of fragile short-term memory are explicitly there in the representational sense (and might thus give rise to metacognitive feelings), and can *become* conscious and available to introspection when attended. But it certainly doesn't follow from this that those contents are *already* conscious in advance of being attended to.

In addition to the failure of arguments supporting the claim that consciousness coincides with fragile short-term memory, there is evidence that people can only report about four items even when the cue for reporting coincides with stimulus offset, thus obviating any need for memory (Tsubomi et al. 2013). People can be shown an array of colored squares for a full second, whereupon just one of the squares remains illuminated. But that square is now divided into two colored halves, one of which is the original color of the square and the other of which is drawn from elsewhere in the display. The task is just to indicate which is the original color. Participants still show the standard four-item limit (two in each hemisphere), which is also present in their neural EEG signatures during the encoding phase that flatten off at that four-item limit. These findings seem plainly inconsistent with the fragile-short-term-memory view. If one's perception of a colored square were already conscious, then one would think that one would immediately know which side of the square had changed when half of it gets replaced by a differently colored rectangle.[7]

Furthermore, there is evidence from a number of different retro-cuing paradigms that seems inconsistent with the fragile-short-term-memory account of consciousness (Sergent et al. 2013; Thibault et al. 2016; Xia et al. 2016). According to the latter, conscious experience should be time-locked to the occurrence of the stimulus, emerging swiftly through a feed-forward sweep of sensory processing, and should be independent of attention. Indeed, attention is merely the gateway to access consciousness, on this view. Moreover, the reason why a cue that follows stimulus offset only enables one to access a subset of one's comparatively rich conscious experience is said to derive from strict limits on the scope of attention and working memory. But in the retro-cuing experiments cited above there was just a single stimulus. It comprised a faint set of oriented lines (a Gabor patch) set near the limits of visual detection occurring in one of two possible locations, where that location could either be pre-cued or post-cued, either validly or invalidly.

The finding was that valid post-cues increased conscious detection, as well as improving people's discrimination of the orientation of the lines. But why, on a short-term-memory account, would a post-cue improve conscious detection? It should *already* be conscious (contained in short-term memory), in which case post-cue attention should be irrelevant. It might be replied that the stimulus was represented in short-term memory, but too weakly to qualify as conscious. It might have fallen below the threshold for consciousness, being boosted over that threshold by attention as a result of the retro-cue. But this reply then undermines the probative value of the original experiments that were held to support the fragile-short-term-memory account in the first place. For in those cases, too, the contents that become reportable as a result of a post-cue

---

[7] Moreover, Buschman et al. (2011) show, using direct neural recordings in monkeys, that the loss of excess information when the number of target objects exceeds four takes place early during sensory encoding (especially in parietal cortex, which is the "business end" of the attentional system), and not just during later retention. It seems that the limits on performance during working-memory tasks are the same as the limits governing perception; and both reflect limits on attention. (The presuppositions behind the use of animals in consciousness research will be discussed in Chapter 5.)

might have previously been below the threshold for consciousness, hence being *un*conscious, just as global-workspace theory implies. Overall, the data suggest quite strongly that, in contrast with the short-term-memory theory, conscious experience is attention-dependent.

It seems there aren't any good reasons for thinking that the fragile-short-term-memory account of phenomenal consciousness is true, whereas there *are* good reasons for taking it to be false. But what would such a view imply about the distribution of consciousness across the animal kingdom? This question is by no means easy to answer (although Block himself takes for granted that all mammals, at any rate, would qualify; Block 2002). This is because it is left unclear which facts about short-term memory are supposed to carry the explanatory burden.

Taken in one way, the implications of the account for animal consciousness become essentially the same as those of the global-workspace theory (see Chapter 7), since fragile short-term memory is partly individuated through its functional relationship with working memory, and hence with reasoning, decision-making, and verbal report. (There are multiple reverberating memory stores in the human mind that don't qualify for consciousness, on Block's account. What is distinctive of fragile short-term memory is that people *report* awareness of its contents, even if they can't describe those contents fully.) But taken in other ways, the implications of the short-term-memory account might be highly restrictive (if something about the neural realization of short-term memory in humans and/or apes is what explains the properties of conscious experience) or quite liberal (if the neural realizations that do the explaining are widely shared). At this point the question of the distribution of phenomenal consciousness in the animal kingdom is wide open, on a fragile-short-term-memory account.

4.4 Actual higher-order thought

We now consider the class of higher-order theories of consciousness. These come in two basic varieties. The first claims that it is the actual presence of a higher-order thought about a perceptual state that renders that state phenomenally conscious (Rosenthal 2005), which will be discussed here. (The second is dual-content theory, to be considered in Section 4.5.) Both varieties of higher-order theory can readily explain the categorical nature of phenomenal consciousness. In the case of the actual-higher-order-thought account, this is because entertaining such a thought seems to be an all-or-nothing matter. Either one is thinking a thought about some aspect of one's current perception, or one is not. There seems no room for *partial* higher-order thought.[8] Dual-content theory, in contrast, is categorical because global broadcasting is categorical in nature (as we will see in Chapter 5). Either a given perceptual content is globally broadcast and hence available as input to the mind-reading system (in which case it acquires a dual first-order/higher-order nonconceptual content), or it is not. This immediately gives higher-order theories an advantage over those considered thus far in this chapter.

The actual-higher-order-thought account faces a number of severe difficulties, however. One is that it is hard to know what one should say when the content of perception and the content of the higher-order thought don't align with one another (Mandik 2009; Weisberg 2011). What happens to one's phenomenally conscious experience if one undergoes a perception of red but *believes* that one is perceiving orange? Notice that this sort of mismatch has to be a live possibility, since the first-order percept and the higher-order belief are distinct (causally linked) existences. Just as one can actually be confronted with a red object while falsely believing it to be orange, so must it be possible to be *perceiving* (perceptually representing) red while falsely believing that one is *perceiving* orange.

One possible view is that in cases of mismatch, the first-order perceptual content dominates. So in the example imagined above, one would have a phenomenal experience as of red. But this would seem to render the higher-order thought redundant. Or at least, the *content* of the higher-order thought would become redundant. (It might still be the case that the first-order perceptual content is only phenomenally conscious if it causes *some* higher-order thought.) It seems to follow that one

---

[8] Recall from Chapter 1, however, that Rosenthal (2018) has recently claimed that the varying degrees of confidence with which a higher-order thought can be entertained correspond to varying degrees in the extent to which the targeted perceptual state is a conscious one. This implication would be a serious strike against higher-order thought theory if it were mandatory. But plainly a higher-order theorist doesn't *need* to make such a claim.

could have a higher-order thought of *any* sort, appropriately caused by a given first-order percept, and yet that percept's content would nevertheless become phenomenally conscious. Suppose, at the limit, that I am actually perceiving red but that this somehow causes me to believe that I feel a tickle on my arm. On the present account, that would be sufficient for my perception of red to become phenomenally conscious. While the idea isn't incoherent, it seems completely bizarre.

A second alternative is that in cases of mismatch one's phenomenally conscious experience falls somewhere between the content of the percept and the content of one's belief. That is, if one is perceiving red while believing one is seeing orange, what one will phenomenally experience is a sort of reddish-orange. So one's phenomenally conscious experience corresponds *neither* to the content of one's perception *nor* to what one thinks it is. This, too, is coherent but bizarre.[9]

Given the unattractiveness of the alternatives, it is perhaps not surprising that higher-order-thought theorists have generally opted for the remaining possibility. They have said that in cases of mismatch, one's phenomenally conscious experience is fixed entirely by one's higher-order belief (Rosenthal 2005, 2011; Weisberg 2011; Brown 2015). If one *believes* that one is seeing orange, then one is, actually, having a phenomenally conscious experience of orange (even if that belief is caused by first-order perception of red, which remains unconscious). Rosenthal (2005) gives the example of someone placing a cube of ice on one's back, the shock of which causes one to *believe* initially that one is experiencing pain, not cold. He claims—not implausibly, in this instance, given that extreme cold is unpleasant—that for that initial moment one *does* have a phenomenal experience as of a feeling of pain.

If the content of phenomenal consciousness is given by the content of one's higher-order belief, however, then the accompanying first-order experience becomes redundant. For this reason, higher-order theorists accept that phenomenally conscious experience is fixed by the content of

---

[9] Notice that this account is quite distinct from what might well be a plausible suggestion, namely that one's higher-order beliefs can have a top-down causal *influence* on the content of one's perception. Even supposing that this can happen, and that one's beliefs or expectation about what one is seeing can interact with perceptual processing to bias the output in the direction of the belief, this would still leave cases of mismatch between the belief and the resulting experience.

higher-order belief even in the complete absence of first-order perception. If one believes that one is seeing orange while one actually has no visual states at all (perhaps one has gone momentarily blind), then one does actually have a phenomenally conscious experience as of orange. But now the difficulty is to explain how higher-order thoughts (which are fully conceptual states, note) can give rise to the distinctive fine-grained character of phenomenally conscious experience (Block 2011b).

As we noted in Chapter 1, perceptual states have fine-grained non-conceptual contents. When one looks at the gradations in shades of color across a rose-petal, or on the palm of one's own hand, one's experiences comprise subtle differences that are impossible to describe or capture with available concepts. This is the element of truth in the claim that consciousness is ineffable. But ineffability isn't anything mysterious, here. It is just representational content that is more fine-grained than any concept one can possess. And of course, it isn't just unconscious perceptual states that have fine-grained nonconceptual contents. The same is true of our phenomenally conscious states. Indeed, the primary evidence we have of nonconceptual content is introspective in nature: it is by reflecting on our phenomenally conscious experiences that we realize their fine-grained ineffability.

In consequence, higher-order-thought theory can't account for what is perhaps one of the defining features of our phenomenally conscious experience: its fine-grained, ineffable character. One's higher-order thought has the conceptual content, *I am seeing orange*, whereas one's phenomenally conscious experience can be as of a range of specific nonconceptual shades of orange. So the latter cannot possibly be *constituted* by the former, as higher-order-thought theorists claim. This is, surely, a very big problem. If all that fixes phenomenally conscious content is a fully conceptual higher-order belief, then where can the fineness of grain of experience possibly come from?

Another major problem with actual higher-order-thought theory is to explain why we should be entertaining multiple higher-order thoughts about our perceptual states at every moment of our waking lives (Carruthers 2000). Given that cortical activity is expensive (with the brain consuming energy at eight times the rate of the rest of the body Aiello & Wheeler 1995), some account needs to be given of what the continuous stream of higher-order thoughts is *for*.

It should be stressed that this point is entirely independent of claims about the richness or sparseness of conscious experience, discussed in Section 4.3. For even on the sparsest of views, one will, at every moment, have conscious experiences of a number of objects or events, together with their properties. It makes sense that *perception* should be ubiquitous. That is, it makes sense that there should always be some significant element of transitive creature consciousness whenever there is *in*transitive creature consciousness (whenever one is awake). For the world (and states of one's own body) need to be continually monitored, one might think. But why should one be *thinking about* one's own perceptual states at every moment of the waking day? What could all these higher-order thoughts possibly be doing, or be for?

Note that on a global-workspace account, in contrast, it is easy to explain why we should always be subject to some or other phenomenally conscious state. This is because the central workspace serves to focus the entire organism on the most relevant stimuli and the most relevant activities whenever one is awake (Carruthers 2015a). But what could possibly be the point of continually entertaining higher-order thoughts about (some subset of) one's current perceptual states? The only available answer seems to be: to provide flexibility in responding. Perhaps it is higher-order awareness of one's perceptual states that enables one to deal with the world in intelligent and flexible ways.

Recall, in this context, our Chapter 3 discussion of what Tye (2017) says about the case of the absent-minded driver. Tye thinks that a driver on "autopilot" has conscious experiences of the road throughout, and "coming to" is just a matter of acquiring higher-order awareness of those experiences. A higher-order theorist needs to say, in contrast, that one's initial perceptions of the road when on autopilot are *un*conscious ones, but *become* conscious when one becomes higher-order aware of them. We also noted in Chapter 3 that "coming to" is what enables flexible, non-habitual responding. If one remained on autopilot one would run down the child who is playing in the road up ahead; but by "coming to" one is able to apply the brakes and slow down. Since in this case it is the transition to conscious experience that enables flexible responding, it might be thought that this supports the higher-order theorist's account of why we should always be undergoing some conscious experience or other: to enable us to deal with the world in a flexible manner.

As we noted in Chapter 3, however, it is quite implausible that it should be the presence of a higher-order belief that enables one to avoid the child. The relevant new content when one "comes to" from one's autopilot reverie is, *a child is in the road*, not *I am seeing a child in the road*. And indeed, we have to hand well-worked-out scientific accounts of how such a shift in first-order content takes place (Carruthers 2015a). There is a distinctive relevance network in the brain (often called the "saliency" network) that continually monitors the contents of unattended, unconscious percepts and memories, assessing their saliency and checking them against current goals and values (Corbetta & Shulman 2002; Corbetta et al. 2008). When something sudden or unexpected occurs (a child is in the road up ahead) attention is shifted from what one had been musing about to the perceptual content in question, rendering it (the first-order content, *a child is in the road*) conscious, and thus engaging executive and decision-making systems. In contrast, we have *no* scientific account of how higher-order thoughts might be caused in these circumstances, nor of how such thoughts might enable flexible responding.

In addition, it should be noted that many different species of animal are capable of making similar shifts from habitual to goal-directed responding when unexpected events intrude. (Indeed, *no* bird or mammal will remain locked in its habitual foraging behavior when a predator suddenly appears, for example.) There is no evidence whatever that these capacities coincide with capacities for higher-order thought. On the contrary, flexible forms of goal-directed decision-making with respect to the perceived environment are generally thought to be first-order processes (van der Meer et al. 2012).

We can conclude from this discussion that the actualist form of higher-order-thought theory of phenomenal consciousness is quite implausible. Before moving on to consider the second sort of higher-order account, however—namely, dual-content theory—we can examine the implications of higher-order theories of consciousness in general for the question of animal consciousness. For these are quite similar, whatever version of higher-order account is adopted.

The implications of higher-order-thought theories are clear: only animals that are capable of higher-order thought will undergo phenomenally conscious experiences (Carruthers 2000). Only animals with concepts resembling those like SEE and HEAR, and who can make first-person applications of those concepts, will be capable of conscious visual or auditory experience, in particular.[10] The concepts in question need not possess the full richness of our human concepts of sight or hearing, of course. But they must at least come embedded in a simplified, perhaps merely tacit, model of the mind as mediator between environment and behavior, together with knowledge of the role that perception plays in effecting that relationship.

I suggested in Chapter 2 that there is very little direct evidence of self-awareness of mental states in nonhuman animals, and that we should expect such awareness to be possible only in highly social creatures capable of third-person mind-reading. The precise extension of the set of species capable of thoughts about their own perceptual states is unknown at this point, of course. But it seems likely that the class of such creatures is quite small. And in that case, according to higher-order theories of phenomenal consciousness, the distribution of consciousness across the animal kingdom will be equally restricted.

4.5 Dual-content theory

I turn now to the other variety of higher-order-thought theory, sometimes known as *dispositional* (as opposed to actual) higher-order-thought theory. On this view, it is by virtue of the *availability* of non-conceptual contents to higher-order thought that they become phenomenally conscious. The availability in question arises through global broadcasting of those contents to a wide range of consumer systems, included among which is the mind-reading system, which is capable of formulating higher-order thoughts about those contents. And by virtue of such availability, together with the truth of a particular kind of consumer semantics, all of those broadcast nonconceptual contents acquire, at the same time, a higher-order nonconceptual content.

---

[10] Note that higher-order-thought theories are to be sharply distinguished from *inner sense* accounts (Lycan 1996), which are formulated in terms of nonconceptual quasi-perceptual meta-awareness of one's own perceptual states. On these accounts, no higher-order concepts are needed. Such theories face deep problems of their own, however (Carruthers 2000), and I am not aware of anyone defending this sort of approach in the recent literature.

(Note that this is said to be so, whether or not any higher-order thoughts about them are actually formulated.) All such broadcast states thus have *dual* contents: a first-order nonconceptual representation of red, for instance, will at the same time be a higher-order nonconceptual representation with the content, *seeming red*, or *experience of red*. Otherwise-unconscious perceptual contents thus become *self-presenting* when they acquire a dual content. In addition to offering a nonconceptual representation of the world (or of one's own body), they also provide a nonconceptual representation of their own first-order content.

Dual-content theory has none of the disadvantages of its actualist cousin. First, there can be no mismatch between the first-order and higher-order contents in question. This is because the relationship between them isn't causal, but constitutive. Given the form of consumer semantics appealed to (according to which the content of a given state depends partly on what the systems that can make immediate use of that state can infer from it or do with it), any first-order nonconceptual content received by the mind-reading system as input will automatically have a higher-order-seeming version of that very first-order content, by virtue of the system's *capacity* to entertain higher-order thoughts about it. Or so the theory claims.

Second, there is no problem about explaining why we should be subject to phenomenally conscious experiences at every moment in our waking lives. This is because at all such moments some nonconceptual content or other will always be being globally broadcast, with the most relevant of the available contents attracting attention and being boosted over the threshold for entry into the global workspace. Since all globally broadcast contents will de facto be received as input by the mind-reading faculty (in creatures that possess such a faculty), all such contents will acquire the sort of dual nonconceptual content said to be constitutive of phenomenal consciousness.

Moreover, dual-content theory can explain the all-or-nothing nature of phenomenal consciousness just as well as its actualist cousin does. This is because dual-content states are all and only those that are globally broadcast, being received by the mind-reading system among others, in virtue of which they acquire dual content; and global broadcasting is all-or-nothing (as we will see in Chapter 5). If there is no such thing as a partially broadcast nonconceptual content, then there can be no such thing as a state with partial dual nonconceptual content, either; and hence no such thing as partial phenomenal consciousness.[11]

Given that dual-content theory piggybacks on a global-workspace account, one needs to know why it should be preferred over the latter. Why not say that phenomenal consciousness is just globally broadcast nonconceptual content? What does the postulation of dual nonconceptual contents, and the hypothesis that phenomenal consciousness only emerges with the latter, really buy one? The question is pressing, because we have no direct evidence of the existence of such dual contents. And it is on this matter that I have changed my mind. I will briefly state the main arguments I once offered in support of dual-content theory over plain first-order global-workspace theory (Carruthers 2000, 2005a), noting why they don't work. But since, to the best of my knowledge, no one other than myself has ever embraced dual-content theory, this discussion can be quite brief. For there is no one remaining who needs to be convinced. (Those interested in a more detailed treatment can consult Carruthers 2017b.)

One argument I used was that mere first-order nonconceptual content couldn't support the sorts of indexical acquaintance-based phenomenal concepts that are necessary to deal with the "hard problem" thought experiments. Supposing that THIS-R is such a concept (applied to an experience of red), I pointed out that there must be something about the use of the concept that explains its higher-order status. What makes THIS-R about the experience of red, rather than just red? What distinguishes it from a first-order color concept? If the answer is that the concept tacitly embeds the concept EXPERIENCE or the concept SEE, then it will be hard to make sense of our capacity to think thoughts like, _This-R might not have been an experience, but might have had the role of a decision instead._ My own suggestion was that THIS-R acquires its higher-order status by applying specifically to the higher-order

[11] Note that this positive implication of dual-content theory depends on assuming that _only_ globally broadcast contents are available as input to the mind-reading system, thereby acquiring a dual content. It is possible to doubt this claim, however. Indeed, one might think that a large part of what the relevance system does, when competing for attentional resources, is evaluate percepts and memories for their _social_ relevance, which would require them to be processed by the mind-reading system while still unconscious (Corbetta et al. 2008). If this is right, then dual-content theory could have the unpalatable implication that there are phenomenally conscious states that one is incapable of reporting, remembering, or using to guide one's decision-making.

nonconceptual content postulated under dual-content theory. As we will see in Chapter 6, however, one can provide a positive account of phenomenal concepts and their application conditions from the perspective of global-workspace theory without needing to appeal to dual contents.

The second main argument I offered was that while global-workspace theory can account for the *co-extension* of globally broadcast nonconceptual content and phenomenal consciousness, it was incapable of explaining *why* broadcast content should be phenomenally conscious. What is it about global broadcasting, I asked, that explains why broadcast content should "light up" and acquire the properties distinctive of phenomenal consciousness? I suggested, in contrast, that dual content *could* explain this. For if broadcast content automatically acquires higher-order nonconceptual content, then in so doing it will acquire a subjective dimension. I now think, however, that in making the original challenge I hadn't fully ridden myself of the allure of qualia realism (despite being explicitly committed to rejecting it). But again discussion is best deferred to Chapter 6, where I will show how global-workspace theory can provide a fully satisfactory reductive explanation of phenomenal consciousness.

4.6 Conclusion

This chapter has outlined and critiqued global-workspace theory's five most plausible competitors. The weakest, in my view, are integrated-information theory and the brain-stem theory, which seem incapable of serving as theories of phenomenal consciousness at all, and might better serve as accounts of some forms of creature consciousness. In contrast, the fragile-short-term-memory account, as well as both forms of higher-order-thought theory, have something to be said for them. All three have significant weaknesses, however. Chapter 5 will show that global-workspace theory can do much better. Indeed, over the course of the next two chapters I hope to show that it provides a successful fully reductive theory of phenomenal consciousness. That will set up the remainder of our discussion thereafter, which will concern the implications of global-workspace theory for the question of animal consciousness.

5

Global-workspace theory

The present chapter outlines and defends the empirical case supporting global-workspace theory as the best account of the functional/neural correlates of consciousness. The more strictly philosophical task of showing that the theory can provide a fully reductive explanation of phenomenal consciousness—and, more particularly, of showing that it can explain the explanatory gap—is deferred to Chapter 6.

5.1 Global-workspace theory: The initial case

A global-workspace account of consciousness was first developed in detail by Baars (1988, 1997, 2002), and was originally formulated in cognitive (rather than neural-network) terms. A close relative of Baars' theory (published subsequently but independently) is Tye's (1995, 2000) PANIC theory. (PANIC stands for Poised Abstract Nonconceptual Intentional Content.) The basic idea of both approaches is that some perceptual and perception-like contents (including visual and auditory imagery) are globally broadcast and received by a wide range of other systems in the mind, whereas others have more specialized or local uses. Conscious states are those that are broadcast to systems for reporting, planning, reasoning, decision-making, and remembering, whereas unconscious states are those that are *not* so broadcast, although they can have a variety of other roles or effects, such as online guidance of movement. In effect, the theory identifies phenomenal consciousness with access consciousness—or rather (at least in Tye's version of it) with access-conscious *nonconceptual* content. And access consciousness, in turn, is generally now identified with the broadcasting function of working memory.

Human and Animal Minds: The Consciousness Questions Laid to Rest. Peter Carruthers, Oxford University Press (2019). © Peter Carruthers.
DOI: 10.1093/oso/9780198843702.001.0001

A couple of qualifications are needed before we proceed further. First, the global workspace is not intended to be truly *global*, of course. Its contents aren't broadcast to *every* subsystem of the mind. Rather, they are broadcast to *many* such subsystems, especially those that can be clustered around the notion of *executive function*. Globally broadcast contents are available for reasoning, reporting, and decision-making; they can give rise to sustained emotional reactions; and they generally issue in long-term memories (which may or may not be consolidated thereafter, of course). Yet while they are available to systems that engage in action *planning*, they don't play a role in the online guidance of action. (This is the role of the dorsal sensorimotor system, as we saw in Chapter 3.)

It is also worth noting that one can draw at least a conceptual distinction between global *broadcasting* and the global *workspace*. The latter corresponds most directly to the notion of working memory. And working memory is, of course, a form of *memory*. In the case of *working* memory, contents are actively sustained by attentional signals. And although global broadcasting of perceptual contents depends on attention too (as we will see), one might think that initial broadcasting of incoming perceptual information and *sustained* broadcasting (in working memory) after the stimuli have disappeared could be distinct. In particular, it is at least a conceptual possibility that more might be capable of being initially broadcast (given the pre-existing strength of incoming sensory signals) than can thereafter be sustained through attention alone (Carruthers 2017c). The finding discussed in Chapter 4, however, that the bandwidth of perception and working memory are the same (Buschman et al. 2011; Tsubomi et al. 2013) seems to imply that this is a *mere* conceptual possibility. In what follows, then, I shall use the terms "global workspace," "working memory," and "global broadcasting" equivalently, unless explicitly discussing alleged differences between them.

Global-workspace theory can of course explain the intuitive distinction between conscious and unconscious states. Conscious contents are those that are globally broadcast, thereby enabling subjects to be aware of them, reflect on them, and report them. Global broadcasting means that they are made directly available to the executive systems that enable verbal reporting and reflection, as well as to the mind-reading system for metarepresenting and referring to them. In contrast, sensorimotor states in the dorsal visual stream are *not* globally broadcast; nor are states in the ventral visual stream that fail to attract attention, although they can thereafter prime a variety of cognitive and behavioral responses.

The theory can also explain the seeming *ineffability* of phenomenal consciousness. I propose to assume (along with Tye 1995, and as was argued briefly in Chapter 1) that phenomenal consciousness is exclusively a property of nonconceptual states and contents. So even if concepts and conceptual information can be globally broadcast (as I believe), only globally broadcast *non*conceptual content is constitutive of the phenomenally conscious properties that result. And as we noted in Chapter 1, what is distinctive of nonconceptual content is its fineness of grain. When made available to executive systems, nonconceptual contents can enable fine-grained *discriminations* ("*that* shade is a little bit yellower than *that*"), but those differences will be inexpressible except using indexicals such as "*that* shade of color." So we end up *aware* of properties that we have no concepts for, and that we can't express, describe fully, or remember in thought or language.

Moreover—and especially important, given the failures of integrated-information theory and fragile-short-term-memory theory to capture this feature of our experience—global-workspace theory can explain why phenomenal consciousness should be all-or-nothing. For one significant finding in the literature has been that global broadcasting in the human brain is likewise all-or-nothing (Dehaene & Naccache 2001; Del Cul et al. 2007; Marti & Dehaene 2017; van Vugt et al. 2018). There is a step-function underlying the global workspace. Either activation levels in the neural populations in question remain below threshold, in which case no global broadcasting occurs (although there can be some additional local or specialized effects as activation levels increase); or those activation levels hit threshold, and full global broadcasting results. By equating phenomenal consciousness with globally broadcast nonconceptual content, then, one can explain the all-or-nothing character of phenomenal consciousness. So in this respect, too, there is a good mesh between the explaining theory and the target to be explained.

Furthermore, global-workspace theory is now embedded in—and gains some indirect support from—a detailed, well-researched account of human cognitive architecture (Carruthers 2015a). There have been extensive investigations of working memory, of perception, and of attention, as well as the relationships between them. We know quite a bit about how attention works, boosting and aligning neural activity in the targeted populations, while suppressing competing representations. We also know that the result is generally conscious availability of the targeted representations in working memory, where they can be sustained, manipulated, reported, and utilized in a variety of further ways. So the proposal that consciousness is globally broadcast nonconceptual content *makes good sense*, given everything else we know about how the human mind operates.

In what follows, we will first consider the relationship between consciousness and attention, before looking at some of the evidence that supports equating consciousness with global broadcasting of information in the brain. Then we will consider objections.

5.2 Consciousness and attention

Psychologists have always known, of course, that the contents of working memory are severely limited (Baddeley & Hitch 1974; Baddeley 1986). Initially that limit was thought to be around seven items (Miller 1956). But when the pure retention capacities of working memory are measured while ruling out rehearsal and chunking strategies, the limit turns out to be about four (Cowan 2001). Moreover, initial models conceptualized working memory as something distinct from perception (Baddeley 1986). But then multiple-object-tracking experiments suggested that the number of items we can keep track of *perceptually* is about four (Pylyshyn 2003). And brain imaging and other forms of evidence showed that working memory operates by sustaining activity in mid-level sensory regions of the cortex through the direction of attention (Postle 2006). In addition, a whole raft of inattentional blindness experiments suggested that the contents of conscious visual perception are much more restricted than we intuitively think (Mack & Rock 1998).

One often-used variety of inattentional blindness is change blindness. People can watch two pictures alternate back and forth without noticing any difference, despite the fact that those pictures actually differ in some notable respect (e.g. the airplane in one of the two pictures is missing its jet engine). Or an entire scene can be totally transformed (in incremental stages) while one watches. People in the scene can be added or removed, curtains can be drawn back, bookshelves can be replaced with shelves of ornaments, and so on. Still, most observers fail to notice any difference. Now, it is a fair criticism of change-blindness experiments that noticing changes requires comparisons over time, and hence memory. So perhaps the failures in question are failures of memory rather than failures of perception (Block 2011a). One indication that this isn't so, however, is that if attention is manipulated to the changed item just before it changes, then the resulting alteration leaps out at one.

Clearer demonstrations of the dependence of conscious perception on attention come from experiments where attention is manipulated across participants. For example, if observers watching a basketball game are tasked with counting the number of times a player in a white T-shirt touches the ball, then most them don't notice a man in a gorilla suit who walks into the center of the court and beats his chest before walking off. (Versions of this video are readily available on YouTube.) Those who are merely told to watch the game, in contrast, see the gorilla immediately. And it seems quite unlikely that observers in the first group would have consciously seen the gorilla but forgotten about him (hence failing to report his presence when probed afterwards). For his presence is both unexpected and quite salient.

Indeed, a direct demonstration that inattentional blindness is a perceptual phenomenon, not a failure of memory, is provided by Ward & Scholl (2015). Participants had to maintain fixation on a dot at the center of a horizontal line across the screen. Items of various sorts moved around randomly above and below the line. The ongoing task was to count the number of times an item of a specific sort touched the line. But participants were also told to *immediately* report if anything unexpected happened. Yet they failed to make any report in trials where a colored letter traveled along the line and right through the point of fixation where their eyes were focused. With attention fully occupied with tracking the items moving around on either side of the line, they simply didn't see it.

While everyone allows that attention is *important* for consciousness (or at least access consciousness), some have denied that it is strictly necessary (Koch & Tsuchiya 2007; Tononi & Koch 2008). In part this is on the grounds that perception of background scenes seems to be conscious independently of attention. For a number of experiments have shown that if the background scene is altered, people instantly notice and report it (Rensink et al. 1997; Simons & Levin 1997). But as we noted in Chapter 4, background scene perception requires very little attention, rather than none at all. If people are placed under high-enough attentional demands, then they *do* become blind to changes in background scene (Cohen et al. 2011). Moreover, Cohen et al. (2011) also employed a dual-task method to show that as the attentional demands of the object-tracking task were ramped up, so people made many more errors in classifying background scenes, suggesting that the two tasks share a common resource (namely, attention).

Evidence has been accumulating, then, that both conscious perception and working memory are attention-dependent, and that the same strict resource limits govern both. It is worth reiterating a point noted in Chapter 4, however: the poverty of conscious perception should not be overly exaggerated. For each of the items actively entered into working memory and sustained there can come with a rich set of fine-grained properties bound into its representation (Luck & Vogel 1997; Zhang & Luck 2009; Ecker et al. 2013; Fougnie et al. 2013).

5.3 Consciousness in the brain

Everyone agrees that the contents of working memory are (at least generally) conscious. However, there is now data that some people interpret as evidence of unconscious working memory, realized in temporary changes in synaptic weights in the neural populations involved, independent of attention (Lewis-Peacock et al. 2012; Trübutschek et al. 2018). This is so different in nature, however, that in my view it shouldn't be classified as a form of working memory. Rather, it should be thought of as a fast-decaying form of long-term memory. And indeed, some theorists have previously introduced a term for such memories: "long-term working memory" (Ericsson & Kintsch 1995). In what follows, then, I propose to restrict use of the term "working memory" for contents that are actively sustained in the global workspace, excluding those that are merely readily recoverable *into* that workspace.

In addition, the neural networks involved in working memory are now quite well understood. (See Carruthers 2015a for a review.) They link together dorsolateral prefrontal cortex, the frontal eye-fields in high-level regions of motor cortex, and regions around the intraparietal sulcus, together with mid-level sensory cortices in the relevant sensory modalities.[1] The dorsolateral prefrontal cortex houses the executive component of the working memory system, and is thought to be the system responsible for activating and sustaining the task goals underlying working memory performance. The intraparietal sulcus is the attentional component of the working memory system, and interacts with the dorsolateral prefrontal cortex via the frontal eye-fields. It issues in attentional signals targeted at the relevant neural populations in mid-level sensory cortices, boosting and coordinating the activity of those populations, while suppressing others. The upshot is to make the targeted contents widely available to be reported, reflected on, or transformed into others through inference.

The neural correlates of conscious perception, too, have been heavily investigated. Much of this work has used minimal contrasts between conscious and unconscious conditions in combination with EEG, MEG, and/or fMRI. (See Dehaene 2014 for a review.) Minimal contrasts are ones where the stimuli remain fixed but where consciousness is sometimes present, sometimes absent. These were described in Chapter 3, and include binocular rivalry, continuous flash suppression, backward masking, and the attentional blink. The general finding in such experiments is that unconscious stimuli give rise to local reverberations in visual cortex and some higher-level association areas of temporal cortex. In contrast, stimuli that are consciously experienced give rise to much more widespread coordinated activity, involving both prefrontal and parietal cortices, with activity overlapping heavily with the attentional network that underlies working memory (Dehaene 2014).

Note that the prefrontal cortex is thought to house the main hubs of the networks responsible for decision-making, reasoning, and verbal report (as well as control of working memory). Moreover, it interacts

---

[1] The dorsolateral prefrontal cortex is situated on either side of the midline between the two hemispheres, forward of motor regions of the frontal cortex (which include the frontal eye-fields that control eye movements as well as shifts of covert attention). The intraparietal sulcus is a long fold within the parietal cortex at the back of the brain, situated above the visual cortex and below the somatosensory cortex, which in turn is situated just behind the central sulcus that divides parietal from frontal cortices.

heavily with the hippocampus and the medial temporal cortex in the formation of long-term memories (Buckner et al. 1999; Preston & Eichenbaum 2013).[2] So we appear to have a neural-network-based account of all of the main components of access consciousness, at least.

Recall, moreover, that the only *evidence* we have of phenomenally conscious states comes from states that are access-conscious—either states that we are aware of in ourselves, or states that others can report and describe. And recall, too, that the concept of phenomenal consciousness is a first-person one. Its extension is fixed in a way that starts from the first-person case, which means starting from states that are accessible to introspection and first-person thought. Without access consciousness, then, it seems there can be no direct evidence of states with the defining first-person character of phenomenal consciousness. So the simplest hypothesis is that phenomenally conscious states *are* those that are access-conscious.

Even those who want to claim that phenomenal consciousness should be identified with the contents of fragile short-term memory (rather than with the contents of working memory) allow that the only direct evidence we have of the existence of such consciousness comes from people's reports—in this case, their reports that they can see more in the briefly presented stimulus than they can thereafter sustain in working memory and identify (Block 2011a).[3] But as we saw in Chapter 4, there are no good options when trying to turn the fragile-short-term-memory account into a fully worked-out theory of phenomenal consciousness. For we know that in priming experiments where people say they see nothing, contents are nevertheless often active in the neural networks that realize such memory (the mid- and high-level sensory cortices) (Dehaene 2014). So we either have to say that they are wrong, insisting that the contents in question are phenomenally conscious despite

[2] The hippocampus is a curved subcortical structure shaped a bit like a seahorse (hence its name, derived from the Latin). It is adjacent to the inside (medial) surface of the temporal lobes, which wrap alongside the lower portions of the two halves of the brain, forward of the primary visual cortex at the back.

[3] Block (2011a) emphasizes that he doesn't think there can be inaccessible phenomenally conscious states. While many conscious states are actually unaccessed (i.e. the rich contents of fragile short-term memory), and thus never enter working memory, all are nevertheless *accessible*—on an individual basis they *would* enter working memory and hence become reportable if attended to.

subjects being unaware of them; or we have to define the short-term-memory system in question functionally, in terms of whether or not attention is *capable* of rendering its contents access conscious. But even that may leave us having to postulate phenomenally conscious states that people are unaware of, as we saw in Chapter 4. So, to repeat: the simplest hypothesis is to *identify* phenomenal consciousness with the nonconceptual contents of working memory/access consciousness.

5.4 Objections and replies

Critics have sometimes objected that the minimal-contrast methodology controls for stimulus factors but not for behavioral or downstream cognitive ones (Michel 2017).[4] For in order to report that a stimulus is visible on a given trial, participants need to say so, or press a button to indicate so, or respond in some other way that differs from how they respond when the stimulus remains unconscious. And as Pitts et al. (2014) point out, although both "seen" and "unseen" conditions may require a behavioral response, thus controlling for mere motor factors, formulating a "seen" response is likely to engage attention to sustain the seen stimulus in working memory while the response is encoded. Hence for this and other reasons there is ongoing debate over the question whether the prefrontal cortex is specifically involved in consciousness itself, as opposed to its causes and effects (Boly et al. 2017; Odegaard et al. 2017). We need to address the main aspects of this debate here.

Michel (2017) cites Frässle et al. (2014) as part of his attempt to challenge global-workspace theory; but in fact that article offers no such support. Frässle and colleagues managed to use binocular rivalry in passive viewing conditions (without requiring a behavioral report) by utilizing objective measures to signal the shifts in perceived content—such as the pupil dilation that happens automatically when one's percept switches from an image with one luminance to another. Using fMRI, they found robust posterior activation associated with image switches

---

[4] Michel has since "switched sides," and now defends the involvement of the prefrontal cortex in conscious experience. See Michel & Morales (2019), which reviews some additional data in addition to that discussed below.

under passive viewing conditions, but much reduced frontal activation compared with the active-report conditions. However, what they were actually investigating were the neural correlates of *shifts* in consciousness, not the neural correlates of consciousness itself. And Frässle and colleagues' own conclusion is merely that—in contrast with some existing theories—frontal activity plays little or no role in *causing* the shifts in perception in binocular rivalry. There is nothing here to conflict with global-workspace theory.

Michel (2017) also cites Pitts et al. (2014), whose findings are a bit more challenging. Pitts and colleagues designed a clever inattentional blindness paradigm that they combined with EEG. This enabled them to contrast brain activity in an unseen condition with both a passive-seen condition (where the stimulus was noticed but task irrelevant) and an active-seen condition (where participants were required to signal that they had seen the stimulus). They were able to do this by presenting the same set of stimuli three times: first with the central shape stimuli irrelevant to an attention-demanding task requiring attention to the periphery (the shapes remained invisible on these trials); then second having drawn attention to the central shapes, while the task remained the same (the shapes were reliably seen once participants knew they were there); and then finally when the task was to report the presence of the central shapes (here, too, the shapes were reliably perceived).

Pitts and colleagues found that conscious awareness correlated well with a mid-latency negative signal involving the parietal and visual cortices at around 200–240 milliseconds, which probably reflects the engagement of attention. But the later frontal EEG signal that has often been found in studies of consciousness that require a behavioral response (the P3b, or "centro-parietal positivity") was present only in the task-relevant trials, and was absent in the passive-seen condition. This might seem inconsistent with a global-workspace account. But it is important to stress that this is not the conclusion that Pitts and colleagues themselves actually draw. On the contrary, they suggest that the role of the mid-latency negativity is to make the stimulus content globally available. (Indeed, how else would people be able to report at the end of the run of trials that they had seen the central shapes in the seen-passive condition?) What the finding really shows is that an EEG signature that has often been *taken* to be a correlate of consciousness isn't actually so, but rather reflects the prerequisites of behavior planning. The data fail to raise any problem for the idea that consciousness comprises those contents that are broadcast to frontal executive systems.

All sides in these debates should accept that specific regions of temporal and parietal cortices are critically involved in processing and representing particular sensory contents, of course—such as faces, houses, colors, and so on—as well as being engaged by attentional processes. But according to global-workspace theory, these contents need to be broadcast more broadly—and to executive regions in the prefrontal cortex, in particular—in order to become conscious. Notice, however, that since these contents are thought to be broadcast quite widely, their representation in the prefrontal cortex is likely to be diffuse and distributed. As a result, one can explain why prefrontal content-related activity sometimes doesn't show up in brain-imaging studies using EEG or fMRI, as Odegaard et al. (2017) point out.

Likewise, the same point can explain why the prefrontal MEG response to a briefly presented stimulus should be less predictive of conscious experience than the MEG signal emanating from visual areas (Andersen et al. 2016). For visual processing of the stimulus is *concentrated* in the visual cortex, of course, and that processing is sharpened and boosted in conditions where the stimulus becomes conscious. In contrast, the resulting contents (when conscious) will be broadcast to multiple cortical sites, distributed in a variety of functionally distinct regions.

What would evidence against global-workspace theory look like, then? It would have to be evidence of consciousness realized in sensory-parietal interactions that *don't* have an effect on prefrontal regions. One type of alleged evidence of this general sort comprises the findings cited in support of "sensory overflow" and the fragile-short-term-memory account, discussed in Chapter 4. If one could show that there is *more* information consciously represented in the mid-level sensory cortices than can be transmitted to the prefrontal cortex for reporting purposes, then that might be taken to show that access consciousness is merely needed to provide *evidence* of phenomenal consciousness, without being either *constitutive* of the latter or the minimal neural correlate of the latter. However, as we saw in Chapter 4, the fragile-short-term-memory view is quite problematic, on a number of grounds.

Boly et al. (2017) offer evidence of a different sort, pertaining to people who have had accidentally induced or surgically caused lesions of all, or almost all, of the prefrontal cortex.[5] Yet these patients are said to remain conscious. This would certainly challenge global-workspace theory if it were true. But Odegaard et al. (2017) point out that it is *not* true. Close examination of the original reports for these patients (most of which derive from the first half of the twentieth century) show that the damage to prefrontal cortex in such cases was far from complete. And in contrast, Odegaard and colleagues report cases of patients with full prefrontal damage who have received comparatively little attention in the literature because they are completely mute and unresponsive, suggesting that they are *not* capable of conscious experience.

Moreover, there are deeper problems with Boly et al.'s (2017) argument. For they provide no evidence that the patients in question were capable of phenomenally conscious experience, as such. Indeed, their exposition seems to confound the various notions of consciousness distinguished in Chapter 1. They say that the patients in question were "fully conscious," which sounds as if it might be a reference to intransitive creature consciousness. (That is, the patients were awake and alert.) And they report that some of these patients were able to move around normally, which seems to be evidence only of transitive creature consciousness of a sensorimotor sort, guided by the affordances of the environment, utilizing forms of action selection that don't require executive decision-making.

Suppose, however, that there were patients with extensive frontal damage who nevertheless manage to display at least simple forms of flexible responding to perceptual stimuli, where that behavior doesn't seem to be merely of a sensorimotor sort. Would that be good grounds for granting that they have conscious experience (and hence for thinking that consciousness doesn't require broadcasting to prefrontal cortex)? It would not. The simplest way to see this is by assuming the truth of qualia realism. (Recall that in the present chapter we are only really investigating the functional and neural *correlates* of phenomenal consciousness.

---

[5] Notice that the other authors of this paper include a number of the main players from the anti-global-workspace camp, including Naotsugu Tsuchiya, Christof Koch, and Giulio Tononi. So it is reasonable to take this paper as presenting their strongest arguments against global-workspace theory.

Chapter 6 will attempt to turn global-workspace theory into a fully reductive account.) In that case there are any number of possible hypotheses about the set of functional and/or neural processes that are sufficient for qualia to become associated with a state. And in particular, it might be that flexible responding is *in*sufficient. The only cases that we know (or at least reasonably believe) to be sufficient are those in which subjects can issue verbal or other reports, and can engage in the kinds of behavior that suggest that one's own first-person concepts would be applicable to their experience. Beyond those central cases, we have no firm grounds for belief.[6]

Boly et al. (2017) also cite the evidence provided by Siclari et al. (2017), concerning the brain activity that takes place during dreaming. Siclari and colleagues found that changes in low-frequency EEG signals in a parietal-visual "hot-zone" reliably correlated with reports of dreaming when participants were wakened moments later. And this remained true whether that activity occurred during rapid-eye-movement (REM) sleep or during non-rapid-eye-movement (NREM) sleep. (One important finding of the study, then, is to demonstrate clearly that dreaming isn't exclusively associated with REM sleep.) Moreover, the same low-frequency EEG signature can be used to *predict* dreaming with high accuracy, discovered by waking participants whenever it occurs and probing them for dream awareness. Boly and colleagues seem to think this supports their view that conscious experience doesn't require broadcasting of information to prefrontal cortex, and that it can be realized entirely by activity in the back of the cortex.

In fact, however, Siclari and colleagues' data provide no such support. In the first place, the authors note that the causal role of low-frequency activity in the hot zone may be to disrupt the formation of the sort of *high*-frequency activity that generally correlates with specific types of conscious experience. Indeed, the cortical location of such high-frequency activity in these experiments could be used to predict whether participants were dreaming of faces or places, for example (via high-frequency activity in the fusiform face area versus a region of right posterior parietal cortex generally associated with spatial attention). In

---

[6] A related point to the one made here will be returned to and developed at length in Chapter 7, when we consider the question of consciousness in creatures that can respond flexibly to the environment, but are incapable of verbal report or reflection on their own perceptual states.

the second place, Siclari and colleagues found evidence of such high-frequency activity in regions of prefrontal cortex during dreaming also. So although it may be low-frequency activity taking place in the back of the brain that is the determining factor for whether or not dreaming of a certain sort takes place, there is no evidence here to show that the dream-states in question don't need to be broadcast to prefrontal regions also, in order to become conscious.

There is, moreover, an important conceptual point to be made here, given that dream reports are necessarily retrospective. Suppose that what had been found was a complete suppression of prefrontal activity during dreaming. Would that have demonstrated the falsity of global-workspace theory? In fact, it would not. For everyone allows, of course, that the specific contents of experience (faces, places, colors, and so on) are generated and represented in the posterior part of the brain. Hence the fact that such contents can exist in the absence of prefrontal activity (and hence in the absence of consciousness, according to global-workspace theory) is not in question. Then let us suppose that, when active and vivid enough, such contents can create at least short-term memories in the absence of consciousness. Still, when recalled on waking, those memories would of course *become* phenomenally conscious. For when one recalls an event—as one does in episodic remembering, for example—it results in the global broadcast of the representations in question, and entry into working memory. The fact that dreams *when recalled* have all the properties of phenomenal consciousness fails to show that dreams *when created* are likewise conscious. The hypothesis that they were wholly unconscious at the time of creation, but that they can be recalled retrospectively and consciously, can fully explain the data.[7]

5.5 Positive evidence

While the arguments against global-workspace theory have failed, it should be noted that proponents of the theory have nevertheless taken up the challenge that prefrontal activity may have to do with the causes

---

[7] Dennett (1976) once proposed an idea much like that described in this paragraph, among other suggestions.

and/or effects of consciousness, rather than consciousness itself. They have developed novel experimental paradigms to address the point. In particular, a recent study attempted to control for both behavioral and attentional factors (Salti et al. 2015). Participants were first trained to use all eight fingers when indicating the spatial position of a stimulus on a clock-face, with a unique finger used for each position. They were then presented with the same stimuli under conditions of backward masking that rendered the stimulus invisible on about 50 percent of the trials, but they were nevertheless required to guess at a location on *every* trial. Since these guesses on invisible trials were accurate at levels well above chance, one can infer that something like "blindsight" was involved (Weiskrantz 1986). Finally, on each trial participants had to indicate (by this time about two seconds following stimulus presentation) whether the stimulus had been seen or not seen.

The investigators then trained pattern classifiers on the resulting EEG and MEG data to determine where in the brain the information about the specific location of the stimulus was represented. The question was whether the pattern classifier could tell, from the location of activity in the prefrontal cortex in particular, in what location in the visual field the stimulus on a given trial had been presented. (The experimenters had selected location as the relevant content parameter because there are known to be retinotopically organized regions of prefrontal cortex, as well as such regions in visual and parietal cortices.) The finding was that in consciously seen trials the spatial content reached much further into the prefrontal cortex, and was processed much more deeply, than in blindsight cases that shared the same motor response.

Notice, first, that the fact that the spatial location of the stimulus on *un*seen trials could be decoded from the prefrontal cortex at all is not a problem for global-workspace theory. For that information would at least need to reach motor and premotor regions of the cortex in order for accurate "blindsight" responses to be selected and implemented. In effect, what may lie behind this finding is the transmission of spatial content through the dorsal (sensorimotor) action-guidance system, rather than the network that underlies conscious experience. In addition, some weak information from unseen stimuli may reach the prefrontal cortex more generally, helping to explain the sorts of priming effects on decision-making that unconscious perception is known to have. Or it might correspond to information transmitted to the prefrontal cortex through the relevance system that enables unconscious contents to compete for attentional resources (Corbetta et al. 2008).

Notice, second, that in this experiment the motor responses on seen trials and blindsight trials were identical. Hence the greater, more deeply processed representation of spatial content in the prefrontal cortex in the seen-condition can't simply be a function of motor planning or motor execution. For the motor properties of the two sorts of trial didn't differ. However, might the difference have reflected the fact that participants were preparing to make a "seen" rather than an "unseen" response at the end of the trial? Perhaps participants deployed extra attentional resources to sustain the representation of the seen location in trials when they were deciding to report "seen." This may well be so. But the increased prefrontal activity can't simply reflect generic attentional processes. Rather, it reflects better, more deeply processed encoding of the spatial location of the stimulus. Hence it must still be the case that the spatial content in question is better represented in the prefrontal cortex when the stimulus is seen. This is just what global-workspace theory would predict.

One further study—in this case employing passive viewing—is also worth considering in some detail (Panagiotaropoulos et al. 2012). This used binocular suppression with monkeys. On the basis of previous work with monkeys, the experimenters were confident that a new stimulus presented to one eye would immediately dominate an existing image being presented to the other, and would be sustained for at least a couple of seconds. Moreover, they were able to confirm this for the present study using an additional monkey who was trained to make a report each time his percept flipped. (He was trained on genuinely alternating stimuli for which the timing was known, and then tested under conditions of bicocular rivalry that matched those used in the current experiment.) This gave them a timing window within which they could be confident that the newly activated stimulus would dominate, despite both images being presented simultaneously to the visual system.

The experimenters then used cellular recording techniques to measure neuronal responses in lateral prefrontal cortex and elsewhere. (Lateral prefrontal cortex was chosen because of its extensive and direct—monosynaptic—connections with the regions of temporal cortex where object identity is extracted and coded.) They first located neurons that preferentially fired when the face of another monkey was perceived, as opposed to the alternative patterned stimulus. They then measured the activity of these content-specific neurons under conditions of binocular suppression, finding that they fired vigorously and in a more coordinated way during the time-period when the image of the monkey face was dominant.

Note that no behavioral demands were placed on the monkeys during this study, beyond the requirement to keep their eyes focused on a central fixation point, for which they were rewarded after each block of trials. So this was a study of entirely passive viewing under conditions in which the external stimulus remained identical across seen and unseen trials resulting from binocular suppression. Yet the finding was that the presence of the seen stimulus was robustly represented in prefrontal neurons, which remained unresponsive when the stimulus was not seen. This implies that the prefrontal activity observed in instances of conscious experience in humans can't just be a matter of action preparation, nor of generalized attention. On the contrary, it seems to be content-specific, just as was found in the study by Salti et al. (2015) discussed earlier. So in this respect, too, global-workspace theory is supported.

5.6 Animals in consciousness research

The study conducted by Panagiotaropoulos et al. (2012) was done with monkeys, of course. Hence it can't provide direct evidence of prefrontal involvement in *phenomenal* consciousness without begging the question of animal consciousness currently being addressed in this book. But that is not the sort of conclusion I think should be drawn from it. Rather, I take the findings to show that the difference between seen and unseen binocular-rivalry stimuli in monkeys (and hence presumably humans) is represented in content-specific activity in prefrontal cortex. And then, since the difference between seen and unseen is a difference between phenomenally conscious versus unconscious experience *in humans*, it supports the view that phenomenally conscious perceptions are those that are "globally broadcast" to prefrontal executive systems, just as global-workspace theory claims.

Is the extent to which monkeys have been used in consciousness research a problem for any view that might deny phenomenal consciousness to nonhumans? Or for the view (to be defended in Chapter 7) that there is no fact of the matter about consciousness in nonhumans? For monkeys have frequently been employed in studies of binocular rivalry (Lehky & Maunsell 1996; Leopold & Logothetis 1996; Tong et al. 2006), and also in studies of blindsight (Humphrey 1974; Cowey & Stoerig 1995; Stoerig & Cowey 1997). Moreover, we noted in Chapter 2 that they have been heavily used in research on the nature and properties of attention and working memory (Luck et al. 1997; Baluch & Itti 2011; Buschman et al. 2011). How are these studies to be interpreted, if not as demonstrating that monkeys, at least, are sometimes phenomenally conscious? Indeed, someone might think that it is a presupposition of this research that monkeys, too, have phenomenally conscious mental states.

A great deal of what we know about the brain networks underlying the global workspace has been derived from animal models, in fact. So we can conclude that the animals in question undergo states that are to some degree *access*-conscious, at least. Indeed, we know that the seen stimulus in a monkey blindsight experiment, as well as the currently dominant stimulus in a binocular-rivalry experiment, are represented in prefrontal cortical activity and can guide executively controlled actions. Such findings can be used to inform our understanding of access-conscious perceptual states in humans, and hence our understanding of phenomenal consciousness if the latter correlates with, or is identified with, access-conscious nonconceptual contents. But those findings don't (or needn't) presuppose that the animals in question are phenomenally conscious, and nor do they support such a view. To achieve the latter, we would need to know how extensive the similarities need to be between the broadcast-to executive systems of an animal and the executive systems found in humans, in order for phenomenal consciousness to be supported in the former as well as the latter. This question will be addressed in Chapter 7.

Notice, too, that a monkey's responses in a blindsight experiment (say) don't need to be interpreted as demonstrating higher-order awareness, despite the fact that humans in the same experiments might well make their reports in those terms. A human blindsight subject might be told, "We want you to guess at the nature of the stimulus on every trial, even if you don't see it; but on each trial we want you to tell us whether or not you saw anything." If the subject reports, "not seen" on a given trial, then that displays higher-order awareness of his own perceptual state. A monkey in a similar experiment will first be trained (in the sighted visual field) to make one response if a stimulus is present and another response if it is absent. When it then signals "absent" to a stimulus presented in its blind field (despite correctly classifying the stimulus in a forced-choice selection), this is most parsimoniously interpreted in first-order terms—as saying something like, "nothing there" rather than "I *see* nothing there."

The key point in all this, however, is as follows. Even if the brain networks underlying phenomenally conscious experience in humans have a great deal in common with those of animals, and even if some behaviors are also common across the two cases, this by no means settles the question of phenomenal consciousness in nonhumans. For the answer to that depends on the precise neural or functional correlates of phenomenal consciousness—and in particular, on whether or not those correlates implicate components of the global workspace that are unique to humans.

5.7 Conclusion

According to global-workspace theory, phenomenal consciousness comprises globally broadcast nonconceptual content—or at least, the theory claims that phenomenal consciousness and global broadcasting are reliable co-correlates. (Recall that the case for saying that global broadcasting can provide a successful *reductive* explanation of consciousness will be taken up in Chapter 6.) The present chapter has laid out the case in support of such a view. It has also responded to a number of recent challenges to the account. In short, global-workspace theory has none of the drawbacks of the competing theories discussed in Chapter 4, while facing no real obstacles of its own; and it can account for all the main properties of phenomenal consciousness, including its all-or-nothing character.

One important point that has emerged from our discussion is how difficult it is to find evidence that could dissociate phenomenal consciousness from reflective awareness and verbal report. This is a consequence of the first-person nature of the very *concept* of phenomenal consciousness. For possession of such a concept seems to constitutively depend on just such capacities. Yet most if not all nonhuman animals, of course, lack those capacities. All are incapable of verbal report; and most if not all are incapable of reflective higher-order thought about their own perceptual states. Somehow, then, we must find a way to project our first-person, introspectively grounded concept of consciousness into the minds of animals who may be incapable of forming or using such a concept. This is the basic challenge involved in ascribing phenomenal consciousness to animals. How can we get third-person evidence that would support the application of a first-person concept, except from cases where people can offer third-person evidence of deploying just the same sorts of first-person concepts as we do? This challenge will be discussed in depth in Chapter 7.

6

Explaining the "hard" problem

This chapter shows how global-workspace theory can be developed into a satisfying, fully reductive, explanation of phenomenal consciousness. It shows how globally broadcast nonconceptual content enables higher-order thoughts about that content, where those thoughts can lack conceptual connections with physical, functional, or representational facts. As a result, zombies are conceivable and an (epistemic) explanatory gap is opened up. But the thoughts in question can themselves be given a fully naturalistic explanation. Hence all of the facts involved in consciousness can be explained.

6.1 The right level of explanation

We noted in Chapter 1 that there are good theoretical reasons for rejecting qualia realism. This is because the guiding assumption of science has been the causal closure of physics. The latter entails that all causally relevant properties are, at bottom, physical properties or are realized in physical properties. So either (1) consciousness is physical, or (2) it makes no causal difference to the world (epiphenomenalism), or (3) it is composed of intrinsic nonphysical properties that somehow ground the laws of physics (Russellian monism). The second alternative is hard to believe. Indeed, it borders on incoherence: if consciousness makes no difference, then how do we even know it exists, and how can we talk about it? The third alternative is equally problematic, postulating properties that do no real explanatory work and that aren't needed for physics itself, while setting up a new version of the explanatory gap.

The physical-closure assumption, in contrast, has given rise to an extraordinarily successful explanatory strategy. This is to seek causal—broadly mechanistic—explanations for all of the phenomena we observe

Human and Animal Minds: The Consciousness Questions Laid to Rest. Peter Carruthers, Oxford University Press (2019). © Peter Carruthers.
DOI: 10.1093/oso/9780198843702.001.0001

in nature, while also seeking explanations of our causal findings that bottom out in physical processes. Again and again through the history of science, nature has given up her secrets to this strategy. So we have good reason to expect that the same will be true of phenomenal consciousness. That is to say, we have reason to expect that phenomenal consciousness should be physically explicable, or explicable in terms that are themselves ultimately physically explicable.

This conclusion leaves open, of course, the right *level* at which to seek an explanation of consciousness (or the right combination of levels, since many successful scientific explanations are multi-level in nature; Craver & Darden 2013). Many assume that the correct explanation should be couched in terms of brain mechanisms and brain processes. Indeed, the problem of consciousness itself—and the explanatory gap, in particular—is often expressed in just such terms. People ask: how can collections of neurons firing off electrical discharges to other neurons give rise to the distinctive smell of cinnamon, or the wash of color-experience as one observes a sunset?

My view is that this is a mistake, for a pair of distinct reasons. The first is that there are a number of potentially explanatory levels located between facts about neurons in the brain, on the one hand, and phenomenally conscious experience, on the other. For example, there are functional accounts (sometimes depicted using boxes and flowcharts) and computa-tional ones, as well as explanations that might be couched in terms of intentional/representational content. And in general, in science it is a bad idea to attempt to jump over too many explanatory levels at once. We don't attempt to explain how cells produce energy, for instance, in terms of quantum mechanical processes, but rather in terms of chemical ones. Nor do we explain biological principles of inheritance directly in atomic terms, but rather by appealing to the properties of chromosomes.[1]

Moreover, just as it is common to explain many biological processes in terms of other—better understood or more basic—biological processes,

---

[1] It is worth noting that Shea (2014) describes how the famous biologist William Bateson once thought that it was inconceivable that inheritance could be explained in terms of properties of chromosomes (Bateson 1916). In part this was because at the time Bateson lacked detailed knowledge of the internal structures and properties of cells. It seems that any claimed identity between properties can strike one as inconceivable if one's conceptions of those properties are too far apart.

so one might expect to understand phenomenal consciousness *in other mental terms*. In particular, I suggest, we might hope to explain it in terms of a certain sort of intentional content playing a certain kind of causal role. And that, in effect, is what global-workspace theory does. It explains phenomenal consciousness in terms of globally broadcast nonconceptual content.

The second reason for thinking that it might be a mistake to explain— or attempt to explain—phenomenal consciousness directly in terms of brain processes is that people already feel intuitively that there is some sort of deep distinction between mind and body. Indeed, as we noted in Chapter 1, there are reasons to think that the appeal of Cartesian dualism is innate or innately channeled, resulting from a clash between two fundamentally different bodies of "core knowledge" concerning the physical and mental domains (Bloom 2004). And, for sure, such beliefs come very naturally to people, since belief in the possibility of mentality after death is virtually universal across human cultures and historical eras. Now, it may be that these beliefs themselves result from the difficulty of explaining phenomenal consciousness in physical terms. But Chapter 1 argued that they don't, on a variety of distinct grounds.

As a result, if one casts the problem of consciousness in terms of a contrast between mind and brain, then one will run into the tacit folk intuition that these are separate existences; and in that case it is no wonder that people should feel there must remain some sort of residual explanatory gap between the two, no matter how much we learn about the brain. This source of resistance can be avoided if we seek to explain one form of mentality (phenomenal consciousness) in terms of another (intentional content and causal role).

Such a strategy presupposes, of course, that intentional content can in turn be reductively explained in lower-level (ultimately physical) terms. Yet the prospects for such a reduction might not appear too bright. For despite more than thirty years of attempted philosophical reductions of intentionality, none of them has (to put it mildly) been greeted with universal acclaim. However, I don't think we actually need in hand a reductive account of intentional content for us to be confident that content is real, and plays a real role in the world (via the work that it does in our psychology). On the contrary, since most theorizing in cognitive science treats both *representation* and *representational content* as theoretical primitives (setting aside a few backwaters that attempt to get by without these notions altogether), it is reasonable for us to do likewise. Since psychological properties are real, and since progress in integrating psychology with neuroscience is ongoing, we can assume that intentional content, too, is real. For *content* is one of the basic postulates of scientific psychology (Botterill & Carruthers 1999; Burge 2010).

There are further disputes surrounding the notion of intentional content, of course, in addition to the question of reduction. Specifically, there is the debate between defenders of *wide* content (according to which content is partly individuated by the worldly individuals and properties that cause it) and *narrow* content (according to which content individuation abstracts from such differences). While I have defended a notion of narrow content for purposes of psychological explanation in the past (Botterill & Carruthers 1999), I don't need to re-engage that debate for our purposes here—or at least, not in its entirety. This is because it is really only nonconceptual content that we need to deal with (together with phenomenal concepts, whose reference is internal to the mind in any case), for which many of these issues don't arise.

Notice, for instance, that there can be no differences in nonconceptual content resulting from the sorts of classic cases that have been thought to support the existence of wide content, such as the difference between water (H_2O) and twin-earth water (XYZ) (Putnam 1975), or the difference between arthritis (a disease of the joints) and twin-earth arthritis (a disease of the limbs generally) (Burge 1979, 1986). For both water and T-water will cause the same nonconceptual representations of watery stuff; and in the arthritis examples both people feel the same nonconceptual pain sensation in the thigh. Nor will there be any differences in nonconceptual content between perceiving Molly and her identical twin, Maud. And this is just as it should be for our purposes: one's phenomenally conscious visual experience will surely remain the same, whether it is Molly or Maud whom one is seeing.[2]

This last example should not be taken to suggest that nonconceptual content is wholly general in nature, however, and abstracted from the

---

[2] Of course, if one knows (or believes) that one is seeing Molly rather than Maud then there may well be overall differences in one's phenomenal experience. These might result e.g. from affective differences in one's attitudes towards the two people. (Perhaps Molly is loved and Maud is hated.)

individual things represented. On the contrary, when one is engaged in multiple object tracking, for example, elements of the visual system lock onto the individual objects involved in an indexical or quasi-indexical manner (Pylyshyn 2003). Likewise, such indexical-like representations are arguably at the heart of the binding process in vision, giving rise to a distinct object-file into which a variety of other forms of property information concerning color, shape, texture, and so forth (both non-conceptual and conceptual) can be bound. But what is nevertheless true is that if one individual is substituted for another without the visual system picking up on the change, then one's nonconceptual representation of the second individual will be the same as the first. A *mere* change in external reference doesn't result in any change in nonconceptual content, any more than would an unnoticed substitution of Maud for Molly.[3]

I propose to assume, then, that the most promising approach, if one is seeking a reductive explanation of phenomenal consciousness, is to cast one's account in intentional/representational terms, rather than directly in terms of brain mechanisms. And that is just what global-workspace theory does: it proposes to reduce phenomenal consciousness to globally broadcast nonconceptual content. As we saw in Chapter 5, such an account can already explain many of the properties of phenomenal consciousness (its ineffability, for example, and its all-or-nothing character). Our task in the present chapter is to extend that account into a reductive explanation of the explanatory gap, explaining the "hard problem" thought experiments.

6.2 The phenomenal-concept strategy

The basic strategy is long-standing and familiar in outline (Loar 1990; Tye 1995, 2000; Balog 1999, 2012; Carruthers 2000; Papineau 2002; Carruthers & Veillet 2007; Prinz 2012). It is to argue that the problems in question

---

[3] Given the fundamental role played by indexical-like representations in perception, it is worth noting that if such indexicals are thought to qualify as concepts, then this means that the content of phenomenally conscious perception is not, strictly, fully nonconceptual in nature. Rather, the sort of content appealed to in global-workspace theory will comprise nonconceptual fine-grained representations of properties like color and shape organized around indexical-like representations of individual things. For simplicity, I will generally ignore this qualification in what follows.

arise, not because our conscious states possess special properties of any sort (qualia), but rather from the distinctive first-person way in which it is possible for us to *think about* those states. It is because these thoughts lack conceptual connections with physical, functional, or even representational ones that we can conceive of the possibility of zombies; and it is also why we can see that even a complete physical/functional/intentional description of ourselves wouldn't entail the truth of those thoughts. But the nature and existence of the thoughts themselves can be explained in a way that doesn't introduce any special nonphysical properties, either.

Three different types of proposal have been made concerning the nature of phenomenal concepts. Some have said that they are *purely recognitional* concepts (Loar 1990; Carruthers 2000). Others have said that they are *quotational* in nature, in that they embed a phenomenally conscious content within their scope (Balog 1999; Papineau 2002). The idea here is that such concepts take the form, THE EXPERIENCE ___,[4] where what fills the gap is an instance of some specific experience or other (or an image thereof, since visual, auditory, and other mental images are also phenomenally conscious). Thirdly, yet others have said that phenomenal concepts are a distinctive class of *indexical* concept, referring nondescriptively to one's attended conscious contents (Perry 2001; Levin 2007; Schroer 2010).

One problem for the recognitional view is that it has difficulty explaining first-time phenomenal thoughts, as when color-deprived Mary leaves her black-and-white room and experiences color for the first time in her life (Jackson 1986). For one can't *recognize* what one has never experienced before. Another is that it has difficulty accounting for thoughts about specific experiences that are too fine-grained for reliable recognition, as Prinz (2012) points out. Thus one can think that *this* experience of a specific shade of red is subtly different from *that* one, even though one would be unable to tell, after closing one's eyes for a moment and finding just one shade presented, which experience of the two one was then undergoing (or whether, indeed, the experience was of a subtly different third shade of red).

---

[4] The term "experience" in the quotational account is not intended to be a phenomenal concept itself, obviously, on pain of vicious circularity. Rather, it should be some functionally characterized concept, perhaps equivalent in content to PERCEPTUAL OR PERCEPTION-LIKE STATE.

A problem for the quotational view, on the other hand, is that it requires one's experiences to actually become embedded within one's phenomenal concepts themselves. A phenomenal concept then doesn't just *refer* to an experience or mental image of some sort, it actually contains the referred-to state within itself. While not incoherent, this seems unnecessarily cumbersome, implying that our phenomenal thoughts have a structure that isn't really propositional.

One thing that the quotational view gets right, however (and in this it contrasts with the recognitional account), is that it entails that phenomenal concepts can only be activated when referring to some current phenomenally conscious state. While one can think about phenomenally conscious states in their absence, one isn't then employing a phenomenal concept in the sense that matters for our purposes here, I suggest. And while one can have recognitional concepts for some of one's own phenomenally conscious states, it isn't *those* concepts that we employ when we entertain thoughts about the conceivability of zombies and the rest. Indeed, as we will see in Section 6.4, there are many ways of thinking and talking about phenomenally conscious states that don't involve the distinctive kinds of concepts that give rise to the "hard problem" thought experiments. Those thought experiments only really get a grip on one when thinking about some current experience or image and thinking that a zombie might lack *that*, or that one could know everything of a physical and functional sort without knowing what *that* is like.[5]

In consequence, I propose to follow Prinz (2012) in taking phenomenal thoughts to involve reference to nonconceptual content via a special sort of acquaintance-based indexical concept.[6] Depending on the context

---

[5] Recall from Chapter 1 that Balog (2009) draws a distinction between *basic* and *non-basic* phenomenal concepts in this connection. The important point for our purposes is that it is basic phenomenal concepts that give rise to an explanatory gap.

[6] The notion of acquaintance employed here is entirely anodyne, as we will see shortly. Moreover, it should be noted that Prinz's (2012) actual focus is on the knowledge argument, and his goal is to give an account of what it is to know what an experience is like. He identifies knowledge of what it is like with a form of nonpropositional acquaintance, one that involves actively sustaining a nonconceptual representation in working memory via an attentional pointer. Plainly, however, although such active maintenance may be a necessary condition for entertaining phenomenal thoughts, it isn't sufficient. One needs to think *about* the sustained content by using an indexical that targets it. Merely sustaining a nonconceptual content can't give rise to the various "hard problem" thought experiments; they need to be thought about for that. So the account that I offer in the text extends what Prinz actually says (which, indeed, he invites the reader to do).

and the intent behind the thought, that concept can be quite specific in content, as when one thinks, "*This* [experience of red] is subtly different from *that*." Alternatively, the content might tacitly track the extension of an existing first-order concept, as when Mary thinks, when she leaves her black-and-white room and sees a ripe tomato, "So *this* is what it is like to see red." Or the content of a phenomenal thought might be wholly general, as when one thinks, while morbidly reflecting on one's own mortality, "When I die, all *this* will disappear"—meaning to refer to one's experience in general. In what follows, partly to emphasize that the concepts in question are purely first-person ones, I propose to use the notation "this-R" for a concept applying to an experience of red (either a specific shade or in general), and "this-E" for a concept that applies to one's phenomenal experience as a whole.

What can be said about the acquaintance relation then? Can this be characterized in a naturalistically acceptable manner? Nothing more mysterious need be involved than global broadcasting of nonconceptual content in general, as well as the ways in which globally broadcast contents are made available to the executive systems that formulate explicit judgments. In my view, though, higher-order thoughts aren't formulated automatically and embedded into globally broadcast non-conceptual contents in the course of perceptual processing. Many perceptual judgments, in contrast, *are* automatic, and they can become components of the globally broadcast contents themselves. When one sees something *as* a cat, or *as* a truck, for example, the concepts CAT and TRUCK get bound into the object-files in question and are broadcast along with them (Carruthers 2015a). Phenomenal concepts, on the other hand, are only deployed in explicit, executively controlled judgments.[7]

Phenomenal thoughts thus belong in the same general category as explicit thoughts like, "*This* is the shade of color I want on the living-room walls." Here, too, one's indexical concept is grounded in acquaintance with a nonconceptual representation of color, made available to

---

[7] In this my view contrasts with that of Picciuto (2011), who argues that phenomenal concepts are routinely bound into the contents of all globally broadcast states. But which concepts? And what would be the point? It is easy to see why first-order concepts like TOMATO should get bound into the contents of perception, since they can then evoke relevant stored knowledge and enter into decision-making processes. But what could be the point of binding THIS-E into each and every access-conscious state?

one's judgment-forming systems through global broadcasting. But in this case the resulting judgment is first-order, whereas when one thinks, "So *this*-R is what it is like to see red," the thought is a higher-order one, being *about* the first-order nonconceptual content in question.

What is it about the acquaintance-based indexical THIS-R that makes it a higher-order one rather than a first-order one, however? (Recall from Chapter 4 that this was one of the challenges presented to global-workspace theory by Carruthers 2000, which was supposed to motivate a move to dual-content theory instead.) Plainly it must be something about the intent with which the concept is employed, or the ways one is disposed to use it and infer things from it, that marks it out as referring to one's *experience* of red, rather than to red itself. And this means there must be at least a tacit use of the concept EXPERIENCE (or the concept PERCEPTION, or something similar) in the background of one's explicit thought. Notice that this implies that phenomenal concepts are not completely conceptually isolated.[8]

If phenomenal concepts aren't entirely isolated from all other concepts of the mental, however, then the problem is to explain how one can entertain some of the more radical "hard problem" thought experiments. It is obvious how one can think, "*This*-R might not have been a brain state," for there are no conceptual connections between phenomenal concepts as characterized here and brain-state concepts. It is equally obvious how one can think, "There could be a being who is physically and functionally just like myself, whose perceptual states play just the roles that mine do, but who nevertheless lacks *this*-R." For even if the phenomenal concept THIS-R tacitly embeds the concept PERCEPTION, this doesn't mean that thinking third-personally of a state that is perceptually just like mine need entail an application of THIS-R. Indeed, it plainly doesn't. However, although this is significantly harder to do, it seems one can also think a thought like, "*This*-R might not have been an experience/ perceptual state at all, but could have had the role of a decision instead."

---

[8] I should emphasize here that the concepts whose tacit use renders the indexical higher-order (about one's experience of red) rather than first-order (about red) are not themselves phenomenal ones. They are just regular concepts like SEE or PERCEIVE, which aren't first-person in nature, and carry no commitments about the presence of qualitative, intrinsic, or directly known properties.

How is this possible if THIS-R embeds the concept EXPERIENCE or the concept PERCEPTION?

A number of answers are possible, in fact (Carruthers 2017b). One is that, since the embedding of the concept EXPERIENCE in one's phenomenal concept is only tacit, one might not notice the incoherence when one thinks that the phenomenal state might not have been an experience. This is similar in spirit to the manner in which one can explain how people can seemingly think things like, "He knows it but he doesn't believe it." Although knowledge arguably entails belief, the connection isn't explicitly represented in thought, and this makes it possible for people to violate the entailment without realizing it. Another possibility, however, is that the tacit causal theory or mind-model deployed by the mind-reading system, in which concepts like EXPERIENCE and DECISION are embedded, doesn't treat the causal roles it assigns to such states as *essential* to them. It might rather treat them as contingent causal generalizations; and plausibly (like causal theories generally) it does.

One final point of elucidation, before we return to the phenomenal-concept strategy as such: how does the extension of a concept like THIS-R or THIS-E get fixed? Some possibilities are easily ruled out. Since these concepts are first-person ones, they plainly can't get their extension by deferring to the usage of others. (This isn't to deny that there might be other nearby concepts that *are* deferential, however. See the discussion in Section 6.4.) There are no public norms governing their use, so one can't be deferring to such norms when employing them in phenomenal thoughts. Neither are they employed as natural-kind terms, getting their reference from whatever turns out to be the underlying explanatory "essence" of the states picked out. For as Kripke (1980) famously pointed out, one's intention when employing a phenomenal concept is merely to track the content of the experience itself, not to refer to some sort of underlying physical or functional essence.

The only remaining possibility, then (if one rejects the reality of qualia), is that the extensions of one's phenomenal concepts get fixed by one's classificatory dispositions when employing them. When one thinks a thought with the content, *this-R is an interesting experience*, the extension of the concept THIS-R will be determined as the set of non-conceptual contents that would evoke the same dispositions-to-judge as those that underlie the thought in question (or something of the sort). This point will prove to be of some importance in Chapter 7.

6.3 Implementing the strategy

With phenomenal concepts thus characterized, we can return to explain the conceivability of zombies. Since the concept THIS-E is first-personal, applications of it won't be entailed by any combination of physical, functional, or representational concepts. As a result, one can coherently think, "There could be a being who is a physical, functional, and representational duplicate of myself, who nevertheless lacks *this*-E." But at the same time, the sort of state picked out by THIS-E is just globally broadcast nonconceptual content. No special properties—no qualia, nothing nonphysical—need to be postulated in order to explain how that thought can be thinkable. Nor do any of the properties often attributed to qualia—such as being intrinsic, private, or infallibly known—need to be built into the concept THIS-E in order for it to play the role that it does in conceiving of zombies.

What *is* true, however, is that in formulating a concept like THIS-R or THIS-E one has to focus just on the nonconceptual content of the experience in question. For as we noted in Chapter 1, an access-conscious perception of a red tomato, say, will likely come with the concepts RED and TOMATO embedded into the visual object-file along with nonconceptual representations of color and shape. And as we also argued briefly in Chapter 1, conceptual contents *don't* give rise to "hard problem" thought experiments (Carruthers & Veillet 2017). One cannot coherently think, for example, "This tomato-experience might not have been about tomatoes." So when formulating a concept like THIS-R or THIS-E one has to bracket off any conceptual content that might be embedded in one's experience, attending just to the latter's fine-grained nonconceptual content. (This might be why one often has to *work* to get people on board with the idea of zombies or inverted spectra. In effect, one has to get them to focus on their own experience in the right sort of way.) Having done so, one can then coherently think, "*This*-R might have been about green rather than red, and might have been reliably caused by the sight of fresh grass." For while nonconceptual red color content would normally warrant, or provide evidence for, an application of the concept RED, it certainly doesn't mandate or entail one.

The explanation of the explanatory gap runs in parallel. When one imagines oneself knowing everything there is to know about the physical, functional, and representational facts involved in color vision, for example, one will nevertheless be inclined to think, "But even if I knew all that, it still wouldn't explain the existence of *this*-R when I look at a red tomato." This is because, given the conceptual isolation of the phenomenal concept *THIS*-R, nothing in all those facts can entail or mandate its application. But the gap here is entirely at the level of thought. All that would remain when all the explaining facts are known, is a true thought that isn't entailed by one's complete naturalistic description. But what that thought picks out (globally broadcast nonconceptual red color content) can be naturalistically explained, as can be one's capacity to think such thoughts in the first place. So nothing in the world is left unexplained. It is merely that the thought entertained when one thinks of the world in a specific way (deploying a phenomenal concept) is left dangling. But we have now explained why this should be so.

Finally, consider Jackson's (1986) color-deprived Mary. By hypothesis, she knows everything there is to know about the neurophysiology, functional organization, and representational contents involved in color vision. Nevertheless, when she leaves her black-and-white room and experiences color for the first time, it seems she would learn something new. For instance, she might come to know the proposition, *this-R is what people undergo when they see a red tomato*. But this is a proposition that she wasn't in a position even to entertain before leaving her room, since it contains a phenomenal concept of color; and that concept, in turn, is grounded in acquaintance with nonconceptual representations of red. But the latter have now entered her mind for the first time. So she learns something new, in the sense of thinking a new true thought. But the fact described by that thought is something she *already* knew, since she already knew all about the nonconceptual content involved and its roles when globally broadcast. So there is novelty at the level of thought, resulting from new nonconceptual representations being broadcast in her mind for the first time (nonconceptual color content). But no new properties need to be added to the world beyond the physical, functional, and representational ones she already knew about.

One might remain puzzled as to why indexical thoughts about one's own experience, grounded in acquaintance with that experience itself, should have such different properties from indexical thoughts about items in the physical world, which are likewise grounded in one's experience. Why does an explanatory gap seemingly remain between all physical facts, on the one hand, and thoughts involving concepts such as THIS-R or THIS-E, but not with thoughts involving world-directed indexical concepts like THIS-[object] or THAT-[type of object]? For in the latter cases, too, one might be entirely ignorant of the nature of what one is thinking about. One might be unsure whether *this* is a physical object of some sort, or a shadow cast by an object, or indeed whether it might merely be a hologram of some kind. And by the same token, there would seem to be no conceptual connections between specific physical facts and concepts, on the one hand, and the bare-indexical thought in question, on the other.

The answer is that the worldly indexical thought, although grounded in a perceptual content of some sort, is directed at the thing *represented in* one's experience, which is located, or is at least represented as located, in the space outside of one's body. (I set aside here, for simplicity, indexical thoughts one might entertain about the causes of one's own interoceptive bodily experiences.) As such, the object of one's thought falls within the domain of facts from which physical explanations can be sought. Hence one cannot coherently think that all physical facts might be as they are, and yet *that* thing be absent or different. Indeed, one is compelled to think that any truths that there are about the object of one's thought would be entailed by the complete physical description of the world.

When one entertains a thought involving a phenomenal concept like THIS-R, in contrast, one is thinking about one's experience itself (the representing event, rather than the thing represented). This isn't presented to one as spatially located at all (except trivially, as being at the location occupied by one's own body, since it is predicated of oneself). One's own experiences aren't presented to one as being *in* objective space, as such (in contrast with locations within a visual field, say). As a result, they don't automatically fall within the domain of physical facts, and a potential explanatory gap is opened up. And indeed, McGinn (1991) puts the nonspatial character of experience at the very heart of his own development the explanatory gap. But of course, from the fact that one's own experiences aren't *represented to oneself* as physical or spatial, it doesn't follow that they *aren't* spatially located. (Nor does it follow that they are represented as *non*-spatial, either.) But it does provide one with an intuitive foothold for the thought experiments that are supposed to motivate an anti-physicalist conclusion.

6.4 In defense of phenomenal concepts

The success of the phenomenal-concept strategy hinges on the existence of phenomenal concepts of the sort described, of course. Yet both Ball (2009) and Tye (2009)—for very similar reasons—argue that there are no such things as phenomenal concepts. Those arguments are fully and carefully rebutted by Veillet (2012). Here I will confine myself to a few general points.

The arguments of both Ball and Tye turn crucially on the fact that we can talk and write publicly about phenomenal consciousness—just as I am doing in this book, indeed. Whether, when doing so, we are employing phenomenal concepts in the intended sense, however, is a moot point. Suppose I assert, for example, "What it is like to see red is more similar to what it is like to experience orange than it is to see green." While the topic, here, is relations among phenomenally conscious states, arguably no phenomenal concepts are employed. Rather, hearers are being invited to reflect on their own phenomenally conscious experiences when seeing red, orange, and green, so as to verify that the first is more like the second than the third. Not all talk about phenomenal experience needs to employ phenomenal concepts.

A similar point can be made about some of Ball's (2009) examples. For instance, he imagines Mary, while still in her black-and-white room, saying, "I don't know what it is like to see red," but then later, after she leaves, saying, "I know what it is like to see red." Since the two thoughts expressed contradict one another, they must involve the same concepts. But (says Ball) phenomenal-concept theorists think that the second involves a phenomenal concept of red whereas the former doesn't. In fact, however, *neither* thought employs a phenomenal concept in the sense outlined in Section 6.2. Both thoughts are *about* the phenomenal experience of red, of course. But neither involves a concept that carves that experience apart from physical, functional, and (especially in this case) intentional notions. For notice that *seeing red* is an intentional notion. Employing a genuine phenomenal concept like THIS-R, one can think: "*This-R* might not have been what it is like to see red." And as we noted in Chapter 1, the language of "what it is like" is intended just to draw our attention to our own phenomenally conscious experience. So none of the concepts in, "I know what it is like to see red" are actually phenomenal concepts.

In addition, both Ball (2009) and Tye (2009) argue that concepts for phenomenally conscious states can be acquired, like other concepts, via deference to the concepts of other people. Suppose one were to tell Mary while she is still in her room that "this-R" is the concept one employs for the phenomenal experience of red. Mary can then defer to that usage, despite never having experienced red for herself, just as someone can acquire the concept BEECH despite never having seen one. She can think thoughts employing that concept, and make assertions that directly contradict the assertions of others. If Mary says, for example, "This-R gives rise to feelings of coolness," that seems to directly contradict one's own assertion when one says, "No, actually, *this*-R gives rise to feelings of warmth." Since they contradict, they must employ the same concepts.

Part of what is at stake, here, is the question of how concepts are individuated. What is true, of course, is that since in this example Mary's concept THIS-R is parasitic on one's own, it is guaranteed to have the same extension, and in that sense they are the same concept. They both "lock on to" the same property, as it were. Nevertheless, the *way in which* Mary is thinking about phenomenal red when she employs that concept is quite different. Some people distinguish concepts from conceptions, in this sort of connection (Rey 1985). For example, one might say that the novice who has never seen a beech and knows nothing about beeches, but who defers to the use of the experienced forester, has the *concept* BEECH, but has a different *conception* of what a beech is. Given this framework, the important point for our purposes can be put like this: it is one's distinctive first-person acquaintance-based *conceptions* of one's own phenomenal states that do the work in explaining the explanatory gap, not the concepts we can acquire via deference to the thoughts of others. Moreover, we can convert those conceptions into distinct concepts by declining to use them in a deferential way.[9]

One should grant that Ball (2009) and Tye (2009) are right, of course, that we *can* form concepts of phenomenal states we have never experienced, and that we *can* have concepts referring to phenomenal states that defer to the judgments of other people. But it simply doesn't follow that these are the only kinds of concepts available for thinking about phenomenal states. Specifically, it is left entirely open that there can also be indexical acquaintance-based concepts of the sort described in Section 6.2, that are *not* used deferentially. And not everyone need always possess such concepts, either, even though they can think about phenomenal consciousness in other ways. Indeed, it has been my experience when trying to get students to grasp the "hard" problem of consciousness that many of them first have to be invited to focus on a specific phenomenal experience and then formulate a thought about it; in effect, requiring them to create a novel phenomenal concept on the fly.

I conclude that there may be multiple ways of thinking about phenomenally conscious states, and not all of them implicate the kinds of phenomenal concepts described in Section 6.2. (In the terminology introduced by Balog 2009, many ways of thinking about phenomenally conscious states don't involve *basic* phenomenal concepts.) All that really matters for our purposes, however, is that people *can* form concepts of that sort. And it is difficult to see how thought-experiments of the "hard problem" type could even get a grip on us if we couldn't. Even those who believe, like Chalmers (2006), that the phenomenal-concept strategy fails, nevertheless think that the hard problem depends on the existence of phenomenal concepts. They just believe that an appeal to such concepts can't do the explanatory work required of them, as we will see in Section 6.5.

---

[9] An alternative way of handling the issue would be to distinguish between two distinct notions of *concept*. One of them would individuate concepts in the way needed to support and explain our communicative practices. The other would individuate them in the manner necessary for successful psychological explanation and generalization (Botterill & Carruthers 1999). Given this sort of framework, the important point is that it is the latter notion of *concept* that is needed to explain the explanatory gap.

6.5 Chalmers' dilemma

Chalmers (2006, 2018) attempts to develop a dilemma for the phenomenal-concept strategy: either phenomenal concepts could be entertained by a zombie, in which case those concepts can't explain our epistemic situation (since by hypothesis, zombies lack phenomenally conscious experiences); or those concepts couldn't be possessed by a zombie, in which case they, too, are part of the "hard" problem. So either way, that hard problem isn't resolved.[10]

One thing right about Chalmers' dilemma is that there are two ways of characterizing phenomenal concepts. One of these is third-personal and broadly functional, as outlined in Section 6.2. On this account, we can say that a phenomenal concept is an indexical acquaintance-based concept activated with respect to some globally broadcast nonconceptual content. Zombies would, of course, possess such concepts, since they are physically, functionally, and representationally indistinguishable from us. But phenomenal concepts can also be given a first-person characterization, when they are *in use*. One can say, for example, "A phenomenal concept appears in the subject position of the following thought: *This-R is warm* [while one attends to an experience of red]." And yet, of course, when one characterizes zombies one might do so by saying that they lack *this*-R, among other states. Since, by hypothesis, zombies lack phenomenal experiences, they can't, it seems, have the very same indexical concept one employs when characterizing what they lack. And in that case, in addition to lacking phenomenal states, a zombie would also lack the concept THIS-R. So the latter concept becomes part of the problem, rather than the solution.

Notice, however, that an exactly parallel distinction between third-person and first-person characterizations of its own concepts would arise for a zombie itself. When *using* its own acquaintance-based indexical concepts, the zombie would be able to conceive of a zombie-zombie—that is, a zombie version of itself. Indeed, it would be capable of thinking

---

[10] It might help to emphasize, here, that while I allow that zombies are *conceivable*, I deny that they are metaphysically possible. My talk in this section of what zombies could or couldn't do is for expository purposes only. My goal is to disentangle the different ways we have of conceptualizing what is conceptually possible for zombies, demonstrating that their imagined possession or lack of possession of phenomenal concepts doesn't reinstate the hard problem.

thoughts of exactly the same *form*, at any rate, as we do when conceiving of zombies, or when we think that Mary will learn something new on first leaving her room, or when judging that no catalog of physical, functional, and representational facts could close the explanatory gap with our own perceptual states (when thought about in an indexical first-person way). But at the same time, a zombie would have no difficulty in conceiving that a zombie-zombie would possess indexical acquaintance-based concepts grounded in globally broadcast nonconceptual content, of course. So a zombie, gripped by "hard problem" thought experiments of exactly the same *form* as us, might likewise lay out Chalmers' dilemma for anyone who proposes that a phenomenal concept-type strategy could resolve the problem.

What this suggests is that it is indeed phenomenal concepts (when used) that are at the heart of the "hard" problem, not any special properties of our phenomenally conscious states themselves. Zombies, too, would be gripped by "hard problem" thoughts of exactly the same form as our own. Moreover, they too could naturally (without any artifice or special programming) present a dilemma that parallels Chalmers' one, directed at any other zombie who proposes to resolve those "hard" problems via a phenomenal-concept strategy. So I submit that the simplest and most plausible explanation is that the differing characterizations of phenomenal concepts are just different ways of referring to the *same* concepts. While we can *conceive of* zombies when *using* phenomenal concepts, in fact any beings that meet the specifications of a zombie (physically, functionally, and representationally indistinguishable from us) would be phenomenally conscious, just as we are. For to be phenomenally conscious is just to be a subject of globally broadcast nonconceptual contents. And any reflective beings who are subject to such contents, and who can form indexical acquaintance-based concepts for them, can find themselves in the grip of "hard problem" thought experiments.

6.6 Phenomenology beyond representation?

Global-workspace theory proposes that phenomenal consciousness simply *is* globally broadcast nonconceptual content. The truth of such a claim requires that there shouldn't be any phenomenal differences among our experiences that aren't accompanied by representational differences. Put differently, any two experiences that share the same nonconceptual representational content must likewise be phenomenally identical, if global-workspace theory is correct.

Numerous counter-examples to this claim have been proposed over the years. One concerns the phenomenal difference between looking at a square shape and looking at the same shape tilted through 45 degrees, so that it presents as a diamond (Peacocke 1983). It is said that the shape represented is the same in the two cases, although one's phenomenal experience differs. Another example concerns seeing a coin lying on a table, presented at an oblique angle (Peacocke 1992). The coin *looks* circular, but one's phenomenal experience is very different from the case where the same coin is held perpendicular to the line of sight, when it also looks circular. Then there is the difference between seeing a blurry image on the screen and seeing a sharp image without one's glasses on, in which case one also has a blurry experience, but without representing the image itself as blurred (Boghossian & Velleman 1989). In addition, there are cross-modal cases, as when one has a peripheral visual or auditory experience of something moving, where the representational content is said to be the same but one's phenomenal experience is very different (Block 1995).

All of these (and other) alleged counter-examples have been discussed at length by Tye (1995, 2000) and others, and shown to be spurious. I don't propose to review those responses here. But just to illustrate, the difference in experience between the same shape seen as a square and seen as a diamond can reduce to a difference in the represented axes of symmetry. When one views a square, one represents it as resting on its base while being symmetrical around the vertical axis. When one views a diamond, in contrast, one represents it as balanced on its point and as being symmetrical around the diagonal axis. Notice that such contents are pregnant with possibilities for action and movement—the square is seen as *solidly* placed whereas the diamond is seen as finely *balanced*. While it is not mandatory to explain the existence of such contents, theories of content that emphasize not just input-information but also the down-stream inferential or cognitive roles of a representation (so-called "dual factor" theories) can easily make sense of them.

Instead of going over old ground, in what follows I propose to discuss just two sorts of case that have gained a purchase in the more recent literature: the phenomenology of mood and emotional valence, on the one hand (Aydede & Fulkerson 2014; Kind 2014), and the ways in which phenomenal experience can be altered by shifting levels of attention, on the other (Block 2010). Before embarking on those discussions, however, it is worth noting that what can be at stake, here, is a sort of qualia *quasi*-realism. One can think that conscious experiences possess properties (quasi-qualia) that don't reduce to any combination of functional and representational ones, while at the same time accepting that these properties are identical with some or other set of lower-level (perhaps neural) physical ones. Indeed, this appears to be Block's own position. So one can believe in qualia-like properties—maintaining that there are private, ineffable, nonrepresentational properties of some of our mental states—while rejecting qualia *realism*, in the sense that I employ the term in this book (that is, while denying that qualia are nonphysical properties of our mental lives).

It seems obvious that there are at least representational *components* of moods and emotions. When one is afraid, for example, one's heart will be pounding, one's breathing will speed up, and one's palms will sweat. All of these bodily properties can be detected through proprioceptive and interoceptive pathways, and can be conscious when attended to. Similarly, when depressed one might be aware of one's slumped bodily posture, as well as of feelings of physical tiredness or lassitude. And when in pain, of course, there are bodily sensations that can be said to represent tissue damage (Tye 2006), one's muscles will likely tense, and one may be aware of an urge to cry out. But all of these cases share something else as well: they are all *negative*. Pain feels bad; so does depression; and fear and anger are generally classified as negative emotions. These negative components of affective states (and positive, in the case of joy, contentment, and pleasure) are generally called "valence" in cognitive science. So the questions before are (1) whether valence contributes to the phenomenal properties of affective states; and (2) if it does, whether it can be explained in representational terms.

It seems plain that differences in valence make a direct phenomenal difference. Some kinds of morphine can suppress the negative-valence component of pain experience, for example, while leaving the sensory aspect intact. People say that the pain is still there, and still feels the same, but that it no longer bothers them: its presence is no longer *bad*.

Intuitively, there is a big phenomenal difference between a pain that feels bad and one that doesn't; and it seems unlikely that this can reduce to differences in the other bodily or behavioral manifestations of pain, such as one's muscles no longer being tense. But what, then, *is* the valence component of pain? Is it a non-representational quale that normally attaches to the experience in question? Or is it a nonconceptual representation of some sort?

In a recent paper I argue at some length that valence is best understood as a nonconceptual representation of value (Carruthers 2018d). Pain *seems bad*, where the seeming badness doesn't embed the concept BAD, but is rather fully nonconceptual. (For comparison, consider the evidence of nonconceptual representations of approximate number in animals and humans. It seems that one can represent *around twenty dots* without embedding the concept TWENTY. See Barth et al. 2003; Jordan et al. 2008.) Similarly, drinking when thirsty or eating when hungry *seem good*, but without embedding the concept GOOD.

If valence is representational, however, then it must be possible for it to represent rightly or wrongly. Is it possible to say what fixes the correctness conditions for nonconceptual representations of value? One possibility would be to generalize the *harmfulness* account of the negative valence of pain proposed by Cutter & Tye (2011). One might say, for example, that positive valence is a nonconceptual representation of *adaptiveness*, whereas negative valence is a representation of *maladaptiveness*. This would be a broadly "externalist" account. But another possibility would be to explain the correctness conditions in terms of a match to the underlying settings of one's valuational systems. It is well known, of course, that affective priming is ubiquitous in our experience. (A sunny day makes one feel that one's life as a whole is going well; a disgusting video can alter one's evaluation of a moral vignette; a frustrating day at work may facilitate anger at one's kids, and so on.) In such cases the *seeming goodness* or *seeming badness* of a thing is out of line with one's underlying values. So one might try saying something minimal like this: valence of degree v directed at an object o correctly represents the value of o just in case nothing other than o contributed to the production of v.

These are, of course, mere initial sketches. But recall that I am taking intentional content for granted throughout this book as a conceptual primitive. So I prefer not to be committed to any specific theory of the determinants of representational content. However, enough has been said, I hope, to make it seem likely that the valence component of our conscious experience, like all the other components, is best understood as a nonconceptual representation of some sort—in this case, as a nonconceptual representation of value.

Let me now turn to Block's (2010) argument for what he calls "mental paint," which is a phenomenal component of experience that can't be reduced to the representational content of experience. Block focuses on a range of well-attested demonstrations of the effects of attention on conscious experience.[11] Increased attention makes objects seem larger, brighter, higher in contrast, deeper in color saturation, and so on. One challenge for a representationalist is to say which of two perceptions of the contrast in a Gabor grating, say (one seen with full attention and one with peripheral attention), is veridical and which illusory. An answer seems to require one to specify the correct, or optimal, or normal degree of attention to be devoted to a stimulus. Yet Block says it is unclear that this idea really makes sense. What one should attend to, and how much, depends on many contextual factors, including one's goals and purposes.

Granted, what one should attend to, in general, depends on one's purposes. But one might still think that the representational content of perception is fixed under conditions of maximal attention. For one of the functions of attention is to *sharpen* the representation of a stimulus, extracting the maximum amount of information from it that the input allows. Why shouldn't one say that *that* fixes the correctness-condition for perception? Admittedly, it would have the corollary that all other ways of perceiving the same stimulus, with less-than-full attention, would have to be counted as illusory. But this doesn't seem so strange when one reflects on how small such effects generally are. If full attention shifts the contrast in a blurry Gabor patch from 24 percent to 28 percent, for example, then the implication is just that many ways of looking at the patch will present it in a *slightly* illusory manner.

---

[11] To be clear, in all of the cases Block discusses there is some degree of attention to the stimulus. (Hence there is no conflict here with the claim endorsed in Chapter 5 that consciousness *requires* attention.) The data concern the effects of *focal* attention or *full* attention, versus peripheral attention.

Notice, too, the kind of thing that people are required to say or describe in these sorts of attention experiments. They have to report an estimate of the orientation of a grating or the contrast of a patch, or they have to say whether one item is darker than another. These are all first-order reports about perceived items in the world, not comments on the quality of their experience. It is how the world appears to them that is impacted by attention and degrees of attention. And that, surely, is a representational notion, not accounted for by postulating intrinsic or "paint-like" aspects of one's experience itself.

Block's (2010) own proposal is designed to avoid any need to say that perception of either the fully attended or the peripherally attended Gabor patches is illusory. He suggests that the representational content is *vague*, fixing a range of possible contrast levels, taking a form something like this: <That: 22 percent–34 percent>. But in addition to a representational content, one's percept also has a *phenomenal* content, which doesn't supervene on the representational one, and which resolves the indeterminacy in particular cases. Consider, for example, a Gabor patch that actually has 22 percent contrast but is perceived when attended to as the same in contrast as a 28 percent patch that is largely *un*attended to. The representational contents associated with the two patches cover different ranges, but the phenomenal content or "mental paint" is the same.

Notice that phenomenal content makes a cognitive and behavioral difference, for Block. It is what explains why one's answers will cluster around 28 percent when viewing a patch with attention, but around a different value without. But then it is puzzling why we should be required to postulate a novel form of content in explanation, rather than a downstream, consumer-system determinant of regular representational content. On a two-factor account, for example, one could think of the input information as specifying an approximate range of possible values, where those values become determinate with the impact of attention and downstream judgment systems.[12]

In conclusion, the fact that the look of a thing can vary depending on one's level of attention is certainly an interesting finding, but not one that

[12] It is quite remarkable that Block (2010), who was once one of the main proponents of conceptual-role semantics (Block 1987), now seems to think we have no option but to adopt some sort of purely input-side account of representational content, postulating phenomenal content as a supplement.

forces us to give up on a representational theory of phenomenal consciousness. Indeed, given all the other advantages of global-workspace theory detailed in this and the previous chapter, mental paint is surely something we should *not* accept. Rather, the look of a thing is nothing other than how that thing is *represented* in one's experience.

6.7 Conclusion

In Chapter 5 we saw that global-workspace theory is (by some distance) the best of the empirical theories of consciousness on offer. It explains the contrast between conscious experience and various forms of unconscious perceptual state. It explains the all-or-nothing character of human phenomenal consciousness. It avoids all of the difficulties that attend its rivals, and it can support convincing replies to objections. Moreover, when framed in terms of globally broadcast nonconceptual content, it can also account for the ineffability of our experience.

In the present chapter we have seen how global-workspace theory can be developed into a fully reductive explanation of phenomenal consciousness. It is pitched at the right level, seeking an explanation in terms of mental contents and roles, rather than directly in terms of brain mechanisms. And when supplemented with an account of our ability to form acquaintance-based indexical thoughts about our experiences, it can explain how we come to feel the force of the "hard problem" thought experiments. Moreover, it does so without needing to postulate any special properties or qualia. In addition, there is no reason to think that such an account leaves anything out.

With the problem of consciousness thus laid to rest (in the human case at least), Chapter 7 will consider the implications of global-workspace theory for the question of consciousness in animals.

7

Consciousness in animals

No fact of the matter

Chapters 4 and 5 argued that global-workspace theory provides the best account of the neural, functional, and representational correlates of phenomenal consciousness. Chapter 6 then argued that the theory can provide a fully satisfying reductive explanation: phenomenal consciousness just *is* globally broadcast nonconceptual content, and the "explanatory gap" arises from the distinctive acquaintance-based indexical concepts that we can employ when thinking about such contents. The present chapter takes up the implications of this account for the distribution of consciousness across the animal kingdom. It argues that there is no fact of the matter.

It is important to reiterate that our topic, here, is *phenomenal* consciousness. Of course it is true that most animals are subjects of transitive and intransitive *creature* consciousness (of varying kinds). Animals perceive the world around them, and have awake/asleep cycles just as humans do. Moreover, aspects of *access* consciousness turn out to be quite widely shared across species, also. (As we will see in Section 7.1, however, access consciousness is a matter of degree.) Our question is about the distribution of first-personal, subjective, "felt," what-it-is-like consciousness.

7.1 Global broadcasting by degrees

Dennett (2001) once defended a theory very much like the global-workspace account, except that it allowed for degrees. He said that consciousness is like fame in the brain. And just as someone can be more or less famous, or can become just a little bit more famous, so a

Human and Animal Minds: The Consciousness Questions Laid to Rest. Peter Carruthers, Oxford University Press (2019). © Peter Carruthers.
DOI: 10.1093/oso/9780198843702.001.0001

mental state can be more or less conscious, or can get just a little bit more conscious. But it seems he was mistaken. Global broadcasting in humans appears to be an all-or-nothing phenomenon. As we noted in Chapter 5, there is a step-function underlying global broadcasting. Either activation levels in the neural populations in question remain below threshold, in which case there is no global broadcasting (albeit some additional local or specialized effects); or those activation levels hit threshold, and full global broadcasting results (Dehaene & Naccache 2001; Del Cul et al. 2007; Marti & Dehaene 2017; van Vugt et al. 2018). Hence global-workspace theory can fully explain the first-person intuition discussed in Chapter 1, that phenomenal consciousness is an all-or-nothing matter. Any given mental state (in humans, at any rate) is either categorically conscious or definitely unconscious.

When we look across species, however, it is obvious that global broadcasting will admit of degrees.[1] Or more accurately (since the term "global workspace" was introduced in the first instance for the human case), processes in the minds of animals will *more or less closely resemble* human global broadcasting. Recall that globally broadcast contents are made available to a wide range of cognitive systems. They are made available for verbal reporting, to give rise to higher-order awareness, to participate in executive functions of reasoning, planning, and decision-making, as well as to memory-forming systems; and they also serve to sustain or modulate full-blown affective reactions to stimuli. As we noted in Chapter 2, some of these capacities seem to be available in one form or another, or to one degree or another, in some species of animal. However, availability for verbal report is unique to human beings, of course. And as we also noted in Chapter 2, it seems likely that there can only be higher-order awareness of one's own mental states in a relatively small class of nonhuman creatures capable of some form of mind-reading (perhaps only great apes, or perhaps primates more generally; or maybe extending to some other social creatures such as dolphins and elephants).

---

[1] This is not to say that *all* aspects of global broadcasting admit of degrees, of course. And in particular, it is possible that the raw limits on broadcasting quantity are the same across primates, at any rate, amounting to a limit of roughly two items per hemisphere (Tsubomi et al. 2013; Luria et al. 2016). It may be that these limits derive from the number of discrete packets of information that it is possible to fit onto a gamma wave, rather than from anything more cognitive in nature (Miller & Buschman 2015).

Moreover, what we refer to collectively as "executive function" is really a set of different capacities that are at least partly independent of one another (Miyake et al. 2000; Diamond 2013). These functions include: selecting from among competing action-schemata, mentally rehearsing actions, inhibiting actions, forming intentions for the future, remembering and implementing intentions, switching between tasks, directing attention, searching memory, and modulating emotion. It seems quite likely that some of these capacities will be present in some creatures (as we discussed in Chapter 2), but absent in others. For example, it seems that capacities for top-down modulation of emotion are likely to vary independently of other components of executive function, as will long-term memory capacities. Moreover, all of the various systems that receive globally broadcast information will admit of degrees of internal complexity across species, and will likewise involve differing degrees of conceptual richness and sophistication.

In addition, given the numbers, complexity, and complex relationships among the set of systems to which phenomenally conscious states are broadcast in humans, it seems almost inevitable that similarities and differences in those systems across species will be complex, multifaceted, and cross-cutting. Indeed, it seems quite unlikely that there is an objective, linearly ordered similarity-space waiting to be discovered. On the contrary, there will be a multidimensional similarity *network*, with the minds of some species resembling our human global-broadcasting architecture in some respects, whereas others resemble it in others.

It seems likely, for example, that capacities for planning might vary independently of the comparative richness of an animal's conceptual capacities. This is because generalist feeders like raccoons and bears will need an extensive body of conceptual knowledge about the edible and inedible things to be found in their local habitats. But in general they might forage without engaging in long-term planning, taking a semi-random walk through the environment, guided by the affordances of situations that present themselves. Predators like wolves and lions that rely mostly on a single source of prey, in contrast, might possess a much more limited conceptual repertoire. But it seems they need to engage in some kinds of planning, while also having the capacity to inhibit their initial impulse to approach their prey directly.

Some of the systems implicated in global broadcasting might be linearly ordered across species, of course. Thus the evolution of capacities for verbal reporting plainly presuppose prior capacities for action selection. And likewise, one might think that if one lacked a capacity to select among competing actions, then one would also be incapable of forming intentions for the future. For to form an intention is, in effect, to select an action for future implementation. But there might be creatures that have no capacity for executive selection among actions (with choices among actions being determined through bottom-up competition among neural accumulator systems) that nevertheless have the capacity to *inhibit* an action. And vice versa, there might be creatures that can select between actions but lack any capacity to inhibit habitual or prepotent ones.

At first glance, then, there is a mismatch between the all-or-nothing nature of phenomenal consciousness (which is explained by global-workspace theory in the human case) and the implications of global-workspace theory for animals. For animals will surely only instantiate that theory to some or other degree. Yet as we noted in Chapter 1, and then again when discussing integrated-information theories in Chapter 4, it seems to make no sense to say of the mental states of an animal that they are *to some degree* phenomenally conscious. One has to insist: either those states are conscious or they aren't; there is no possibility of an in-between.

One possible response to this mismatch would be to reject the theory. One could claim that, given such a mismatch, whatever else global-workspace theory is, it can't be a theory of phenomenal consciousness. However, there isn't any mismatch between our conception of phenomenal consciousness and global broadcasting in the human case. This is because global broadcasting in humans is all-or-nothing, as we noted above. There is only a mismatch in so far as the systems that get broadcast to vary across species. But as we also noted in Chapter 1, all investigations of consciousness have to take their start from the human case, since *phenomenal* consciousness is a first-person notion. And as we have seen, there is no conflict between first-person (human) applications of that concept and global-workspace theory. Indeed, as we saw in Chapter 6, there are grounds for thinking that the latter theory (when suitably supplemented to include acquaintance-based indexical concepts) can explain everything that needs to be explained about human phenomenal consciousness.

Moreover, although many people have intuitions about which species of animal are likely to enjoy conscious experiences, such intuitions aren't among the possession-conditions for the concept of phenomenal consciousness. This follows from the first-person nature of the concept. Hence one could possess that concept while denying that *any* animals are phenomenally conscious, or while claiming that they *all* are. Indeed, some philosophers even claim that every single physical particle in the universe possess a little bit of phenomenal consciousness (Strawson 2006). So there would appear to be no conceptual constraints on the extension of the concept. As a result, it can't be a condition of adequacy for a theory of human consciousness that it should be able to accommodate our intuitions about animals—especially since those intuitions vary quite widely across people.

Another way to put the point is this: from our point of view there are no definite, first-person-accessible instances of phenomenal consciousness that are left unexplained by global-workspace theory. The fact that the theory is of little help to us in settling the question of phenomenal consciousness in animals isn't a legitimate reason for rejecting it. While we might have *hoped* for such help from a theory of consciousness, consciousness in animals isn't among the first-person facts that an adequate theory of phenomenal consciousness is required to explain.

If there were facts about which animal species enjoy phenomenally conscious experiences and which don't, and if we knew of those facts, then we could use our knowledge of them to triangulate an improved, more precise and more general theory of consciousness. We could look for just those aspects of global broadcasting that are common to all creatures capable of phenomenal consciousness, which would presumably be a subset of those involved in human consciousness. But we have no direct, theory-independent access to phenomenal consciousness in animals. And yet to repeat: phenomenal consciousness is a first-person notion. Moreover, I will suggest in due course that it is a mistake to think that there exists some further fact of the matter regarding animal consciousness or its lack, over and above what we can in principle discover about their cognitive organization.

7.2 Broadcasting as a natural kind

It might be urged that while the sets of systems that receive and consume globally broadcast nonconceptual content admit of degrees across species, global broadcasting itself is categorically present or absent. There are two ways in which this idea might be advanced. One would be to claim that global broadcasting is individuated by its *function*, which remains constant across species, rather than by the set of systems broadcast to. The other would be to identify global broadcasting with a core component of the network involved in humans (most likely *attention*, or perhaps *working memory*, or both combined), and to claim that this component is a natural psychological kind, remaining the same, and being largely homologous, across multiple species and animal groups. Let us take these ideas in turn.

Functions can either be *current* functions ("what role does this component *actually play* in the operations of the overall system?") or they can be *evolutionary* functions ("what role was this component *selected to play*?"). Taken in the first way, global broadcasting can't be separated from the set of systems that are broadcast to—for all will enter into a description of what global broadcasting actually does in the human mind. But taken in the second way, it might well be the case that the adaptive function of global broadcasting can be specified without mention of the human-specific set of consumer systems. Indeed, I have argued elsewhere that the evolutionary function of the network underlying the global workspace is to provide a (virtual) "center" for the mind, enabling multiple subsystems to have their activities coordinated around a single set of representations (Carruthers 2015a). Mightn't one then say that any creature that has such a "centered mind" can qualify as having globally broadcast—and hence phenomenally conscious—mental states?

If phenomenal consciousness can be reductively explained by global-workspace theory (as we are now assuming), then the question before us is whether the workspace, for these purposes, should be identified with the more-general "centered mind" property, or rather with the human-specific set of consumer systems that we have experimental evidence of in the human case (systems for reporting, reasoning, decision-making, and remembering). To answer this question, we need to examine what does the actual explanatory work in reductively explaining phenomenal consciousness. And it seems obvious that no explanatory role is played by the claim that conscious states play a "centering" role in the mental lives of people. Rather, what does the explanatory work is the fact that the contents of the global workspace are made available to systems for reflective higher-order awareness and discursive thought. For it is these that give rise to the "hard" problem of consciousness, the conceivability of zombies, and so on.

Of course, if we had independent evidence of phenomenal consciousness in a wide range of creatures, then that might require us to focus on the centering function of global broadcasting for our explanation. But we have no such evidence—the distribution of consciousness across species is precisely what is at stake in the current discussion. The only species for which we have direct evidence of consciousness is the human species. This is hardly surprising, when we recall that phenomenal consciousness has an essentially first-person characterization. We have first-person access to our own phenomenally conscious states. And we have good evidence for the presence of phenomenal consciousness in other people (albeit not conclusive evidence, given the conceivability of zombies; note that the case against zombies developed in Chapter 6 is an inference to the best explanation, not any sort of entailment). For other people can talk about and reflect on the nature of their experiences in the same kinds of ways that we do. As we noted in Chapter 1, this gives us good reason to think that they, too, have a first-person perspective on their experiences of the same sort that we do ourselves.

What, then, of the suggestion that the global workspace might be identified with one of its key components (specifically attention), rather than with availability to the full suite of receiving systems? One problem for such a suggestion is that attention can either be individuated in network terms, as the mechanism that normally issues in global broadcasting of attended representations (this is the standard notion employed in cognitive science), or it can be individuated computationally, in terms of its function in boosting the targeted neural activity while suppressing competing populations (Mole 2011; Wu 2014). Understood in the first way, the idea seems to become almost a notational variant of the global-workspace account we have been discussing thus far. But understood in the second way, it would plainly be inadequate as a theory of consciousness. For there are multiple boosting-while-suppressing mechanisms in the human brain that remain unconscious. For instance, the mechanism that selects between competing motor plans is thought to operate in just this manner (Wu 2014).

A similar problem arises for the suggestion that the presence of working memory might be sufficient for global broadcasting across species, abstracting somehow from the actual human consumer systems for the contents of working memory. For there are lots of reverberating short-term memory systems in humans and other animals that have nothing to do with consciousness. Now admittedly, we know that there are working-memory-*like* systems in multiple creatures, including mammals and birds, as we saw in Chapter 2. And in some of these creatures, the contents of those systems are made available to simple executive-like systems for reasoning and decision-making. But one way of putting our present difficulty is to know whether phenomenal consciousness is confined to the contents of *actual* (human) working memory, or extends also to the contents of these working-memory-*like* systems in animals also.

One might try combining these suggestions with previous ones. Perhaps the global workspace can be identified with those attention-like networks across species that play the "centering" role in the species in question. (These appear to be homologous in mammals and birds at least, as we noted in Chapter 2; see Carruthers 2015a for discussion.) This would be to identify the global workspace with a biologically individuated natural kind. But a similar problem arises here as before: it is not *this* notion that carries the explanatory burden in the reductive explanation of phenomenal consciousness in humans outlined in Chapter 6, but rather one that implicates availability to reflective forms of discursive thinking.

Moreover, as we have noted before, one thing that everyone has agreed on since Kripke (1980) is that terms referring to phenomenally conscious mental states aren't used as natural-kind terms. In contrast, it is generally agreed that our concepts for substances like water *are* natural-kind ones. Even before we knew anything about chemistry, we used the concept WATER to refer to the underlying nature or essence of the recognizable stuff that fills our lakes and rivers (H_2O); and it turned out that it was that very same stuff that presents as ice in some circumstances (frozen water) and as mist in others (evaporated water). But our phenomenal concepts aren't like that. We don't use them with the intention of referring to whatever natural kind underlies our experiences, whatever that might turn out to be, and however that kind might be presented in other creatures. On the contrary, we mean to refer just to the qualities we are aware of in ourselves. (These turn out to be globally broadcast nonconceptual contents, if the arguments of Chapters 5 and 6 are correct, but they aren't conceptualized as such when we deploy concepts like THIS-E.)

So we still face the same problem. Given that phenomenal consciousness is successfully explained in our own case by full-blown global broadcasting, what reason is there to identify it with the operations of some much more minimally described system or natural kind? This challenge is especially acute, since many of the remaining components of human-like global broadcasting might *also* be natural kinds. This might be true of the language faculty, for example, or the mind-reading network. So why shouldn't we say that it is availability of nonconceptual content to one of *these* kinds that fixes the extension of consciousness? There would appear to be nothing in our first-person conception of phenomenal consciousness that rules this out.

7.3 Stipulating a categorical boundary

As we noted in Chapter 1, we can't really make sense of degrees of phenomenal consciousness. But perhaps we don't have to. An obvious suggestion is to say that a creature will enjoy phenomenally conscious experience if it undergoes states that are more similar to human global broadcasting than they are similar to any form of human *un*conscious mental state. We can set up a categorical concept that will reach beyond the human case, while staying true to the all-or-nothing first-person nature of the concept, by fixing its extension in terms of relative closeness to the two poles drawn from the human case: the global broadcasting architecture that underlies human phenomenally conscious experience, on the one hand, and the sorts of content availability that underlie *un*conscious forms of perception in humans, on the other.

The resulting concept will be vague, of course (which arguably our concept of phenomenal consciousness isn't—see Simon 2017; but we can set this aside). There are bound to be cases that aren't determinately more similar to global broadcasting than they are to dorsal-network sensorimotor guidance, for example. In part this is because any concept defined in terms of two poles in a continually varying domain will leave cases that are indeterminate between the two. (Think of defining shades of color as *red* provided they are more similar to scarlet than they are to some central instance of yellow.) But it is also because of the complex and cross-cutting nature of the similarity space, noted in Section 7.1. Some creatures will enjoy states that are more similar to globally broadcast ones along one dimension, but more similar to sensorimotor states along another.

Moreover, not only are the receiver systems for global broadcasting in humans multifaceted, but so too are the causal roles of *un*conscious perceptual states. The states involved in online and habitual forms of motor control are one thing (Lisman & Sternberg 2013; Goodale 2014; Wood & Rünger 2015), whereas the perceptual states that issue in direct affect-expressive behavior are another (Panksepp 1998; LeDoux 2017); and both are quite different again from unattended states in the ventral visual and auditory systems that have a variety of priming effects independently of global broadcasting (Dehaene 2014). So both poles of the proposed category contain significant (and potentially independently varying) internal complexity.

Are some aspects of global broadcasting more important, or more relevant to the question of consciousness, than others? We have evidence from the human case that some of the consumer systems for global broadcasts aren't *necessary* for someone to have phenomenally conscious experience. Thus a person with complete amnesia, or someone with completely flattened affect, can nevertheless describe their experiences to us and engage in "hard problem" thought experiments. So that would leave us with the broad class of higher-order thought, semantic-memory, and executive-function systems (including verbal report) as the relevant components of global broadcasting when we make comparisons across species.

It might be claimed that executive systems aren't necessary for consciousness, either, however. For dreams are phenomenally conscious states, but during dreaming, one's capacities for executive function are suppressed. It remains unclear, however, whether a creature that *had no* executive-function capacities (rather than suppressed ones) could have phenomenally conscious dreams. For our only direct evidence of the phenomenally conscious status of dreaming derives from the reports and reflections that we can make about our dreams when we recall them on waking, as we noted in Chapter 5. Moreover, a recent study found that dream reports were predicted by gamma-band EEG activity in the prefrontal cortex (Siclari et al. 2017), suggesting that dream contents *reach* prefrontal cortex, even if the latter is largely suppressed and incapable of responding to them further.

What if one could completely knock out capacities for language and higher-order thought on a temporary basis, however? (Perhaps one might use some future and more effective form of transcranial magnetic stimulation; or one might employ some future sort of invasive but temporary chemical or thermal enervation of the neural systems involved.) If, on recovery, people reported that they continued to enjoy phenomenally conscious experience, then wouldn't that demonstrate that language and reflective thought aren't necessary for consciousness? No, it would not. For these reports would, of course, be retrospective ones, grounded in memory of one's perceptual contents while capacities for reporting were knocked out. But in order to report the contents of a memory, that memory needs to be activated and globally broadcast. It thereby becomes available to linguistic report and higher-order thought. So on the hypothesis that it is these, specifically, that are necessary for a content to become phenomenally conscious, those memory contents will thereby *become* phenomenally conscious, even if they hadn't been when originally undergone.

Some components of global broadcasting are *epistemically* more important than others, of course. In particular, capacities for verbal report combined with capacities for higher-order forms of reflective thinking (of the sort that are required for one to become puzzled by the "hard problem" thought experiments) provide the most direct evidence that we have of phenomenally conscious experience in other people. But on a global-workspace account, these capacities aren't *constitutive* of phenomenal consciousness. (That would involve a shift to some kind of higher-order-thought theory of consciousness, discussed in Chapter 4.) So we can't conclude that these capacities are metaphysically necessary for consciousness to occur.

Given the multicomponent and multifaceted nature of global broadcasting, what would it take for there to be a fact of the matter about whether or not a given mental state in an animal is more similar to a human globally broadcast one than to a human unconscious one? There will inevitably be greater similarity along some dimensions of comparison than there are along others. So on some ways of weighting the importance of the various dimensions, the state in question will come out as conscious, whereas on other ways of weighting those dimensions it will be classified as *un*conscious. How could we decide between these possibilities in a manner that doesn't just stipulate the outcome? I suggest that we can't. Given that there are no real qualia (as we argued in Chapters 1 and 6), there is no fact of the matter concerning the relevant dimensions of comparison.

We could, however, borrow an idea from the supervaluation literature on vague concepts (Fine 1975; Lewis 1982). We could say that definitely conscious states are ones whose similarity to human globally broadcast states are greater on any reasonable way of weighting the different components and dimensions. If phenomenal consciousness in the mind of a monkey, or a chicken, or a honey bee is not to be something that we *stipulate* but rather *discover*, then greater similarity to human global broadcasting would have to survive any reasonable precisification of the concept of global broadcasting. This sort of maneuver might well imply that *some* other animals would qualify as phenomenally conscious. But the class of such animals is likely to be quite small.

One reason for this is that a multifaceted set of executive functions is at the heart of global broadcasting in humans, and yet it is widely agreed that human executive function capacities are uniquely well-developed in comparison even to the other great apes, as well as containing components such as verbal report that are wholly unique to humans.[2] So there will already be a considerable gulf between the nature of human and

---

[2] Indeed, the size of prefrontal cortex in humans is *proportionately* greater than in other primates (Donahue et al. 2018). Yet the differences between human brains and those of our nearest relatives, the chimpanzees, are already quite large. This is true whether one measures absolute brain-size (the human brain is about three to four times larger), or considers the encephalization quotient (which corrects for body size), which is also more than three times as great (Roth & Dicke 2005). Recall from Chapter 2, too, that executive inhibition capacities among primates in the A-not-B task seem roughly equivalent to those of a ten-month-old human infant.

animal global broadcasting. In addition, the conceptual repertoire of an ordinary human will be orders of magnitude richer than even the most sophisticated of animals. (Human concepts are thought to number in the tens if not hundreds of thousands; Bloom 2002.) Hence the vast majority of creatures in the animal kingdom will either determinately lack consciousness (because their states are more similar to human *un*conscious states on all ways of stipulating the weights in the similarity space), or there will be no fact of the matter whether or not they are phenomenally conscious (because their states are more similar to global broadcasting given some ways of stipulating the weights in the similarity space, but are more similar to human *un*conscious states given others, and thus fail to be classified as conscious under all reasonable weightings of the dimensions).

There is another reason for thinking that the class of animals capable of consciousness will be quite small, if this is the set of creatures that would satisfy all reasonable precisifications of the notion of global broadcasting. This is because both philosophers (Dennett 1978) and psychologists (Kurzban 2012) have claimed—seemingly reasonably— that conscious mental states are all and only those that can be verbally reported. Likewise, both philosophers (Rosenthal 2005) and psychologists (Graziano 2013) have claimed—again, not unreasonably—that consciousness requires capacities for higher-order thought. On the former approach, consciousness will be restricted to humans; on the latter, it will likely be restricted to a small set of highly social and intelligent species.[3]

We can conclude that although global-workspace theory *could* provide the basis for a categorical concept to employ across species, it seems likely that only a small subset of species (perhaps a set restricted to humans) would qualify as determinately phenomenally conscious, on this approach. In connection with the vast majority of species, the phenomenally conscious status of their perceptual states would have to be something that we stipulate rather than discover.

---

[3] Note that the argument here isn't an argument from authority. I am not saying that the restrictions in question are supported because famous people have endorsed them. Rather, the point pertains to the supervaluation process that can be used to fix definite truth-conditions for the vague concept of global broadcasting. This defines definite truth as what would survive all possible ways of sharpening the concept. The views in question provide evidence that there are reasonable sharpenings that would exclude most if not all species of animal.

7.4 The negative semantic argument

Section 7.3 has sketched how one might construct a categorical concept of global broadcasting centered on the human case. It should be emphasized that such a concept would need to be *constructed*, however. It isn't somehow implicit in our conception of phenomenal consciousness. On the contrary, the latter concept is first-personal, as we have stressed throughout. Although it applies to states that are, as a matter of fact, globally broadcast ones (given the truth of global-workspace theory), there is nothing in one's first-person use that entails that the consciousness concept should also have in its extension any states that are more similar to human globally broadcast states than to human unconscious ones. Likewise, as we pointed out in Section 7.2, there is nothing in our first-person conception of phenomenal consciousness that ties the extension of the concept to one or another natural psychological kind underlying global broadcasting. In fact, there is nothing about our first-person concept of phenomenal consciousness that fixes its extension across the mental states of other species. Hence there is no fact of the matter whether members of any those species have phenomenally conscious states or not.

Call this "the negative semantic argument." There is nothing in the intentions with which first-person phenomenal concepts like THIS-E or THIS-R are employed that settles how similar the functional role of an animal's perceptual states must be to human global broadcasting to count as "the same," or that even constrains our answers. For, as already noted, the concepts one uses to think about one's own conscious experiences aren't natural-kind ones, and when we think about our own experiences in this sort of distinctive first-person way we aren't intending to designate the underlying explanatory property, whatever that might turn out to be.

Note that the negative semantic argument isn't an argument from *vagueness*. (Nor, of course, is the claim that attributing consciousness to animals is some sort of category mistake.) The claim isn't that there fails to be a fact of the matter about phenomenal consciousness in animals because their states fall somewhere within the vague boundary of our concept of consciousness. On the contrary, our phenomenal concepts are *sharp*, in the sense defended in Chapter 1—any candidate mental state of ours is either definitely phenomenally conscious and is *like something* to undergo, or it definitely isn't. Nevertheless, the argument does turn on a kind of semantic indeterminacy. For I have argued that there is nothing in our first-person concept of phenomenal consciousness that fixes how physically or functionally similar an animal must be to the human case to qualify as conscious.

But how *could* there be no fact of the matter whether another animal has phenomenally conscious experiences or not? How is this even possible? Recall that we are now supposing that globally broadcast nonconceptual content is what phenomenal consciousness *is*. Hence there is no special property that gets added when a perceptual state is globally broadcast—there are no qualia. As we transition from species whose states are more similar to some variety of human unconscious state than they are to human globally broadcast states, through to species for which the reverse is true, nothing lights up, and nothing magical appears. There is just nonconceptual content that is available to a greater range of systems, or to systems with greater internal complexity or conceptual sophistication. There will be functional differences between the two sets of contents of course. But then there will likewise be functional differences among the mental states of two species that fall closer toward the unconscious end of the spectrum, or two species whose states fall closer to the human-global-broadcasting end. The differences in question don't differ in kind in any deep way.

In the human case there is a big introspective difference between states that are phenomenally conscious and states that aren't, of course, and the difference is akin to "lighting up." For globally broadcast states are ones that we are immediately aware of having, whereas un-broadcast states are ones that we aren't aware of having at all (except through third-person-type interpretative inferences). But introspective availability is just one facet of global broadcasting in humans. It isn't *constitutive* of phenomenal consciousness (that would turn the global-workspace account into a higher-order theory, rather than a first-order one). And more important, "lighting up" is fully explained (we are supposing) by functional differences between the two types of state, not by the appearance of any new kind of property (qualia).

Suppose we had complete knowledge of the functional and representational components of the mentality of a monkey, or a salmon, or a honey bee. Suppose we knew everything of a third-person sort that there is to know about what happens to the animal's perceptual states under various conditions, how those states interact with its valuational ones, and how the resulting behavior is determined. Would it add anything to our knowledge to have done the comparative work needed to know whether states in these animals are more like globally broadcast ones in humans (on all reasonable ways of precisifying the concept of global broadcasting, perhaps) than they are similar to any of the various kinds of unconscious state that humans undergo, or vice versa? I suggest not. That comparison, and the resulting classification of the state as conscious or unconscious, wouldn't add anything to what we already knew. There is no extra property of the mind of the animal that accrues to it by virtue of its similarity or dissimilarity to the human global workspace. As a result, there is no substantive fact of the matter concerning consciousness in nonhuman animals.

7.5 The positive semantic argument

Section 7.4 presented a negative semantic argument for the claim that there is no fact of the matter about animal consciousness. That argument turned especially on claims about what our concept of phenomenal consciousness is *not*. The present section will develop a second way of coming to the same conclusion. This is the positive semantic argument, which turns on a positive account of the truth-conditions of judgments attributing phenomenal consciousness to other creatures.

Recall, again, that the concept of phenomenal consciousness is a first-person one, grounded in one's capacities for thought about one's own globally broadcast perceptual states. For instance, while undergoing an experience of redness one might think about it using the acquaintance-based indexical concept THIS-R. Or when contemplating one's own mortality, one might think, "When I die, all *this* will disappear," meaning to refer to one's phenomenal experience in general. Here one employs an acquaintance-based indexical concept such as THIS-E.

What, then, are the truth-conditions of thoughts employing concepts of this kind when thinking about the mental states of an animal? Since the concepts are first-person ones, the truth-conditions will presumably have to take a first-person-based form, somewhat along the lines of, "Species X undergoes perceptual states of the *same sort* as *this-E*." If one were a realist about experiential qualia, then it would be clear what "same sort" amounts to here: it would mean that there are qualia properties present in the mind of the animal in question. And there would be a fact of the matter (whether knowable by us or not) concerning whether or not that is true. But on the view defended in Chapters 5 and 6, in contrast, THIS-E picks out globally broadcast nonconceptual content in general. And then the question is, what counts as *sameness of sort* in fixing the truth-conditions of one's thoughts about the animal?

Plainly, the sameness relation can't just be a matter of sameness of nonconceptual content. This is because unconscious perceptual states, too, have nonconceptual content—including color content. Now admittedly, perceptual states in the dorsal visual (sensorimotor) system are thought to be coded in limb-centered and body-centered coordinates, whereas conscious visual contents are generally allocentric (Milner & Goodale 1995). But there can be unconscious perceptual states in the ventral visual system too (Dehaene 2014). And other forms of conscious experience can be coded in body-centric ways, as are proprioceptive experiences of the position and movements of one's own body-parts. In consequence, the sameness relation that forms our target must somehow implicate the functional roles of the contents in question—which is to say, global broadcasting.

In Sections 7.2 and 7.3 we noted that concepts like THIS-E aren't used as natural-kind terms, nor with the intention of tracking the underlying explanatory properties, whatever they turn out to be. Nor, of course, are they used with the intention of deferring to the practices of other speakers, as we noted in Chapter 6. Phenomenal concepts aren't taught to us, and aren't directly part of public discourse. Rather, as we noted in Chapter 1, they emerge out of first-person acquaintance with one's own experiential states. They are, in a sense, private, in that they aren't beholden to other people's judgments or usage, and their truth-conditions aren't fixed by public usage-norms. Rather, when we communicate about phenomenal consciousness, we do so by drawing the attention of other speakers to states within themselves.

Consider an analogy, in this case with a first-order concept, but one that plainly isn't intended to track any natural kind and is also (in the required sense) private, not intended to defer to the usage of others. Moreover, it is a concept whose extension hasn't been fixed by previous usage or public norms. While looking around neighborhoods in an unfamiliar city to which one is relocating, one might exclaim, "Now *this* is the sort of place we should live!" In the case I imagine, the referent of the term "this sort of place" isn't a single feature (like houses with picket fences), nor would one be able to articulate all the factors that enter into one's judgment. And plainly one isn't intending to refer to the underlying essence of the place, whatever that might turn out to be. (One isn't using "this sort of place" as a natural-kind term.) Now consider another neighborhood in the same city, and ask, "Is that neighborhood of *this sort*?" And if one asserts that it is, what fixes the truth-condition for one's judgment?

The answer to the latter question is surely something like this: that if one were to visit that other neighborhood under the same conditions with the same precursors (thus creating the same set of dispositions-to-judge) then one would (or would not) count that other neighborhood as the same in the relevant respect. Or, somewhat more abstractly: if someone with the exact same dispositions-to-judge that were involved in one's judgment about the first neighborhood were to be exposed to the second, then the second neighborhood would evoke a judgment that it belongs to the relevant sort.

The truth-conditions of thoughts employing phenomenal concepts that are about the mental states of other beings must be something like this. The meaning of the concept is fixed in the first-person case (just as the meaning of "this sort of place" is fixed by an individual thinker in a specific neighborhood), but is then applied beyond it. By analogy, then, the truth-condition of a judgment like, "Creature C has perceptual states that are *this-E*" might be this: "If I were to be aware of creature C's perceptual states, then I would judge them to be *this-E*." Or more plausibly (since the antecedent of this conditional is impossible to fulfil), this: "If the dispositions-to-judge that underlie my use of the concept THIS-E were to be instantiated in creature C, then they would issue in a judgment that some of the creature's perceptual states are *this-E*." Indeed, it is hard to see any other way in which the truth-condition for a phenomenal judgment about another being could be fixed (given qualia irrealism, of course).

On this account it is fairly easy to understand how one can think that another human has a color experience of the same sort as *this-R*, or that another human is phenomenally conscious more generally, undergoing states that are *this-E*. And there is surely a fact of the matter in the human case. One just has to suppose that classificatory dispositions exactly like those underlying one's use of the concepts THIS-R or THIS-E might exist in the mind of another. Moreover, the behavior of other people (especially their verbal behavior when talking about their experiences, expressing puzzlement about the explanatory gap, and so on) can provide us with sufficient evidence that one's thoughts about phenomenal consciousness in others are true. But when extended to the case of other animals, the corresponding counterfactual is no longer evaluable. And in that case, I suggest, it must be neither true nor false.

To suppose that one's own classificatory dispositions underlying a phenomenal concept like THIS-R or THIS-E might exist in the mind of an animal is to suppose that the animal has a completely different kind of mind from the one that it *actually* has—it attributes to the animal a mind capable of formulating concepts referring to its own experiences and engaging in reflective thought about them. But the intended target of one's thought, of course, is the mind of the animal as it actually is. Suppose one thinks that macaque monkeys, for instance, have states that are *this-E*. Here one is making a judgment about macaque minds as they actually are. But the truth-condition of this thought is that, if the dispositions underlying *my* use of THIS-E were instantiated in the mind of the monkey, then those dispositions would be evoked by the monkey's states. But the antecedent of this conditional entails that I am no longer thinking about a monkey's mind, but the mind of another sort of creature altogether, with cognitive capacities like those of humans. As a result, there is no fact of the matter about how human first-person concepts of experience would or would not apply if instantiated in the mind of the animal.

Not all counterfactuals that suppose a target entity to be other than it is are unevaluable, of course. One can judge the truth of a statement like, "If 260-pound John were to weigh 160 pounds, then he would be capable of climbing the stairs more quickly." The problem arises when one is using the truth of the counterfactual to determine some *further* truth about the thing mentioned in the antecedent as it *actually is*. If we want to know, for example, whether someone weighing 260 pounds is in principle capable of running a four-minute mile, then offering the following counterfactual is plainly of no help: "If someone weighing 260 pounds were to weigh 160 pounds, then he would in principle be capable of running a four-minute mile."

In the case just described, of course, we think there is some fact of the matter whether a person weighing 260 pounds could run a four-minute mile. This is because the truth-condition for the statement, "Someone weighing 260 pounds can in principle run a four-minute mile" are fixed independently of the counterfactual proposed (mistakenly) to help one adjudicate its truth. In the case of statements about phenomenally conscious experience in beings who only satisfy global-workspace theory to some *degree*, in contrast, the counterfactual in question is precisely the one we need to fix the truth-condition for the statement. For as we noted above, the truth-condition for the statement, "Creature C undergoes states that are *this*-E" (i.e. creature C is phenomenally conscious), is given by the counterfactual, "If the disposition-to-judge underlying my use of the concept THIS-E were to be instantiated in the mind of creature C, then C would judge that some of its states are *this-E*." Here it is none other than the counterfactual needed to fix the truth-condition for an attribution of phenomenal consciousness to an animal that at the same time requires the mind of the creature in question to be other than it is.

Suppose this argument is resisted, however. Suppose someone were to insist that it is allowable for the counterfactuals that fix the truth-conditions for thoughts like, "Creature C is *this*-E" or, "Creature C is *this*-R" to require us to suppose that the mind of C is quite other than it actually is. In that case the truth-value of those judgments when applied to a macaque monkey, say, would presumably be *true*. For it is presumably true that if the monkey's attended percept of a red tomato were presented to a disposition-to-judge just like that underlying my use of the concept THIS-R, then that percept would be judged to be *this*-R.

But now this line of thought can be reduced to absurdity. For it is equally true that if an *un*attended percept of red in my own ventral visual stream were presented to a disposition-to-judge like that underlying my use of the concept THIS-R, then it would be judged to be *this*-R. And in the same way, it will be true that if a nonconceptual content in my own dorsal—sensorimotor—visual stream were presented to a disposition-to-judge like that underlying my use of the concept THIS-E, then it would be judged to be *this*-E. But these are paradigmatic instances of perceptual states in myself that *aren't* phenomenally conscious. It is plainly illegitimate to use counterfactuals to project my own phenomenal concepts into unconscious regions of my own mind. For doing so presupposes that those unconscious contents have a role other than they do. By the same token, then, it must be illegitimate to project my own phenomenal concepts into minds that are significantly different from my own. For doing so presupposes that the minds in question are other than they really are.

We can conclude, then, that there is no fact of the matter about phenomenal consciousness in most animals, at least. This is because the counterfactuals that fix the truth-conditions for our first-person concept of phenomenal consciousness are unevaluable when extended to minds that are too much unlike our own. But how much unlike is *too* unlike? What degree of dissimilarity must there be, for the counterfactual that fixes the truth-condition for statements attributing phenomenal consciousness to others to become unevaluable? The answer depends on what set of capacities underlies our use of the phenomenal concepts that are employed to formulate those counterfactuals. Plainly, since such concepts are about one's own experiences, they require capacities for higher-order thought. But do they also require capacities for language and for executively controlled sequences of reflective thinking?

If capacities for higher-order thought were the only ones necessary for phenomenal concepts to be possible, then that would imply that there is a fact of the matter about phenomenal consciousness in all creatures capable of such thought. But in fact the *kinds* of higher-order-thought capacities that are required for one to have phenomenal concepts are rather special ones. Regular higher-order concepts are deeply embedded in predictive and explanatory networks linking mental states with circumstances and behavior. This will surely be true of the higher-order concepts possessed by other primates; and it is equally true of human higher-order concepts, except when we do philosophy and become puzzled by "hard"-problem thought experiments. Recall that in order to form a phenomenal concept one has to set aside one's regular set of concepts for mental states of various sorts, focusing just on a globally broadcast nonconceptual content that one is acquainted with (but not described as such, of course), and formulating a thought with the intention of referring just to that. These capacities appear to go well beyond those that are required for higher-order thought in general.

In fact, the dispositions underlying one's phenomenal concepts would seem to require capacities for intentionally controlled concept formation and reflective thinking. And they might well require linguistic ability as well. This will be true if, as seems plausible, the capacity for this kind of controlled reflective thought is language-dependent. And if so, then the positive semantic argument outlined in this section will imply that there is no fact of the matter about phenomenal consciousness in any creature outside of the human species. (The question of phenomenal consciousness in human infants and young children will be discussed in Chapter 8.) But in the absence of a more careful analysis of the cognitive prerequisites of phenomenal concepts than I can provide here (as well as a more detailed account of the cognitive powers of animals than I was able to give in Chapter 2), the issue of the precise extension of cases where there is a fact-of-the-matter about phenomenal consciousness must be left undecided. What we can be quite confident of, however, is that the extension in question is a highly restricted one.

7.6 A diagnosis

I have claimed that there is no fact of the matter about the presence or absence of phenomenally conscious states in most if not all nonhuman animals. This should come paired with a diagnosis for why almost everyone who has addressed the topic previously has assumed that there *is* a fact of the matter, whether known or unknown. Why does everyone assume that there is a substantive question here with a determinate answer, if in reality (as I claim) there isn't?[4]

---

[4] One exception to this generalization is Papineau (2003), who develops an argument similar to the negative semantic argument of Section 7.4. He claims that there is nothing in our use of the first-person concept of phenomenal consciousness that fixes its extension beyond the human case, concluding that there is no fact of the matter whether the mental states of other creatures count as instances of that concept. Moreover, Papineau's diagnosis for why people naturally assume that there *is* a fact of the matter is also quite similar to my own. However, the indeterminacy he focusses on concerns the right level of description of our conscious states—functional, neuronal, chemical, and so on—whereas my own argument operates at the

Part of the answer is that many people are qualia realists of one sort or another. If our phenomenal concepts pick out realworldly properties of some kind, that don't reduce to functional and representational ones, then there must be facts about how those properties are distributed across the animal kingdom. Moreover, even those people who are officially qualia irrealists might find it hard to shake the intuition that something "lights up" with the arrival of phenomenal consciousness in the world, and hence that there should exist answers to the question where in the world that something is to be found. Indeed, I count my own past self in this category. For recall from Chapter 4 that I once objected against a form of global-workspace theory that it doesn't really *explain* why first-order contents should "light up" and acquire a subjective dimension when globally broadcast.

The deeper and more general answer, though, is that I suspect people lose sight of the first-person character of the concept of phenomenal consciousness. We (some of us) talk about phenomenal consciousness on a regular basis, of course, and hence deploy public, shared concepts that we use in the course of such talk. This is, in effect, an alternative—third-personal—concept of phenomenal consciousness. It treats consciousness as whatever properties of experience give rise to thought experiments of the "hard problem" type. We naturally assume that this talk, like almost all other public discourse, issues in thoughts that have definite truth-conditions (albeit vague ones, perhaps). It is easy to forget that the point of this talk is just to draw attention to our own conscious experience, and that the critical concepts that get the problem of consciousness going in the first place are first-person ones. It is these that can't issue in determinate truth-conditions when projected across species.

Indeed, it is worth noting that although I have presented both the negative and positive semantic arguments given in Sections 7.4 and 7.5 within the framework of global-workspace theory, versions of those arguments could equally well be employed by any theorist who takes

---

functional level itself. It turns on indeterminacy in the set of systems globally broadcast to that are necessary for conscious experience. My view is that this is the right level at which to explain consciousness, as I argued in Chapter 6; hence differences in underlying physical constitution that make no functional or representational difference are irrelevant to the question of consciousness.

seriously the first-person character of phenomenal consciousness while denying the existence of qualia. For example, consider someone who endorses the fragile-short-term-memory view discussed in Chapter 4, but who thinks (as Block 1995 actually does), that the public concept PHENOMENAL CONSCIOUSNESS is intended just to draw people's attention introspectively to their own experiential states. Then there will be nothing in the use of that concept that prioritizes one rather than another of the physical or functional factors that accompany fragile-short-term-memory contents in humans (the negative semantic argument). And the truth-conditions for thoughts employing that concept across species will require projecting one's own conceptual dispositions into the mind of the animal in question while nevertheless trying to hold the nature of that mind fixed (the positive semantic argument).

7.7 Conclusion

Our first-person concept of phenomenal consciousness is an all-or-nothing one; and applications of that concept in our own case are fully explained by global-workspace theory, as we saw in Chapters 5 and 6. But when we shift our gaze to the question of consciousness across species, we confront a mismatch. While our concept of phenomenal consciousness is all-or-nothing, the minds of other animals will only resemble the human global workspace more or less closely, to some or other *degree*. Moreover, because that concept is a first-person one, it can find no determinate application when applied to minds that are significantly unlike our own. The upshot, I have argued, is that there is no fact of the matter whether animals have phenomenally conscious states or not.

Let me reiterate what I emphasized at the outset of the chapter: the upshot here pertains just to the question of *phenomenal* consciousness in animals. It is important that phenomenal consciousness shouldn't be confused with any of the other uses of the term "conscious" that we distinguished in Chapter 1. For of course it is definitely *true* that many animals have perceptual states that are (to some degree) *access*-conscious. And of course it is *true* that animals are often conscious rather than unconscious (i.e. they are sometimes *intransitively creature-conscious*; they are sometimes awake). Moreover, it is undeniably true that they are often conscious *of* objects and events in their environment (i.e. they are frequently *transitively creature-conscious* in some form or another; they perceive the world). My claim is just that the first-person concepts that give rise to the "hard problem" thought experiments (phenomenal concepts) can't be projected into the minds of nonhuman animals except by stipulation (although they *can* be projected into the minds of other people).

If one embraces the fully reductive nature of global-workspace theory, however, then the question of animal consciousness is no longer of any factual significance. There are many facts to be discovered about the minds of nonhuman animals; and among those facts will be dimensions of similarity to, and difference from, the human global workspace. But supposing we knew all of those facts, inquiring in any given case whether there is *enough* similarity for an animal's mental states to qualify as phenomenally conscious could add nothing further to what we already knew. Nor would trying to figure out what judgments the dispositions underlying our own phenomenal concepts would issue in if transplanted into the mind of the animal. So these aren't questions that comparative psychologists should spend any time on. What I suggest, then, is that the nature and functioning of animal minds should be studied; but phenomenal consciousness in animals doesn't deserve to be. This is because there are no further facts to discover.

8

Does consciousness matter?

Chapter 7 concluded that there is no fact of the matter concerning phenomenal consciousness in animals, while also arguing that that this conclusion is of no importance for science. The present chapter inquires whether it is nevertheless important in other ways, specifically for our ethical treatment of animals. The chapter also considers what should be said about the phenomenally conscious status of humans who, like animals, only partially share a full global-broadcasting architecture, such as infants and people suffering from age-related cognitive impairments.

8.1 Consciousness and ethics

Chapter 6 argued that global-workspace theory provides a complete reductive explanation of phenomenal consciousness. Consciousness just *is* globally broadcast nonconceptual content, and the various "hard problem" thought-experiments only arise because we can formulate first-person acquaintance-based indexical thoughts about our access-conscious states that lack any conceptual connections to physical, functional, and representational facts.

Chapter 7 then argued that if this conclusion is correct, there is no fact of the matter about phenomenal consciousness in animals. As one surveys the variety of animal minds, containing greater or lesser degrees of resemblance to human global broadcasting, there is no extra property (phenomenal consciousness) that manifests itself, whether at any particular stage or by degrees. For there *is* no extra property. (There are no qualia.) Hence there is nothing further for comparative psychologists to study. Cognitive scientists will want to understand how *all* minds work, not just the human mind, of course. But once we understand the systems and functional networks involved across various different species, and

Human and Animal Minds: The Consciousness Questions Laid to Rest. Peter Carruthers, Oxford University Press (2019). © Peter Carruthers.
DOI: 10.1093/oso/9780198843702.001.0001

the ways in which contents are processed in members of those species to issue in other contentful states and behavior, then there is nothing further to know or understand.[1]

While the question of animal consciousness turns out to be of no importance for science, it might be thought that it is nevertheless important for other domains of human inquiry—specifically, for ethics. This seems to have been the background assumption of *The Cambridge Declaration on Consciousness* (Low et al. 2012), for instance. And it appears to be the reason why the Humane Society Institute for Science and Policy would sponsor a scientific journal, *Animal Sentience*, which describes itself on its website as devoted to the question whether (and which) animals can *feel*. In addition, utilitarians such as Singer (1981, 1993) plainly think that consciousness is the "magic bullet" that will settle the question of moral standing for each animal species. Indeed, the founding father of utilitarianism, Bentham (1789), famously remarked, "The question is not, can they *reason*? nor, can they *talk*? but, can they *suffer*?" Notice, moreover, that although consciousness isn't mentioned here, there is every reason to think that it is nevertheless intended. In part this is because prior to the rise of cognitive science, philosophers (and others) drew no distinction between conscious and unconscious mental states. On the contrary, mentality was almost universally equated with consciousness. But it is also because, even in our own era, people often assume that pains and other forms of suffering are necessarily conscious.

Utilitarianism isn't the only game in town, of course. For instance, Regan (1985) argues that all and only creatures who are "subjects of a life"—which means having a sense of their own past and future—qualify as having moral rights. And it is by no means clear that such a view implies that consciousness is a necessary condition for having rights. On the other hand, it isn't clear that it *doesn't*, either. Can one have a "sense of one's own past" of the required sort without it being a *conscious* sense, and without it being *like anything* to revisit one's past? Regan doesn't say. Yet one widely held view about the nature of episodic memory implies

---

[1] Of course I just mean: nothing further to know or understand about their mental lives as such. One may still need to understand how mental states and their contents are realized in neural ones, for example.

that one can't (Tulving 1985; Mahr & Csibra 2018). This is the "auton-oetic consciousness" view of episodic memory.[2]

Likewise, Nussbaum (2006), in extending her "capabilities approach" to argue for moral rights in animals, nevertheless says that she shares with utilitarians the belief that *sentience* is a minimum necessary condition for a creature to have moral status. But it is left unclear whether this is sentience in the sense of *phenomenal* consciousness or merely sentience as a form of transitive creature consciousness (which can arguably exist in the absence of phenomenal consciousness). The same difficulty infects a recent paper by Sebo (2017), who argues that animals are owed duties of a sort appropriate for their form of what he calls "perceptual agency." For in explaining this notion he, too, asserts that sentience is presupposed; and the language in which he couches his descriptions of perceptual agency is riddled with talk of *experience*. So again we may wonder whether he really intends (or should intend, given the structure of the theory) a commitment to the idea that phenomenal consciousness is a necessary condition for perceptual agency, or whether mere transitive creature consciousness would do (and if so, of what sort).

There is a general moral here, which I will return to again in Section 8.5. This is that philosophers who have proposed ethical theories that grant rights or moral standing to animals—or that imply duties towards animals more generally—need to revisit those theories to ask themselves whether the accounts they have offered require animals to be phenomenally conscious or not. In fact, the point I am urging here is pretty much exactly parallel to the one advanced by King & Carruthers (2012, 2020) for theories of moral responsibility. We argue that theorists in that domain, too, need to take much more seriously the reality of unconscious mentality. For there is a widespread prescientific assumption that *all* mentality is conscious mentality. Moreover, that same view is likely to be tacitly assumed whenever humans—even scientifically literate humans—theorize about topics that implicate the mind without explicitly reminding themselves of the reality of unconscious mental states of all kinds. Hence, it is quite likely that the theories developed

---

[2] I happen to think such a view is wrong (Carruthers 2018c). While human episodic memories are actually phenomenally conscious (because globally broadcast), one can characterize forms of modality-specific perspectival event-memory without presupposing anything about consciousness.

may end up presupposing consciousness by default. Those theories will then need to be revisited to see whether or not they can survive being prized apart from their assumption of consciousness.

Moreover, many views, even views of a broadly Kantian or contractualist sort, can maintain that one basic sort of duty we have towards animals is to be *kind* and avoid *cruelty* (Carruthers 1992). And that then immediately raises the question whether consciousness is a prerequisite of kindness and cruelty. Is cruelty restricted to the infliction of *phenomenally conscious* suffering, for example? Or can one be cruel to creatures that lack conscious mental states altogether? And then what about creatures for whom there is no fact of the matter whether or not they possess conscious states, as I claim is true of most animals?[3] This will form the topic of Section 8.2.

8.2　Do animals feel pain?

Conceptually, this question is a mess. This is because the term "feel" plays two quite different roles in the present context, which are frequently not distinguished from one another. Philosophers often use the term when attempting to characterize phenomenal consciousness in general. Consciousness is said to comprise the *felt qualities* of experience, or the "feely" component of experience. In this sense of "feel" one can talk about the *feel* of a perception of vivid red, or what listening to the sound of a trumpet *feels like*. But "feel" is also the term we use for bodily forms of perception, in particular. We talk about feeling the shape of an object with our hands, feeling the warmth of a fire, feeling a tickle on the arm, and feeling a pain in the toe. What links the two uses is that whenever one is in a position to report feeling a bodily state of some sort, the content of that state will have attracted attention and been

---

[3] I say "most animals" because I assume that creatures whose lives are entirely governed by lifecycle-triggered fixed-action routines, where the execution of those routines is under direct sensorimotor guidance, and who are incapable of evaluative learning, are definitely *not* conscious. This is because all of the states of such creatures will be closely similar to the sensorimotor states in humans that provide one of our paradigms of *un*conscious perception, as we saw in Chapter 3. Perhaps wasps and some ants fit this description, as Godfrey-Smith (2016) seems to suggest. But honey bees definitely do not.

globally broadcast, perforce becoming phenomenally conscious and acquiring "feel" in the other sense also.

Given this distinction, it makes perfectly good sense to think that there can be felt states that lack feel. One way this can happen is that there might be feelings of bodily states that *don't* attract attention and become conscious, while nevertheless playing other roles in cognition. In particular, there might be feelings of pain that lack feel. Indeed, I will argue shortly that this *sort* of dissociation is a common occurrence in humans (even if it isn't that common for pain specifically). But a second possibility arises in connection with the feelings of animals especially. There might be perceptions of bodily states (of warmth, touch, pain, and so on) that attract attention, and whose role is *more or less similar* to that resulting from human global broadcasting of similar contents. At the least-similar end of the spectrum, the result might be bodily feelings that lack feel altogether (i.e. that are definitely not phenomenally conscious). In other cases, there will be bodily feelings for which there is no fact of the matter whether or not they have feel—or so the arguments of Chapter 7 imply.

In the human case, feelings of pain that lack feel because they fail to attract attention are comparatively rare. For it is part of the very function of pain to attract attention, alerting the agent to a likely source of bodily damage. But anecdotally, at least, there are such cases. These are instances where attentional focus is so firmly fixed on other things that pain—although present, and influencing behavior in other ways—remains unconscious. For example, there are cases of wounded soldiers who don't notice their wounds until the battle is over, and football players who continue to play without noticing any injury (although perhaps they limp or favor their shoulder in consequence). And for sure we know that levels of consciously experienced pain can be *modulated* by attention. This is the point of the distraction techniques doctors employ with children, and it may be part of what underlies placebo effects on pain. For if you *believe* you won't have much pain, you may attend to it less, and consequently *feel* less pain (Buhle et al. 2012).

Although unconscious pains are rare, unconscious instances of other forms of bodily perception are legion. One may shift one's posture, for example, to better accommodate the shape of the chair on which one is sitting, but without noticing that one has done so, or why. One may draw one's coat more closely around one's shoulders to alleviate the cold, but without noticing that one feels cold. And of course one's hands will often adjust themselves to the shape and texture of items one is grasping or carrying without one being aware of the perceptions of touch that guide the adjustments. When seen in the company of these other forms of unconscious perception of states of the body, cases of unconscious pain are just what one might expect (albeit rarely, given pain's attention-grabbing function).

We can ask, now, whether unconscious pains (in contrast with the bodily damage that they signal) are appropriate objects of moral concern. It seems plain that they aren't. While we should want to help with the soldier's injury, this is because of its likely effects on his future life, not because it is causing him unconscious pain. And although (if we could find a way to do it while he continues to fight) we might give him an analgesic, this would be in anticipation of the pain that he will surely feel as soon as the battle stops, not in order to reduce his current level of (unconscious) pain.

Suppose, then, that there are animals who are capable of forms of nociception, but whose resulting perceptions of bodily damage are never made available to anything resembling decision-making processes, with the result that their perceptions of pain are definitely unconscious ones (perhaps influencing withdrawals of a merely sensorimotor sort). In that case their pains should *not* be objects of moral concern, and to cause such an animal pain will not be cruel—although of course it might be wrong for other reasons or in other ways.

If conscious pains matter morally (as plainly they do, at least in humans) and unconscious pains don't, then what are we to say of pains that are neither determinately conscious nor determinately unconscious? What are we to say of pains (likely the majority, as one surveys the range of animal species) for which there is no fact of the matter whether they are phenomenally conscious or not? This question will be tackled, in part, in Section 8.4. But before that, in Section 8.3, we need to discuss *why* pains are bad. What is it that makes them appropriate objects of moral concern even in our own case?

The answer to the question that forms the title of the present section, however ("Do animals feel pain?"), should now be obvious. Yes, many animals do feel pain, probably including all mammals and birds, many species of fish (excepting sharks, who lack nociceptors altogether), as well as other vertebrates, and some species of invertebrate like octopus and squid. These are animals that perceive bodily states of tissue damage, where those perceptual states are *not* merely sensorimotor in their cognitive function. But as for whether these feelings of pain *have feel* and are phenomenally conscious: there is no fact of the matter, according to the views defended in Chapter 7.

8.3 What makes pain bad?

This question has already been answered, in part, in Chapter 6, when we discussed the representational character of negative valence. Recall that pain, like other affective states, comprises a number of potentially dissociable components. It has a sensory element, representing the location of the sensory quality of pain (stabbing, throbbing, or whatever) in some specific region of the body. It has an arousal component, increasing one's heart rate, releasing cortisol and other stress-related chemicals into the bloodstream, and so on. It has a behavioral aspect, causing one to become physically tense, and activating motor routines (which may get suppressed prior to execution) for nursing the injured part and/or removing it from the offending stimulus. And then there is negative valence directed at the sensory component of the pain. I suggested in Chapter 6 that this is best seen as a nonconceptual representation of the badness of that component. The role of negative valence is to directly motivate forms of executive planning and decision-making to improve one's situation.

The question for us now is whether pain sensations are only bad when there is *conscious*—globally broadcast—negative valence directed at them. This is a question that can't be answered introspectively, of course. For in our own case it is, as a matter of fact, always conscious negative valence that we experience when our pains seem bad. We can't dissociate the pain *seeming bad to us* from it *consciously* seeming bad to us. Note that if pains are only bad when conscious, and if there is no fact of the matter about consciousness in most species of animal, then this will mean that there is likewise no fact of the matter whether their pains are bad or not.

Perhaps a different perspective can help, however. Valence is a reflection of the underlying value placed on a thing, event, or property by our affective/valuational systems. In the case of pain, it is a bodily sensation (a secondary quality of the body caused by underlying tissue damage) that is evaluated as bad. And that sensation and the negative valence directed at it are always both of them phenomenally conscious in the cases that matter. But other kinds of affective state are different. When a bear looms out of the bushes while one is hiking and one feels fear, the negative valence is directed at the bear, not at one's own experience of the bear—or so I have argued (Carruthers 2018d). It is the presence of *the bear* that seems bad to one, not the fact that one is *experiencing* a bear. (After all, if it were the latter, one could just close one's eyes and stop one's ears to make the badness end.) So although one does have phenomenally conscious experience of the bear, a component of which is negative valence, what is evaluated as bad is something external. And such evaluating can surely take place in a creature whether or not it is capable of consciousness (or whether or not there is a fact of that matter about the conscious status of its perceptual states).

In general, our value systems are outward-looking. It is worldly items and worldly events that get appraised as good or bad, and are thus seen as nonconceptually good or bad. Such appraisals don't depend on the presence of a full global broadcasting architecture, and are surely possible in creatures that lack such an architecture. So there will be things that are good or bad *for the bear*, or *from the perspective of the bear's values*, even if there is no fact of the matter whether the bear has phenomenally conscious experiences. And by parity of reasoning, then, one should say the same about the bear's pains. When the bear feels pain, it is the property represented in its body that is seen as bad, and hence that *is* bad, from the bear's own perspective.

It may be helpful to express this point in the language of folk-psychology rather than scientific psychology—specifically, using the language of "desire" or "want." (From a cognitive-science perspective, a current or felt desire comprises positive valence directed at the prospect of obtaining a thing or outcome, or else negative valence directed at the presence of something one wants to avoid.) Even if there is no fact of the matter whether or not the bear's mental states are phenomenally conscious, it can still be true that the bear *wants* its pain to stop, just as it can still be true that it *wants* to eat when hungry. And although active desires in humans are phenomenally conscious whenever we are aware of them, it seems reasonable to judge that their importance derives, not from the phenomenally conscious nature of their content, but rather from their status *as* desires, as reflecting one's underlying values and needs.

How can it be true that animals actually have desires while at the same time there is no fact of the matter whether they have phenomenally conscious states? Whence the difference? Recall that phenomenal consciousness is first-personal, and is either definitely present or definitely absent. It doesn't admit of degrees (although other nearby notions like access consciousness *do* admit of degrees). In contrast, our notions of desire, belief, intention, and the rest get their sense from their position in a folk-psychological and/or scientific-psychological theory of the mind. These theories may place rather minimal demands on the extent to which a creature has to satisfy the postulates of the theory in order to qualify as having desires.[4] But in any case, there is no conceptual difficulty in describing the states of an animal as "desire-*like*" or "belief-*like*." (In contrast, it makes no sense to describe its states as "conscious-like," at least if it is phenomenal consciousness that is intended.) And that may be all that is needed for us to be able to say that the bear's pains *matter*, from the bear's own perspective.

It seems plain, then, that preference-utilitarians, at any rate (who think that the value to be promoted is one of preference satisfaction), should have no difficulty in extending moral importance to animals. For many animals definitely have desires or desire-like states, even if there is no fact of the matter whether their desires and other mental states are phenomenally conscious. (Hedonic-utilitarians, in contrast, confront the question whether the hedonic states that matter in ourselves only matter because they are phenomenally conscious.) And for the same reason, one might think that any moral theory that finds a place for the duty of beneficence and the vice of cruelty could find a way to extend those

[4] This isn't to say that there are *no* constraints on what it takes to be a believer/desirer, of course. My view is that the states in question need to possess compositional structure (albeit not necessarily propositional in nature; the structures can be map-like or tree-like), and need to interact with one another in ways that are sensitive to those structures. This allows bees and some other navigating insects to count as having beliefs and desires, while ruling out plants, despite that naturalness of saying that a sunflower "wants" to turn toward the sun.

virtues and vices to embrace our relationships with animals. For beneficence can be thought of as giving a creature what it values or wants; and
cruelty can be conceptualized as willful frustration of those wants.

8.4 Empathy versus sympathy

It is beginning to seem that the main finding from Chapter 7—that there
is no fact of the matter about the presence or absence of phenomenal
consciousness in most animals—*needn't* matter for ethics, any more
than it matters for science. Whether it *does* matter may depend on the
specific commitments of any given moral theory, of course. But it seems
there are at least reasonable accounts of what makes human pains and
desire-frustrations bad that enable us to pull those things apart from
phenomenal consciousness, in a way that might equally apply to the case
of an animal.

Any theorist who places important moral weight on feelings of
empathy, however, may have good reasons to disagree. For empathy
requires first-personal identification with the feelings of the subject
empathized with. To empathize with someone means imagining, in a
first-person way, what that person is feeling—thereby, to a degree,
sharing that feeling (or at least *aiming* to share that feeling, since
empathy may miss its target and go awry). Because any state that we
consciously imagine in this way will perforce be phenomenally conscious, that raises the question whether it is *appropriate* to feel empathy
for any given species of animal. If that animal is capable of phenomenally
conscious experience, then it will be; but if it isn't, then it won't. And if
there is no fact of the matter, this would seem to fall into the same
category as definite *lack* of phenomenally conscious status. It would
appear to require the definite presence of phenomenal consciousness
for empathy for the states of a creature to be appropriate. For one might
think that it can only be appropriate to take a first-person perspective on
the simulated states of a creature if the creature, too, can take just such a
perspective.

Empathy can be morally problematic even in the human case, however
(Bloom 2016). One reason is that it is highly *partial*. It is much easier to
generate empathy for a family member, a loved one, or a friend than it is

to feel empathy for a stranger or an out-group member. Moreover, the accuracy of one's empathic feelings (i.e. their degree of resemblance to the feelings of the target) is highly dependent on one's knowledge of the other person, as well as on the degree to which one's psychological profiles are similar.[5]

Empathy is especially problematic in connection with nonhuman animals, even setting aside the question of consciousness. For imagination is likely to be a highly unreliable guide to the mental life of an animal. This is because anything we imagine, and any set of images we form, will be globally broadcast to our own set of consumer systems and emotional systems, which differ quite significantly from those of the target animal. So the result will be a distinctively human emotional state, rather than a strictly animal one. Empathizing with an animal held in captivity, for example, one might feel that its situation is a terrible one. But that might not reflect the perspective of the animal at all (and will vary on a species-by-species basis). Likewise, empathizing with a circus animal, one might feel that its situation is degrading. But I am pretty confident that no animal ever feels degraded. That presupposes forms of social embeddedness and a concern for reputation that are arguably uniquely human. And in the opposite direction, empathizing with a mouse that remains motionless while one holds it gently in one's hands, one might think that it is enjoying the comforting warmth, when in fact it is frozen in fear.

Empathy should be distinguished from *sympathy*, however. When empathizing, one simulates in the first person the presumed situation of the other, and enters into an emotional state that is (if everything goes well, and one is sufficiently similar in nature to the other) the same as the emotional state of the other. In empathizing with someone's grief at the death of a loved one, for example, one ends up in a grief-like state oneself. Sympathy, in contrast, can be grounded in a third-personal understanding of the situation and emotional state of the other. Understanding that the other person is grieving, and caring about how they feel, one comes

---

[5] Another problem with empathy is that its long-term use can be self-defeating. Doctors and nurses who feel more empathy for their patients tend to "burn out" more frequently, and consequently have reduced abilities to help future patients. Yet another problem, as Bloom (2016) points out, is that empathy is insensitive to numbers: a single starving child can evoke empathy, whereas widespread famine doesn't.

to see their grief as bad. (That is, one experiences negative valence directed at their state of grief; one *wants* them to feel better.) This then motives one to do what one can to alleviate their grief.

Sympathy *can* be grounded in imagination, of course. Imagining what it is like to lose a loved one, one enters a grief-like state. This provides one with knowledge of what the other person is likely feeling. One then comes to see that what the other is feeling is bad, and consequently one wants to help. Plainly, however, one should *not* use imagination to ground one's sympathy directed at the plight of an animal. For what one imagines will be broadcast to one's own affective and valuational systems, not the animal's. So the resulting affective response is likely to be quite wide of its target, and one will end up with false beliefs about what the animal feels. If one thinks that it might be important to be sympathetic towards the situation of an animal, one should seek an accurate third-person understanding of its needs and affective states, not project one's own feelings onto it.

Indeed, it seems plain that sympathy can be independent of questions of consciousness. I have previously argued for this conclusion while assuming the strong claim that the mental states of most animals are *not* conscious ones (Carruthers 1999, 2004). But the conclusion is surely the same if, as I have now argued, there is no fact of the matter. To be sympathetic towards the plight of a creature is to be motivated to help it, grounded in a third-person appreciation of its needs and mental states. Then provided one cares about a given animal or type of animal, one can still feel sympathy for it, even if one is convinced that the mental states of the animal aren't phenomenally conscious ones, or that there is no fact of the matter.

I conclude that while empathy for animals may be impossible or inappropriate if there is no fact of the matter whether the mental states of animals are phenomenally conscious, attempts to empathize with animals are best avoided in any case. Moreover, empathy shouldn't have a foundational position in ethical theory anyway (Bloom 2016). In contrast, sympathy for animals remains possible, while also being preferable on grounds of greater accuracy, and therefore greater appropriateness. Whether one *should* feel sympathy for animals (or accord them rights, come to that) is a distinctively moral question, about which something should now be said.

8.5 The task for moral philosophy

One can ask whether, and on what grounds, animals have moral standing, thus having moral rights or being owed duties in their own right. And one can ask whether, and on what grounds, one should be sympathetic for the plight of an animal, and should try to improve its situation. These are difficult questions for moral theory. While I have published views on this topic (Carruthers 1992, 2011b), I aim to remain neutral on those questions here. My goal is rather to explore the significance, for moral philosophy, of the thesis that there is no fact of the matter about animal consciousness.

Our conclusion thus far has been that much can remain unchanged. Sympathy rather than empathy should be one's preferred mode of responding to animal suffering in any case (supposing that one responds, or should respond, at all); and sympathy should be grounded in third-person understanding of the needs and mental life of the creature in question. The question of phenomenal consciousness needn't arise. Likewise, feelings of pain and other negative mental states can exist in the absence of phenomenal consciousness (i.e. while *lacking feel*), and also if there is no fact of the matter. And such states can still be bad from the perspective of the animal. So anyone who thinks, for whatever reason, that one is obliged to prevent bad things from happening to animals can continue with their views unchanged.

Some aspects of moral philosophy *should* change, however, as a result of our conclusions. Since there is no answer to the all-or-nothing question on which philosophers have traditionally focused ("Are members of species X sentient and capable of conscious experience?"), we have no option but to confront the vast variety of animal mental life. The mind of any given species will resemble the human mind in some respects while differing from it in others. And as we noted in Chapter 6, as one looks across species from a comparative perspective one will see a complex, multidimensional, crosscutting similarity *network*. Moreover, the same will be true for even a single type of mental state, like pain.

Singer (1993) famously claimed that "pain is pain, no matter who feels it." But this is false. Distinct species of animal will undergo negatively valenced states caused by tissue damage that play a variety of different roles in their mental lives. Those roles will be more or less similar to one another depending on the differences that exist in the conceptual abilities of the animals in question, as well as in a broad range of executive functions that may be sensitive to the presence of such states. To his credit (and despite the misleading nature of the slogan quoted above), Singer recognizes some of this complexity. He notes, for example, that the pains that humans undergo can thereafter be recalled and ruminated upon, thus continuing to have a negative impact on the life of the individual well beyond the scope of the sensation itself. The same may not be true at all in some animals, while holding to a much lesser degree in others. But this is just to scratch the surface of the differences that likely exist across species.

Since an all-or-nothing question about the relevant form of animal mentality (assumed to be consciousness) is no longer appropriate, moral theorists of various stripes need to ask which dimensions of similarity and difference are most relevant. One might think that for utilitarians, for example, the most important dimension would concern the presence of desire-like and emotion-like states. This may necessitate the presence of simple forms of executive decision-making; but the latter can be limited to a sort of bottom-up competitive interaction among drives and goals. Whether an animal can reason or plan will seem much less relevant. In contrast, those who are Kantians or neo-Kantians might be expected to think the reverse. The most important dimensions of similarity will concern an animal's abilities to reason and plan, as well as to make top-down higher-order evaluations of its own goals and desires when making a decision.

Questions about the moral treatment of animals should also take an empirical turn, as Dawkins (2012, 2017) argues at length. Dawkins, too, urges that we should drop the question of animal consciousness, focusing instead on animal health, welfare, and emotional wellbeing. (In Dawkins' case, however, this is because she thinks we can never *know* whether animals have conscious states, whereas I have argued that there is no fact of the matter—there is nothing for us to know.) We should ask what causes members of different species stress and distress; we can ask what they want, by giving them choices and seeing what they choose; and so on. (And we should be alive, too, to individual differences among members of a single species. Animals differ in their individual personalities, just as humans do.)

Chapter 7 argued that the question of animal consciousness—and the fact that it has no answer—doesn't matter for scientific purposes. We have now seen that it doesn't matter much for questions about the ethical treatment of animals, either. Most of the same issues will arise, and most of the same debates can continue as before. However, greater attention needs to be paid to the varieties of animal mentality with which we have to deal. Moral theorists need to be much more alive to the varying dimensions of similarity and difference that exist between human minds and the minds of other animal species, explicitly addressing which of those dimensions are most theoretically important, in what respects, and to what degree.

8.6 Of empathy, infants, and the old

We now turn to consider what should be said of humans whose mental lives can be animal-*like*—to varying degrees—namely infants and people suffering from dementia or other forms of brain damage.

Chapter 6 argued that phenomenal consciousness *is* globally broadcast nonconceptual content. But Chapter 7 pointed out that global broadcasting varies by degrees across species, whereas the first-person concept of phenomenal consciousness entails that it is all-or-nothing. This then set up the argument that there is no fact of the matter about phenomenal consciousness in most other species of animal. Similar issues then arise in connection with human beings, of course. The process of fetal, infant, and child development is plainly one that begins with a being that doesn't have phenomenally conscious states (because there is no global broadcasting of any sort) and ends with one that does.

At what point does phenomenal consciousness emerge in child development? Since the concept of consciousness is all-or-nothing, we can't say that it emerges gradually. Yet it seems unlikely that there is some all-or-nothing tipping point, either. Likewise, there will be people whose mental powers gradually fade as they become senile, or develop Alzheimer's disease; and there are people with a variety of forms of brain damage that impact their executive function capacities, language use, capacities for reflective thought, and higher-order thought.

In some of these cases a claim that the human being in question has phenomenally conscious experience might have determinate truth-conditions, and there may be good reason to believe such a claim to be true (as in a child with specific language impairment, for example), or false (as in a first-trimester fetus). In other cases, however, this won't be so. For as Chapter 7 suggested, we have to ask under what conditions the following counterfactual judgment is evaluable: "If creature C were to have the disposition-to-judge that I employ when I think about states as being *this*-E, then C would judge that its states are *this*-E." Cases that *aren't* evaluable are ones where the description of the person C implies that C is incapable of any dispositions-to-judge of the sort required—because C is either incapable of reflective thinking generally or incapable of higher-order thought in particular. For the counterfactual would then have as its antecedent something that entails, "If a being that is incapable of the disposition-to-judge *this*-E were to have the disposition-to-judge *this*-E, ..." But this is just to suppose that the being in question is other than it is.

It follows, then, if we are wondering which components among various executive functions, language ability, and higher-order thought are necessary (or not) for phenomenal consciousness—in such a way that someone who has these capacities damaged, lost, or not yet developed will become incapable of phenomenally conscious experience—then setting up a counterfactual that (in effect) reinstates those abilities can't help. As a result, there will be numerous cases where there is no fact of the matter whether a given human has phenomenally conscious experience or not.

One might think—quite reasonably—that the two cases of infant development and human aging are significantly different from cross-species comparisons. After all, a human infant's brain contains at least nascent versions of all of the main systems involved in global broadcasting in adults. So there will surely be stages in development (or in someone's slide into senility) where it makes sense to suppose that the infant (or adult) could possess the disposition-to-judge that underlies my use of the concept THIS-E, even if she can't manifest such a concept in speech. Whether, and when, this becomes true would seem to depend on subtle issues regarding the evaluation of the counterfactual that fixes the truth-conditions of the thought that the infant has *this*-E. At what point can one suppose that the disposition-to-judge that underlies the first-person phenomenal-consciousness concept can be activated in the mind of the infant without fundamentally altering that mind? Indeed, it seems likely that the answer is at least partly a matter of stipulation. (What counts as a "fundamental" alteration, here?)

However, even if there are stages in development where supposing the infant to possess the disposition-to-judge underlying the concept THIS-E doesn't fundamentally change the existing architecture in any way, that still leaves open the question of yet earlier stages of development. And likewise, even if there are stages in the progress of Alzheimer's disease, for instance, where something similar is true, for sure there are later stages where there would seem to be no fact of the matter.

The important point is that none of this *matters*, however. The question whether or not a newly born infant, a two-year-old child, or a grandmother with severe dementia have phenomenally conscious mental states is of merely classificatory interest. Nothing substantive turns on the answer. So we shouldn't waste time addressing it. For the question just concerns whether the dispositions-to-judge underlying the first-person concept THIS-E could find application in the mind of the infant, say, as that mind actually is; but we now know that what that concept picks out is just globally broadcast nonconceptual content. So as a human infant develops into a phenomenally conscious adult, there is no point at which a light gets turned on (nor does any light get turned on gradually, come to that), and no special properties emerge. There is just broadcast nonconceptual content that gets made available to more and increasingly sophisticated executive function capacities (decreasing, in the case of dementia).

What *is* important is to understand the range of mental states and processes undergone by a newborn, a two-year-old, and a dementia patient. Some of these targets of understanding will bear on the extent of the resemblance between the mentality in question and full-blown global broadcasting. We can ask, for example, about attention and working memory in newborns, or about preserved executive functions in dementia. But equally, we can seek to understand processes that have little bearing on consciousness, such as categorical visual processing and sensorimotor control.

One way in which these issues might matter is for our capacity for empathy, however. We noted in Section 8.4 that empathy—as a form of mental-state *sharing*—seems to presuppose the phenomenally conscious status of the person empathized with. So if there isn't a fact of the matter whether an infant has pains that are phenomenally conscious, then that might seem to stand in the way of empathizing with its suffering. But as we also noted in Section 8.4, the proper home of empathy is among friends and loved ones. Indeed, empathy may play an important role in *building* emotional connections between people, as well as reflecting such connections that antecedently exist. (Certainly we know that *behavioral* mirroring plays such a role; see Tunçgenç & Cohen 2016. So it makes sense that emotional mirroring would do so too.) But if this is so, then all that needs to happen is that one should suppress or ignore one's knowledge that there is no fact of the matter, allowing oneself to empathize *as if* with a normal adult.

Let me illustrate with an anecdote. Many years ago when I was in college, I had a teacher who remarked that mothers seem to suffer from a useful form of temporary insanity when they have children: they talk to their babies as if their babies could understand them.[6] Yet such talk has a point: it facilitates language-learning (as we now know: Kuhl 2007; Newman et al. 2016). I am suggesting something similar here. We empathize with babies—and *should* empathize with them—to build strong and loving bonds with them. This can remain true, even though empathy itself might not be strictly appropriate because there is no fact of the matter about the phenomenally conscious status of infants' mental states. In the same way, one should empathize with the sufferings of one's grandma who has dementia in order to *maintain* such bonds.

Importantly, however, one should rely on mind-reading-based sympathy, and not on first-personal empathy, when taking important decisions on behalf of infants or the aged. Otherwise empathy for grandma when she becomes incontinent may lead one to consider euthanasia in jurisdictions that allow it, since fellow-feeling may lead one to think that she is deeply embarrassed and humiliated. But in reality she may be

---

[6] This was in the context of discussing Wittgenstein's famous remark that if a lion could talk, we wouldn't understand him. And it was long before we knew anything about the extraordinarily sophisticated cognitive abilities of human infants, who understand much more than one might think.

comfortable in the care of a kindly nursing staff, while still being able to connect emotionally with her family.

8.7 Of mice, men, and Martians

I have argued on a combination of empirical and explanatory grounds over the course of this book that there is no fact of the matter whether nonhuman animals—or at any rate, most animals—have phenomenally conscious mental states. But philosophers love their thought experiments, and before concluding we should consider one that has been used as a counter-example to my view on more than one occasion. Suppose that there is a species of alien creature—they might as well be Martians—whose intelligence and executive-function abilities outstrip ours by as much as we exceed the intelligence and executive-function capacities of a mouse. If my view entails that there is no fact of the matter concerning the presence or absence of phenomenal consciousness in the mouse, then couldn't these Martians argue just the same with respect to us? But if they did, we know they would be mistaken. So by the same token, how can we be confident that we aren't making a mistake in denying that there is a fact of the matter about consciousness in mice?

To get this example going, we have to suppose that Martians have introspective access to some of their own nonconceptual states, and that they can form first-person acquaintance-based concepts for those states. Suppose that THIS-M is an example of such a concept. We also have to suppose that when they deploy concepts like THIS-M, Martian philosophers can conceive of zombie-Martians, and can entertain the other "hard problem" thought experiments. But since they are so smart, perhaps the problem doesn't trouble them for long. Indeed, perhaps it is a developmental milestone that infant Martians pass through, just as passing the A-not-B task (discussed in Chapter 2) is an early milestone for human toddlers. They swiftly realize that the apparent explanatory gap isn't really a gap at all, but is just a product of switching among third-person and first-person concepts and perspectives. Still, when they conquer Earth and begin to study its creatures, it might occur to some of them to entertain thoughts like, *I wonder if any of these humans have states that are THIS-M?* Deploying arguments parallel to those used in this book, they might conclude that there is no fact of the matter. But they would be wrong. So perhaps I am wrong to make the equivalent claim about mice.

There are two distinct ways in which the Martian example can be developed, however, and neither is troubling for the view defended here. Suppose, first, that Martian executive-function and conceptual capacities are a super-set of our own. That is, suppose that their minds share essentially the same overall architecture as ours (just as I allow that mice share the same "centered mind" architecture as humans). They, too, have globally broadcast nonconceptual states. But the systems these states are broadcast to, while encompassing ours, include some novel capacities we lack, while greatly extending and enhancing others. Now recall from Chapter 7 that when a Martian asks whether humans have states like *this*-M, the truth-condition needed for a positive answer amounts to this: "If the dispositions-to-judge that underlie my use of the concept THIS-M were to be instantiated in the mind of a human, then those dispositions would issue in a judgment that the human's mental states are *this-M*."

In a case of the sort envisaged, however, this counter-factual thought will be *true*, rather than unevaluable. For although human and Martian minds differ in many respects, we are supposing that they nevertheless share the capacities needed to instantiate the relevant disposition-to-judge (namely, capacities for higher-order acquaintance-based reflective thoughts about globally broadcast nonconceptual contents). For we are supposing that Martian capacities are a super-set of our own. And yet it is the capacities just mentioned that issue in "hard problem" thought experiments. Since these are capacities that both species share, from the Martian's perspective it will be *true* that humans have states like *this*-M. Put differently: although they otherwise differ greatly, human and Martian minds are alike in the ways necessary to project a first-person phenomenal concept into the mind of another being.

Notice that it follows from this that global-workspace theory needn't *just* be a theory of human phenomenal consciousness, and that consciousness is in principle multiply realizable. But our first-person conception of phenomenal consciousness places severe constraints on the extent to which this can be so. The reason for this should by now be familiar: it is because that first-person concept, when projected into the mind of another, presupposes that the mind in question contains the wherewithal to formulate and deploy just such a concept. For recall that the truth-condition for "Creature C has states that are *this*-E" is given by the counterfactual, "If the dispositions underlying my use of THIS-E were instantiated in the mind of C, then C would judge that its states are *this*-E." This counterfactual is unevaluable if the mind of creature C is actually incapable of supporting such dispositions.

Now suppose, on the other hand, that the Martian mind has a completely different architecture from our own. Perhaps their minds differ from ours even more radically than our minds seem to differ from that of the octopus (Godfrey-Smith 2016).[7] In that case, the counterfactual that fixes the truth-condition for the Martian's thought about consciousness in humans really will be unevaluable. For when the Martian supposes that a human might instantiate the dispositions-to-judge underlying the Martian's first-person phenomenal concepts, it is in fact supposing that the mind of the human is quite other than it actually is. But this isn't really a problem for my view. One reason is that the same thing holds in reverse: given that Martian minds are so wholly different from our own, *we* cannot sensibly project *our* first-person concept THIS-E into *their* minds, either. So from our perspective, there is no fact of the matter whether Martians—despite their manifest smartness—have phenomenally conscious experiences.

Another point is that if Martian minds are so completely different in organization from our own, then it is far from clear that the familiar notions of *judgment* and *thought* will even make sense when applied to them. For these notions belong within a network of causal and architectural beliefs about the way our minds (and the minds of many other animals) function. In which case we can't even suppose that Martians might wonder about—that is, entertain thoughts about—the possibility of consciousness in us. Hence the alleged counter-example can't really get started.

---

[7] The octopus is a species of mollusk, which split from the line leading to vertebrates such as fish, birds, and mammals around 600 million years ago. The octopus' brain organization is quite different from ours, with separate sensory and motor controller systems for each of its eight arms, and with two large optic lobes located outside of its central brain. Moreover, the central brain contains only a small proportion of the overall number of neurons in the octopus' nervous system (Hochner et al. 2006).

More importantly, however, nothing of any significance turns on these failures of projection, and nothing important follows from them. There are no magic properties missing from Martian minds (and none from ours, from the Martian perspective, as they would surely be smart enough to appreciate). There are just broadcast nonconceptual contents, together with first-person acquaintance-based concepts that can't sensibly be projected into minds that are too much unlike the minds of their possessors.

8.8 Conclusions

I have argued that the conclusion reached in Chapter 7—that there is no fact of the matter concerning phenomenal consciousness in most species of animal—should not be deeply disturbing. Sympathy for animal suffering can still be appropriate (even if empathy isn't), and things that happen to an animal can still be perceived as good or bad (wanted or unwanted) by the animal itself. Two things should change, however. First, no one should now think that the question of consciousness in animals is any sort of magic bullet for resolving issues about their moral status. And second, moral theorists need to take much more seriously the varied roles that pain perception can play in the minds of different species of animal, as well as the differences among animal minds more generally. Finally, I have argued that although the conclusion reached in Chapter 7 extends also to some humans (especially infants and those experiencing severe age-related declines), this should not be disturbing, either. Indeed, for practical purposes it can generally be ignored.

* * *

This book as a whole has sought to lay the consciousness questions to rest. Nothing mysterious entered the world with phenomenal consciousness: there are no qualia. Rather, phenomenal consciousness just *is* globally broadcast nonconceptual content. Humans are capable of thinking about such contents in a distinctive acquaintance-based way, however, and when they do, they fall prey to the various "hard problem" thought experiments (zombies, color-deprived Mary) and the explanatory gap. But our capacity to think such thoughts is a perfectly natural phenomenon, one that can be naturalistically explained. So nothing is left in need of explanation.

As many have noted, the very notion of phenomenal consciousness is tied up with the first-person perspective on our own mental states, and all investigations of consciousness have to start from that perspective. The result of those investigations is the form of global-workspace theory defended in this book. But the global workspace studied in the human mind will only be present in the minds of nonhuman animals to some or other degree. That creates a problem when put together with the fact that our first-person notion of consciousness is all-or-nothing, and doesn't admit of degrees. Since there is no extra property that enters the world with the emergence of phenomenal consciousness, however, it can only be by *stipulation* that some particular degree of resemblance to the human global workspace is sufficient for consciousness. This isn't a factual matter. The various forms of resemblance to, and difference from, human global broadcasting are what they are; there is no *further* fact about whether they support phenomenal consciousness or not.

In addition, since phenomenal consciousness is a first-person notion, it should be characterized in terms of the same acquaintance-based indexical concepts that give rise to the "hard problem" thought experiments—concepts like THIS-R and THIS-E. And the only way one can specify the truth-conditions of such first-person concepts when applied *across* subjects is in terms of the dispositions-to-judge that underlie their first-person use. As a result, the truth-condition of the statement, "Creature C has states that are *this*-E" becomes, "If the dispositions-to-judge that underlie my use of THIS-E were to be instantiated in the mind of C, then C would judge that some of its states are *this*-E." However, as we have seen, when applied to animals such counterfactuals fail to fix any truth-condition for the mind of the animal *as that creature actually is*. This will be so whenever the antecedent of the conditional requires us to suppose that the mind of the creature in question is significantly other than it actually is. This is likely to be the case for all (or almost all) animals, and for some humans.

The larger point, however, is that none of this matters. People can stop worrying about the problem of consciousness because that problem is solved by global-workspace theory. It only *seemed* deep and intractable because of philosophical thought experiments grounded in the distinctive first-person way we can think about our conscious states. Similarly, people can stop worrying about the question of consciousness in animals. This is because there is no fact of the matter waiting to be discovered. There is much to learn about the *minds* of nonhuman animals, of course, and there are numerous deep problems waiting for comparative psychologists to solve. But facts about phenomenal consciousness (or its absence) aren't among them.

References

Aiello, L. & Wheeler, P. (1995). The expensive tissue hypothesis. *Current Anthropology*, 36, 199–221.

Aleman, B. & Merker, B. (2014). Consciousness without cortex: A hydranencephaly family survey. *Acta Paediatrica*, 103, 1057–65.

Allen, T. & Fortin, N. (2013). The evolution of episodic memory. *Proceedings of the National Academy of Sciences*, 110, 10379–86.

Alter, T. & Nagasawa, Y. (2012). What is Russellian monism? *Journal of Consciousness Studies*, 19(9–10), 67–95.

Andersen, L., Pedersen, M., Sandberg, K., & Overgaard, M. (2016). Occipital MEG activity in the early time range (<300 ms) predicts graded changes in perceptual consciousness. *Cerebral Cortex*, 26, 2677–88.

Armstrong, D. (1968). *A Materialist Theory of the Mind*. Routledge.

Avarguès-Weber, A., d'Amaro, D., Metzler, M., & Dyer, A. (2014). Conceptualization of relative size in honeybees. *Frontiers in Behavioral Neuroscience*, 8, 80.

Avarguès-Weber, A., Dyer, A., Combe, M., & Giurfa, M. (2012). Simultaneous mastering of two abstract concepts by the miniature brain of bees. *Proceedings of the National Academy of Sciences*, 109, 7481–6.

Aydede, M. & Fulkerson, M. (2014). Affect: Representationalists' headache. *Philosophical Studies*, 170, 175–98.

Baars, B. (1988). *A Cognitive Theory of Consciousness*. Cambridge University Press.

Baars, B. (1997). *In the Theatre of Consciousness*. Oxford University Press.

Baars, B. (2002). The conscious access hypothesis: Origins and recent evidence. *Trends in Cognitive Sciences*, 6, 47–52.

Baddeley, A. (1986). *Working Memory*. Oxford University Press.

Baddeley, A. & Hitch, G. (1974). Working memory. In G. Bower (ed.), *The Psychology of Learning and Motivation*, vol. 8. Academic Press.

Ball, D. (2009). There are no phenomenal concepts. *Mind*, 118, 935–72.

Balog, K. (1999). Conceivability, possibility, and the mind-body problem. *The Philosophical Review*, 108, 497–528.

Balog, K. (2009). Phenomenal concepts. In B. McLaughlin, A. Beckermann, & S. Walter (eds), *The Oxford Handbook of Philosophy of Mind*. Oxford University Press.

Balog, K. (2012). In defense of the phenomenal concept strategy. *Philosophy and Phenomenological Research*, 84, 1–23.

Baluch, F. & Itti, L. (2011). Mechanisms of top-down attention. *Trends in Neurosciences*, 34, 210–24.

Barrett, L. & Bar, M. (2009). See it with feeling: Affective predictions during object perception. *Philosophical Transactions of the Royal Society B*, 364, 1325–34.

Barron, A. & Klein, C. (2016). What insects can tell us about the origins of consciousness. *Proceedings of the National Academy of Sciences*, 113, 4900–4908.

Barth, H., Kanwisher, N., & Spelke, E. (2003). The construction of large number representations in adults. *Cognition*, 86, 201–21.

Bateson, W. (1916). Review of *The Mechanism of Mendelian Heredity*, by Morgan et al. *Science*, 44, 536–43.

Bayne, T. & Montague, M. (eds) (2011). *Cognitive Phenomenology*. Oxford University Press.

Beck, J. (2019). Perception is analog: The argument from Weber's law. *Journal of Philosophy*, 116(6), 314–49.

Bentham, J. (1789). *An Introduction to the Principles of Morals and Legislation*. Oxford University Press.

Beran, M., Smith, J.D., & Perdue, B. (2013). Language-trained chimpanzees name what they have seen, but look first at what they have not seen. *Psychological Science*, 24, 660–66.

Bergelson, E. & Swingley, D. (2012). At 6–9 months, human infants know the meanings of many common nouns. *Proceedings of the American Academy of Sciences*, 109, 3253–8.

Bering, J. (2006). The cognitive psychology of belief in the supernatural. *American Scientist*, 94, 142–9.

Bering, J. & Bjorklund, D. (2004). The natural emergence of reasoning about the afterlife as a developmental regularity. *Developmental Psychology*, 40, 217–33.

Bermúdez, J. (2003). *Thinking without Words*. Oxford University Press.

Bermúdez, J. (2015). Nonconceptual mental content. In E. Zalta (ed.), *Stanford Encyclopedia of Philosophy*, https://plato.stanford.edu/archives/fall2015/entries/content-nonconceptual.

Bird, C. & Emery, N. (2009). Rooks use stones to raise the water level to reach a floating worm. *Current Biology*, 19, 1410–14.

Block, N. (1987). Advertisement for a semantics for psychology. *Midwest Studies in Philosophy of Science*, 10, 615–78.

Block, N. (1995). A confusion about the function of consciousness. *Behavioral and Brain Sciences*, 18, 227–47.

Block, N. (2002). The harder problem of consciousness. *Journal of Philosophy*, 99, 391–425.

Block, N. (2007). Consciousness, accessibility, and the mesh between psychology and neuroscience. *Behavioral and Brain Sciences*, 30, 481–99.

Block, N. (2010). Attention and mental paint. *Philosophical Issues*, 20, 23–63.

Block, N. (2011a). Perceptual consciousness overflows cognitive access. *Trends in Cognitive Science*, 12, 567–75.

Block, N. (2011b). The higher-order approach to consciousness is defunct. *Analysis*, 71, 419–31.

Bloom, P. (2002). *How Children Learn the Meaning of Words*. MIT Press.

Bloom, P. (2004). *Descartes' Baby: How the Science of Child Development Explains What Makes Us Human*. Basic Books.

Bloom, P. (2016). *Against Empathy: The Case for Rational Compassion*. Ecco Press.

Boghossian, P. & Velleman, D. (1989). Color as a secondary quality. *Mind*, 98, 81–103.

Boly, M., Massimini, M., Tsuchiya, N., Postle, B., Koch, C., & Tononi, G. (2017). Are the neural correlates of consciousness in the front or in the back of the cerebral cortex? Clinical and neuroimaging evidence. *Journal of Neuroscience*, 37, 9603–13.

Botterill, G. & Carruthers, P. (1999). *The Philosophy of Psychology*. Cambridge University Press.

Botvinick, G., Wang, J., Cowan, E., Roy, S., Bastianen, C., Mayo, P., & Houk, J. (2009). An analysis of immediate serial recall performance in a macaque. *Animal Cognition*, 12, 671–8.

Boyer, P. (2001). *Religion Explained: The Evolutionary Origins of Religious Thought*. Basic Books.

Brady, T., Störmer, V., & Alvarez, G. (2016). Working memory is not fixed-capacity: More active storage capacity for real-world objects than for simple stimuli. *Proceedings of the National Academy of Sciences*, 113, 7459–64.

Breitmeyer, B. & Ogmen, H. (2000). Recent models and findings in visual backward masking: A comparison, review, and update. *Perception & Psychophysics*, 62, 1572–95.

Brentari, D. & Goldin-Meadow, S. (2017). Language emergence. *Annual Review of Linguistics*, 3, 363–88.

Broadway, J. & Engle, R. (2010). Validating running memory span: Measurement of working memory capacity and links with fluid intelligence. *Behavior Research Methods*, 42, 563–70.

Bronfman, Z., Ginsburg, S., & Jablonka, E. (2016a). The evolutionary origins of consciousness: Suggesting a transition marker. *Journal of Consciousness Studies*, 23 (9–10), 7–34.

Bronfman, Z., Ginsburg, S., & Jablonka, E. (2016b). The transition to minimal consciousness through the evolution of associative learning. *Frontiers in Psychology*, 7, 1954.

Brown, R. (2015). The HOROR theory of phenomenal consciousness. *Philosophical Studies*, 172, 1783–94.

Buckner, R. (2010). The role of the hippocampus in prediction and imagination. *Annual Review of Psychology*, 61, 27–48.

Buckner, R., Kelley, W., & Petersen, S. (1999). Frontal cortex contributes to human memory formation. *Nature Neuroscience*, 2, 311–14.

Buhle, J., Stevens, B., Friedman, J., & Wager, T. (2012). Distraction and placebo: Two separate routes to pain control. *Psychological Science*, 23, 246–53.

Burge, T. (1979). Individualism and the mental. *Midwest Studies in Philosophy*, 4, 73–121.

Burge, T. (1986). Individualism and psychology. *Philosophical Review*, 95, 3–45.

Burge, T. (2010). *The Origins of Objectivity*. Oxford University Press.

Burton, A., Nakamura, K., & Roesch, M. (2015). From ventral-medial to dorsal-lateral striatum: Neural correlates of reward-guided decision-making. *Neurobiology of Learning and Memory*, 117, 51–9.

Buschman, T., Siegel, M., Roy, J., & Miller, E. (2011). Neural substrates of cognitive capacity limitations. *Proceedings of the National Academy of Sciences*, 108, 11252–5.

Buttelmann, D., Buttelmann, F., Carpenter, M., Call, J., & Tomasello, M. (2017). Great apes distinguish true from false beliefs in an interactive helping task. *PLoS One*, 12(4), e0173793.

Byrne, R., Cartmill, E., Genty, E., Graham, K., Hobaiter, C., & Tanner, J. (2017). Great ape gestures: Intentional communication with a rich set of innate signals. *Animal Cognition*, 20, 755–69.

Byrne, R. & Whiten, A. (eds) (1988). *Machiavellian Intelligence*. Oxford University Press.

Call, J. & Tomasello, M. (2008). Does the chimpanzee have a theory of mind? 30 years later. *Trends in Cognitive Sciences*, 12, 187–92.

Camp, E. (2004). The generality constraint, nonsense, and categorical restrictions. *Philosophical Quarterly*, 54, 209–31.

Carruthers, P. (1992). *The Animals Issue*. Cambridge University Press.

Carruthers, P. (1999). Sympathy and subjectivity. *Australasian Journal of Philosophy*, 77, 465–82.

Carruthers, P. (2000). *Phenomenal Consciousness*. Cambridge University Press.

Carruthers, P. (2004a). On being simple minded. *American Philosophical Quarterly*, 41, 205–20.

Carruthers, P. (2004b). Suffering without subjectivity. *Philosophical Studies*, 121, 99–125.

Carruthers, P. (2005a). *Consciousness: Essays from a Higher-Order Perspective*. Oxford University Press.

Carruthers, P. (2005b). Why the question of animal consciousness might not matter very much. *Philosophical Psychology*, 18, 83–102.

Carruthers, P. (2006). *The Architecture of the Mind: Massive Modularity and the Flexibility of Thought*. Oxford University Press.

Carruthers, P. (2007). Invertebrate minds: a challenge for ethical theory. *Journal of Ethics*, 11, 275–97.

Carruthers, P. (2008). Meta-cognition in animals: a skeptical look. *Mind and Language*, 23, 58–89.

Carruthers, P. (2009a). Invertebrate concepts confront the Generality Constraint (and win). In R. Lurz (ed.), *The Philosophy of Animal Minds*. Cambridge University Press.

Carruthers, P. (2009b). How we know our own minds: The relationship between mindreading and metacognition. *Behavioral and Brain Sciences*, 32, 121–38.

Carruthers, P. (2011a). *The Opacity of Mind: An Integrative Theory of Self-Knowledge*. Oxford University Press.

Carruthers, P. (2011b). Animal mentality: Its character, extent, and moral significance. In R. Frey and T. Beauchamp (eds), *Handbook on Ethics and Animals*. Oxford University Press.

Carruthers, P. (2013a). Evolution of working memory. *Proceedings of the National Academy of Sciences*, 110, 10371–8.

Carruthers, P. (2013b). Animal minds are real, (distinctively) human minds are not. *American Philosophical Quarterly*, 50, 233–47.

Carruthers, P. (2015a). *The Centered Mind: What the Science of Working Memory Shows Us about the Nature of Human Thought*. Oxford University Press.

Carruthers, P. (2015b). Perceiving mental states. *Consciousness and Cognition*, 36, 498–507.

Carruthers, P. (2017a). Are epistemic emotions metacognitive? *Philosophical Psychology*, 30, 58–78.

Carruthers, P. (2017b). In defense of first-order representationalism. *Journal of Consciousness Studies*, 24(5–6), 74–87.

Carruthers, P. (2017c). Block's overflow argument. *Pacific Philosophical Quarterly*, 98 S1, 65–70.

Carruthers, P. (2018a). The causes and contents of inner speech. In P. Langland-Hassan & A. Vicente (eds), *Inner Speech: Nature, Functions, and Pathology*. Oxford University Press.

Carruthers, P. (2018b). Basic questions. *Mind & Language*, 33, 13–147.

Carruthers, P. (2018c). Episodic memory isn't essentially autonoetic. *Behavioral and Brain Sciences*, 41, e6.

Carruthers, P. (2018d). Valence and value. *Philosophy and Phenomenological Research*, 97, 658–80.

Carruthers, P., Fletcher, L., & Ritchie, J. B. (2012). The evolution of self-knowledge. *Philosophical Topics*, 40, 13–37.

Carruthers, P. & Ritchie, J. B. (2012). The emergence of metacognition: affect and uncertainty in animals. In M. Beran, J. Brandl, J. Perner, & J. Proust (eds), *Foundations of Metacognition*, Oxford University Press.

Carruthers, P. & Schechter, E. (2006). Can panpsychism bridge the explanatory gap? *Journal of Consciousness Studies*, 13(10–11), 32–9.

Carruthers, P. & Veillet, B. (2007). The phenomenal concept strategy. *Journal of Consciousness Studies*, 14(9–10), 212–36.

Carruthers, P. & Veillet, B. (2011). The case against cognitive phenomenology. In T. Bayne & M. Montague (eds), *Cognitive Phenomenology*. Oxford University Press.

Carruthers, P. & Veillet, B. (2017). Consciousness operationalized, a debate realigned. *Consciousness and Cognition*, 55, 79–90.

Chalmers, D. (1996). *The Conscious Mind*. Oxford University Press.

Chalmers, D. (1997). Availability: The cognitive basis of experience. *Behavioral and Brain Sciences*, 20, 148–9.

Chalmers, D. (2006). Phenomenal concepts and the explanatory gap. In T. Alter & S. Walter (eds), *Phenomenal Concepts and Phenomenal Knowledge*. Oxford University Press.

Chalmers, D. (2018). The meta-problem of consciousness. *Journal of Consciousness Studies*, 25(9–10), 6–61.

Cheeseman, J., Millar, C., Greggers, U., Lehmann, K., Pawley, M., Gallistel, C., Warman, G., & Menzel, R. (2014). Way-finding in displaced clock-shifted bees proves bees use a cognitive map. *Proceedings of the National Academy of Sciences*, 111, 8949–54.

Childress, A., Ehrman, R., Wang, Z., Li, Y., Sciortino, N., Hakun, J., Jens, W., Suh, J., Listerud, J., Marquez, K., Franklin, T., Langleben, D., Detre, J., & O'Brien, C. (2008). Prelude to passion: Limbic activity by "unseen" drug and sexual cues. *PLoS One*, 1, e1506.

Chudek, M., McNamara, R., Birch, S., Bloom, P., & Henrich, J. (2018). Do minds switch bodies? Dualist interpretations across ages and societies. *Religion, Brain & Behavior*, 8, 354–68.

Clayton, N., Yu, K., & Dickinson, A. (2001). Scrub jays (*Aphelocoma coerulescens*) form integrated memories of the multiple features of caching episodes. *Journal of Experimental Psychology: Animal Behavior Processes*, 27, 17–29.

Clayton, N., Yu, K., & Dickinson, A. (2003). Interacting cache memories: Evidence for flexible memory use by western scrub-jays (*Aphelocoma californica*). *Journal of Experimental Psychology: Animal Behavior Processes*, 29, 14–22.

Cohen, E., Burdett, E., Knight, N., & Barrett, J. (2011). Cross-cultural similarities and differences in person-body reasoning: Experimental evidence from the United Kingdom and Brazilian Amazon. *Cognitive Science*, 35, 1282–1304.

Cohen, M.A., Alvarez, G., & Nakayama, K. (2011). Natural-scene perception requires attention. *Psychological Science*, 22, 1165–72.

Cohen, M.A. & Dennett, D. (2011). Consciousness cannot be separated from function. *Trends in Cognitive Sciences*, 15, 358–64.

Cohen, M.A., Dennett, D., & Kanwisher, N. (2016). What is the bandwidth of perceptual experience? *Trends in Cognitive Sciences*, 20, 324–35.

Coleman, S. (2012). Mental chemistry: Combination for panpsychists. *Dialectica*, 66, 137–66.

Conway, A., Kane, M., & Engle, R. (2003). Working memory capacity and its relation to general intelligence. *Trends in Cognitive Sciences*, 7, 547–52.

Coppola, M. & Newport, E. (2005). Grammatical subjects in home sign: Abstract linguistic structure in adult primary gesture systems without linguistic input. *Proceedings of the National Academy of Sciences*, 102, 19249–53.

Corbetta, M., Patel, G., & Shulman, G. (2008). The reorienting system of the human brain: From environment to theory of mind. *Neuron*, 58, 306–24.

Corbetta, M. & Shulman, G. (2002). Control of goal-directed and stimulus-driven attention in the brain. *Nature Reviews Neuroscience*, 3, 201–15.

Cowan, N. (2001). The magical number 4 in short-term memory: A reconsideration of mental storage capacity. *Behavioral and Brain Sciences*, 24, 87–185.

Cowey, A. & Stoerig, P. (1995). Blindsight in monkeys. *Nature*, 373, 247–49.

Craver, C. & Darden, L. (2013). *In Search of Mechanisms: Discoveries across the Life Sciences*. University of Chicago Press.

Cutter, B. & Tye, M. (2011). Tracking representationalism and the painfulness of pain. *Philosophical Issues*, 21, 90–109.

D'Aloisio-Montilla, N. (2017). Imagery and overflow. *Philosophical Psychology*, 30, 545–70.

Dally, J., Emery, N., & Clayton, N. (2006). Food-caching Western scrub-jays keep track of who was watching when. *Science*, 312, 1662–5.

Davidson, D. (1975). Thought and talk. In S. Guttenplan (ed.), *Mind and Language*. Oxford University Press.

Dawkins, M. (2012). *Why Animals Matter*. Oxford University Press.

Dawkins, M. (2017). Animal welfare with and without consciousness. *Journal of Zoology*, 301, 1–10.

De Brigard, F. (2014). Is memory for remembering? Recollection as a form of episodic hypothetical thinking. *Synthese*, 191, 155–85.

De Gelder, B., Tamietto, M., van Boxtel, G., Goebel, R., Sahraie, A., van den Stock, J., Steinen, B., Weiskrantz, L., & Pegna, A. (2008). Intact navigation skill after bilateral loss of striate cortex. *Current Biology*, 18, 10.1016/j.cub.2008.1011.1002.

Dehaene, S. (2014). *Consciousness and the Brain*. Viking Press.

Dehaene, S. & Changeux, J-P. (2011). Experimental and theoretical approaches to conscious processing. *Neuron*, 70, 200–27.

Dehaene, S. & Naccache, L. (2001). Towards a cognitive neuroscience of consciousness: Basic evidence and a workspace framework. *Cognition*, 79, 1–37.

Dehaene, S., Naccache, L., Le Clec'H, G., Koechlin, E., Mueller, M., Dehaene-Lambertz, G., van de Moortele, P.-F., & Le Bihan, D. (1998). Imaging unconscious semantic priming. *Nature*, 395, 597–600.

Del Cul, A., Baillet, S., & Dehaene, S. (2007). Brain dynamics underlying the nonlinear threshold for access to consciousness. *PLOS Biology*, 5, e260.

Dennett, D. (1976). Are dreams experiences? *Philosophical Review*, 73, 151–71.

Dennett, D. (1978). Toward a cognitive theory of consciousness. In his *Brainstorms*. Harvester Press.

Dennett, D. (1996). *Kinds of Minds*. Basic Books.

Dennett, D. (2001). Are we explaining consciousness yet? *Cognition*, 79, 221–37.

Diamond, A. (2013). Executive functions. *Annual Review of Psychology*, 64, 135–68.

Dijkerman, H. C. & de Haan, E. (2007). Somatosensory processes subserving perception and action. *Behavioral and Brain Sciences*, 30, 189–239.

Donahue, C., Glasser, M., Preuss, T., Rilling, J., & Van Essen, D. (2018). Quantitative assessment of prefrontal cortex in humans relative to nonhuman primates. *Proceedings of the National Academy of Sciences*, 115, E5183–92.

Drayton, L. & Santos, L. (2016). A decade of theory of mind research on Cayo Santiago: Insights into Rhesus macaque social cognition. *American Journal of Primatology*, 78, 106–16.

Eacott, M. & Easton, A. (2010). Episodic memory in animals: Remembering which occasion. *Neuropsychologia*, 48, 2273–80.

Ecker, U., Maybery, M., & Zimmer, H. (2013). Binding of intrinsic and extrinsic features in working memory. *Journal of Experimental Psychology: General*, 142, 218–34.

Engle, R. (2010). Role of working-memory capacity in cognitive control. *Current Anthropology*, 51, S17–S26.

Ericsson, A. & Kintsch, W. (1995). Long-term working memory. *Psychological Review*, 102, 211–45.

Evans, G. (1982). *The Varieties of Reference*. Oxford University Press.

Evans, J. (2010). *Thinking Twice: Two Minds in One Brain*. Oxford University Press.

Evans, J. & Stanovich, K. (2013). Dual-process theories of higher cognition: Advancing the debate. *Perspectives on Psychological Science*, 8, 223–41.

Feigenson, L. & Halberda, J. (2008). Conceptual knowledge increases infants' memory capacity. *Proceedings of the National Academy of Sciences*, 105, 9926–30.

Fine, K. (1975). Vagueness, truth and logic. *Synthese*, 54, 235–59.

Forstmann, M. & Burgmer, P. (2015). Adults are intuitive mind–body dualists. *Journal of Experimental Psychology: General*, 144, 222–35.

Fougnie, D., Cormiea, S., & Alvarez, G. (2013). Object-based benefits without object-based representations. *Journal of Experimental Psychology: General*, 142, 621–26.

Frankish, K. (2004). *Mind and Supermind*. Cambridge University Press.

Frankish, K. (2009). Systems and levels. In J. Evans & K. Frankish (eds), *In Two Minds*. Oxford University Press.

Frankish, K. (2016). Illusionism as a theory of consciousness. *Journal of Consciousness Studies*, 23(11–12), 11–39.

Franklin, A. Giannakidou, A., & Godin-Meadow, S. (2011). Negation, questions, and structure building in a homesign system. *Cognition*, 118, 398–416.

Frässle, S., Sommer, J., Jansen, A., Naber, M., & Einhäuser, W. (2014). Binocular rivalry: frontal activity relates to introspection and action but not to perception. *The Journal of Neuroscience*, 34, 1738–47.

Geach, P. (1957). *Mental Acts*. Routledge.

Gilbert, D. & Wilson, T. (2007). Prospection: Experiencing the future. *Science*, 317, 1351–4.

Giurfa, M., Zhang, S., Jenett, A., Menzel, R., & Srinivasan, M. (2001). Concepts of "sameness" and "difference" in an insect. *Nature*, 410, 930–33.

Godfrey-Smith, P. (2016). *Other Minds*. Farrar, Straus, and Giroux.

Goff, P. (2009). Why panpsychism doesn't help us explain consciousness. *Dialectica*, 63, 289–311.

Goldin-Meadow, S. (2003). *The Resilience of Language*. Psychology Press.

Goldman, A. (2006). *Simulating Minds*. Oxford University Press.

Goldman-Rakic, P. (1995). Cellular basis of working memory. *Neuron*, 14, 477–85.

Goldman-Rakic, P., Funahashi, S., & Bruce, C. (1990). Neocortical memory circuits. *Quarterly Journal of Quantitative Biology*, 55, 1025–38.

Goodale, M. (2014). How (and why) the visual control of action differs from visual perception. *Proceedings of the Royal Society B*, 281, 0337.

Goodale, M. & Milner, D. (2018). Two visual pathways: Where have they taken us and where will they lead in future? *Cortex*, 98, 283–92.

Gould, J. & Gould, C. (1988). *The Honey Bee*. Scientific American Library.

Graziano, M. (2013). *Consciousness and the Social Brain*. Oxford University Press.

Gross, H., Pahl, M., Si, A., Zhu, H., Tautz, J., & Zhang, S. (2009). Number-based visual generalization in the honeybee. *PLoS One*, 4, e4263.

Hameroff, S. & Penrose, R. (1996). Orchestrated reduction of quantum coherence in brain microtubules: A model of consciousness. *Mathematics and Computers in Simulation*, 40, 453–80.

Hampton, R. (2001). Rhesus monkeys know when they remember. Proceedings of the National Academy of Sciences, 98, 5359–62.

Hampton, R. (2005). Can Rhesus monkeys discriminate between remembering and forgetting? In H. S. Terrace and J. Metcalfe (eds), The Missing Link in Cognition. Oxford University Press.

Hanus, D., Mendes, N., Tennie, C., & Call, J. (2011). Comparing the performances of apes (*Gorilla gorilla, pan troglodytes, Pongo pymaeus*) and human children (*Homo sapiens*) in the floating peanut task. *PLoS One*, 6, e19555.

Haun, A., Tononi, G., Koch, C., & Tsuchiya, N. (2017). Are we underestimating the richness of conscious experience? *Neuroscience of Consciousness*, 1, niw023.

Hauser, M. (1997). *The Evolution of Communication*. MIT Press.

Hauser, M., Carey, S., & Hauser, L. (2000). Spontaneous number representation in semi-free-ranging rhesus monkeys. *Proceedings of the Royal Society of London B: Biological Sciences*, 267, 829–33.

Henrich, J. (2016). *The Secret of our Success: How Culture Is Driving Human Evolution, Domesticating Our Species, and Making Us Smarter*. Princeton University Press.

Hickok, G. & Poeppel, D. (2004). Dorsal and ventral streams: A framework for understanding aspects of the functional anatomy of language. *Cognition*, 92, 67–99.

Hochner, B., Shomrat, T., & Fiorito, G. (2006). The octopus: A model for a comparative analysis of the evolution of learning and memory mechanisms. *Biological Bulletin*, 210, 308–17.

Horgan, T. (2011). From agentive phenomenology to cognitive phenomenology: A guide for the perplexed. In T. Bayne & M. Montague (eds), *Cognitive Phenomenology*. Oxford University Press.

Howard, S., Avarguès-Weber, A., Garcia, J., Greentree, A., & Dyer, A. (2018). Numerical ordering of zero in honey bees. *Science*, 360, 1124–6.

Hrdy, S. (2009). *Mothers and Others*. Harvard University Press.

Huang, L. & Awh, E. (2018). Chunking in working memory via content-free labels. *Nature Scientific Reports*, 8, 23.

Humphrey, N. (1974). Vision in a monkey without striate cortex: A case study. *Perception*, 3, 241–55.

Jackendoff, R. (1987). *Consciousness and the Computational Mind*. MIT Press.

Jackendoff, R. (2012). *A User's Guide to Thought and Meaning*. Oxford University Press.

Jackson, F. (1982). Epiphenomenal qualia. *Philosophical Quarterly*, 32, 127–36.

Jackson, F. (1986). What Mary didn't know. *Journal of Philosophy*, 83, 291–5.

Januszko, P., Niemcewicz, S., Gajda, T., Wolynczyk-Gmaj, D., Justyna, P., Gmaj, N., Piotrowski, T., & Szelenberger, W. (2016). Sleepwalking episodes are preceded by arousal-related activation in the cingulate motor area: EEG current density imaging. *Clinical Neurophysiology*, 127, 530–6.

Jeannerod, M. (2006). *Motor Cognition*. Oxford University Press.

Jordan, K., MacLean, E., & Brannon, E. (2008). Monkeys match and tally quantities across the senses. *Cognition*, 108, 617–25.

Jozefowiez, J., Staddon, J., & Cerutti, D. (2009). Metacognition in animals: How do we know that they know? *Comparative Cognition and Behavior Reviews*, 4, 29–39.

Kabadayi, C., Taylor, L., von Bayern, A., & Osvath, M. (2016). Caledonian crows and jackdaws parallel great apes in motor self-regulation despite smaller brains. *Royal Society Open Science*, 3, 160104.

Kahneman, D. (2011). *Thinking, Fast and Slow*. Farrar, Straus, and Grioux.

Kahneman, D., Slovic, P., & Tversky, A. (eds) (1982). *Judgment Under Uncertainty: Heuristics and Biases*. Cambridge University Press.

Kahneman, D. & Triesman, A. (1984). Changing views of attention and automaticity. In R. Parasuraman, R. Davies, & J. Beatty (eds), *Varieties of Attention*. Academic Press.

Kaminski, J., Call, J., & Tomasello, M. (2008). Chimpanzees know what others know, but not what they believe. *Cognition*, 109, 224–34.

Kaunitz, L., Rowe, E., & Tsuchiya, N. (2016). Large capacity of conscious access for incidental memories in natural scenes. *Psychological Science*, 27, 1266–77.

Kidd, C., Palmeri, H., & Aslin, R. (2013). Rational snacking: Young children's decision-making on the marshmallow task is moderated by beliefs about environmental reliability. *Cognition*, 126, 109–14.

Kind, A. (2014). The case against representationalism about moods. In U. Kriegel (ed.), *Current Controversies in Philosophy of Mind*. Routledge.

King, M. & Carruthers, P. (2012). Moral responsibility and consciousness. *Journal of Moral Philosophy*, 9, 200–28.

King, M. & Carruthers, P. (2020). Responsibility and consciousness. In D. Nelkin & D. Pereboom (eds), *Handbook of Moral Responsibility*. Oxford University Press.

Koch, C. & Tsuchiya, N. (2007). Attention and consciousness: Two distinct brain processes. *Trends in Cognitive Sciences*, 11, 16–22.

Kouider, S. & Dehaene, S. (2007). Levels of processing during non-conscious perception: A critical review of visual masking. *Philosophical Transactions of the Royal Society B*, 362, 857–75.

Kouider, S. & Dehaene, S. (2009). Subliminal number priming within and across the visual and auditory modalities. *Experimental Psychology*, 56, 418–33.

Kripke, S. (1980). *Naming and Necessity*. Blackwell.

Krupenye, C., Kano, F., Hirata, S., Call, J., & Tomasello, M. (2016). Great apes anticipate that other individuals will act according to false beliefs. *Science*, 354, 110–14.

Kuhl, P. (2007). Is speech learning "gated" by the social brain? *Developmental Science*, 10, 110–20.

Kuhlmeier, V., Bloom, P., & Wynn, K. (2004). Do 5-month-old infants see humans as material objects? *Cognition*, 94, 95–103.

Kurzban, R. (2012). *Why Everyone (Else) is a Hypocrite: Evolution and the Modular Mind*. Princeton University Press.

Landman, R., Spekreijse, H., & Lamme, V. (2003). Large capacity storage of integrated objects before change blindness. *Vision Research*, 43, 149–64.

Lauterbach, E., Cummings, J., & Kuppuswammy, P. (2013). Toward a more precise, clinically-informed pathophysiology of pathological laughing and crying. *Neuroscience and Biobehavioral Reviews*, 37, 1893–1916.

Le Pelley, M. (2012). Metacognitive monkeys or associative animals? Simple reinforcement learning explains uncertainty in nonhuman animals. *Journal of Experimental Psychology: Learning, Memory, and Cognition*, 38, 687–708.

LeDoux, J. (1996). *The Emotional Brain*. Simon and Schuster.

LeDoux, J. (2017). Semantics, surplus meaning, and the science of fear. *Trends in Cognitive Sciences*, 21, 303–6.

Lehky, S. & Maunsell, J. (1996). No binocular rivalry in the LGN of alert macaque monkeys. *Vision Research*, 36, 1225–34.

Leopold, D. & Logothetis, N. (1996). Activity changes in early visual cortex reflect monkeys' percepts during binocular rivalry. *Nature*, 379, 549–53.

Levin, J. (2007). What is a Phenomenal Concept? In T. Alter & S. Walter (eds), *Phenomenal Concepts and Phenomenal Knowledge*. Oxford University Press.

Lewis, D. (1982). Logic for equivocators. *Noûs*, 16, 431–41.

Lewis-Peacock, J., Drysdale, A., Oberauer, K., & Postle, B. (2012). Neural evidence for a distinction between short-term memory and the focus of attention. *Journal of Cognitive Neuroscience*, 24, 61–79.

Lin, Z. & Murray, S. (2014). Unconscious processing of an abstract concept. *Psychological Science*, 25, 296–8.

Lisman, J. & Sternberg, E. (2013). Habit and nonhabit systems for unconscious and conscious behavior: Implications for multitasking. *Journal of Cognitive Neuroscience*, 25, 273–83.

Loar, B. (1990). Phenomenal states. In J. Tomberlin (ed.), *Philosophical Perspectives: Action Theory and Philosophy of Mind*. Ridgeview Press.

Low, P., Panksepp, J., Reiss, D., Edelman, D., Van Swinderen, B., & Koch, C. (2012). The Cambridge Declaration on Consciousness. Signed by the participants in the Francis Crick Memorial Conference on Consciousness in Human and Non-Human Animals, Churchill College, Cambridge, July 7, 2012. fcmconference.org/img/CambridgeDeclarationOnConsciousness.pdf

Luck, S., Chelazzi, L., Hillyard, S., & Desimone, R. (1997). Neural mechanisms of spatial selective attention in areas V1, V2, and V4 of macaque visual cortex. *Journal of Neurophysiology*, 77, 24–42.

Luck, S. & Vogel, E. (1997). The capacity of visual working memory for features and conjunctions. *Nature*, 390, 279–91.

Luria, R., Balaban, H., Awh, H., & Vogel, E. (2016). The contralateral delay activity as a measure of visual working memory. *Neuroscience and Biobehavioral Reviews*, 62, 100–108.

Lycan, W. (1996). *Consciousness and Experience*. MIT Press.

Mack, A. & Rock, I. (1998). *Inattentional Blindness*. MIT Press.

MacLean, E., Hare, B., Nunn, C., Addessi, E., Amici, F., Anderson, R., Aureli, F., Baker, J., Bania, A., Barnard, A., Boogert, N., Brannon, E., Bray, E., Bray, J., Brent, L., Burkart, J., Call, J., Cantlon, J., Cheke, L., Clayton, N., Delgado, M., DiVincenti, L., Fujita, K., Herrmann, E., Hiramatsu, C, Jacobs, L., Jorndan, K., Laude, J., Leimgruber, K., Messer, E., Moura, A., Ostojic, L., Picard, A., Platt, M., Plotnik, J., Range, F., Reader, S., Reddy, R., Sandel, A., Santos, L., Schumann, K., Seed, A., Sewall, K., Shaw, R., Slocombe, K., Su, Y., Takimoto, A., Tan, J., Tao, R., van Schaik, C., Viranyi, Z., Visalberghi, E., Wade, J., Watanabe, A., Widness, J., Young, J., Zentall, R., & Zhao, Y. (2014). The evolution of self-control. *Proceedings of the National Academy of Sciences*, 111(20), E2140–48.

Maginnity, M. & Grace, R. (2014). Visual perspective taking by dogs (*Canis familiaris*) in a guesser-knower task: Evidence for a canine theory of mind? *Animal Cognition*, 17, 1375–92.

Mahr, J. & Csibra, G. (2018). Why do we remember? The communicative function of episodic memory. *Behavioral and Brain Sciences*, 41, e1.

Mandik, P. (2009). Beware of the unicorn: Consciousness as being represented and other things that don't exist. *Journal of Consciousness Studies*, 161 (1), 5–36.

Marcovitch, S. & Zelazo, P. (1999). The A-not-B error: Results from a logistic meta-analysis. *Child Development*, 70, 1297–1313.

Marti, S. & Dehaene, S. (2017). Discrete and continuous mechanisms of temporal selection in rapid visual streams. *Nature Communications*, 8, 1955.

Marti, S., Sigman, M., & Dehaene, S. (2012). A shared cortical bottleneck underlying Attentional Blink and Psychological Refractory Period. *NeuroImage*, 59, 2883–98.

Marticorena, D., Ruiz, A., Mukerji, C., Goddu, A., & Santos, L. (2011). Monkeys represent others' knowledge but not their beliefs. *Developmental Science*, 14, 1406–16.

McClelland, T. (2016). Gappiness and the case for liberalism about phenomenal properties. *Philosophical Quarterly*, 66, 536–58.

McDowell, J. (1994). *Mind and World*. Harvard University Press.

McGinn, C. (1991). *The Problem of Consciousness*. Blackwell.

Mendes, N., Hanus, D., & Call, J. (2007). Raising the level: Orangutans use water as a tool. *Biology Letters*, 3, 453–5.

Menzel, R. & Giurfa, M. (2001). Cognitive architecture of a mini-brain: The honeybee. *Trends in Cognitive Sciences*, 5, 62–71.

Menzel, R., Greggers, U., Smith, A., Berger, S., Brandt, R., Brunke, S., Bundrock, G., Hülse, S., Plümpe, T., Schaupp, F., Schüttler, E., Stach, S., Stindt, J., Stollhoff, N., & Watzl, S. (2005). Honey bees navigate according to a map-like spatial memory. *Proceedings of the National Academy of Sciences*, 102, 3040–45.

Menzel, R., Kirbach, A., Haass, W-D., Fischer, B., Fuchs, J., Koblofsky, M., Lehmann, K., Reiter, L., Meyer, H., Nguyen, H., Jones, S., Norton, P., & Greggers, U. (2011). A common frame of reference for learned and communicated vectors in honeybee navigation. *Current Biology*, 21, 645–50.

Mercier, H. & Sperber, D, (2017). *The Enigma of Reason*. Harvard University Press.

Merker, B. (2007). Consciousness without a cerebral cortex: A challenge for neuroscience and medicine. *Behavioral and Brain Sciences*, 30, 63–134.

Michel, M. (2017). Methodological artefacts in consciousness science. *Journal of Consciousness Studies*, 24 (11–12), 94–117.

Michel, M. & Morales, J. (2019). Minority reports: Consciousness and the prefrontal cortex. *Mind & Language*.

Miller, E. & Buschman, T. (2015). Working memory capacity: Limits on the bandwidth of cognition. *Daedalus*, 144, 112–22.

Miller, G. A. (1956). The magical number seven, plus or minus two: some limits on our capacity for processing information. *Psychological Review*, 63, 81–97.

Milner, D. & Goodale, M. (1995). *The Visual Brain in Action*. Oxford University Press.

Mischel, H. & Mischel, W. (1983). The development of children's knowledge of self-control strategies. *Child Development*, 54, 603–19.

Miyake, A., Friedman, N., Emerson, M., Witzki, A., Howerter, A., & Wager, T. (2000). The unity and diversity of executive functions and their contributions to complex "frontal lobe" tasks: A latent variable analysis. *Cognitive Psychology*, 41, 49–100.

Mole, C. (2011). *Attention Is Cognitive Unison*. Oxford University Press.

Mulcahy, N. & Call, J. (2004). Apes save tools for future use. *Science*, 312, 1038–40.

Mysore, S. & Knudsen, E. (2013). A shared inhibitory circuit for both exogenous and endogenous control of stimulus selection. *Nature Neuroscience*, 16, 473–8.

Newman, R., Rowe, M., & Ratner, N. (2016). Input and uptake at 7 months predicts toddler vocabulary: The role of child-directed speech and infant processing skills in language development. *Journal of Child Language*, 43, 1158–73.

Nicholson, T., Williams, D., Grainger, C., Lind, S., & Carruthers, P. (2019). Relationships between implicit and explicit uncertainty monitoring and mindreading: Evidence from autism spectrum disorder. *Consciousness and Cognition*, 70, 11–24.

Nisbett, R. & Wilson, T. (1977). Telling more than we can know. *Psychological Review*, 84, 231–95.

Nussbaum, M. (2006). *Frontiers of Justice: Disability, Nationality, Species Membership*. Harvard University Press.

Odegaard, B., Knight, R., & Lau, H. (2017). Should a few null findings falsify prefrontal theories of conscious perception? *Journal of Neuroscience*, 37, 9593–9602.

Olofsson, J., Nordin, S., Sequeira, H., & Polich, J. (2008). Affective picture processing: An integrative review of ERP findings. *Biological Psychology*, 77, 247–65.

Osvath, M. (2009). Spontaneous planning for future stone throwing by a male chimpanzee. *Current Biology*, 19, R190–91.

Osvath, M. & Karvonen, E. (2011). Spontaneous innovation for future deception in a male chimpanzee. *PLoS One*, 7, e36782.

Osvath, M. & Osvath, H. (2008). Chimpanzee and orangutan forethought: Self-control and pre-experience in the face of future tool use. *Animal Cognition*, 11, 661–74.

Oudiette, D., Smaranda, L., Pottier, M., Buzare, M-A., Brion, A., & Arnulf, I. (2009). Dreamlike mentations during sleepwalking and sleep terrors in adults. *Sleep*, 32, 1621–7.

Overgaard, M., Rote, J., Mouridsen, K., & Ramsoy, T. (2006). Is conscious perception graded or dichotomous? A comparison of report methodologies during a visual task. *Consciousness and Cognition*, 15, 700–708.

Panagiotaropoulos, T., Deco, G., Kapoor, V., & Logohetis, N. (2012). Neuronal discharges and gamma oscillations explicitly reflect visual consciousness in the lateral prefrontal cortex. *Neuron*, 74, 924–35.

Panksepp, J. (1998). *Affective Neuroscience*. Oxford University Press.

Papineau, D. (2002). *Thinking about Consciousness*. Oxford University Press.

Papineau, D. (2003). Could there be a science of consciousness? *Philosophical Issues*, 13, 205–20.

Peacocke, C. (1983). *Sense and Content*. Oxford University Press.

Peacocke, C. (1992). *A Study of Concepts*. MIT Press.

Pepperberg, I. (1999). *The Alex Studies: Cognitive and Communicative Abilities of Grey Parrots*. Harvard University Press.

Perry, C. & Barron, A. (2013). Honey bees selectively avoid difficult choices. *Proceedings of the National Academy of Sciences*, 110, 19155–9.

Perry, J. (2001). *Knowledge, Possibility, and Consciousness*. MIT Press.

Persaud, N., Davidson, M., Maniscalco, B., Mobbs, D., Passingham, R., Cowey, A., & Lau, H. (2011). Awareness-related activity in prefrontal and parietal cortices in blindsight reflects more than superior visual performance. *NeuroImage*, 58, 605–11.

Pessoa, L. (2013). *The Cognitive-Emotional Brain*. MIT Press.

Picciuto, V. (2011). Addressing higher-order misrepresentation with quotational thought. *Journal of Consciousness Studies*, 18(3–4), 109–36.

Pitt, D. (2004). The phenomenology of cognition, or What is it like to think that P? *Philosophy and Phenomenological Research*, 69, 1–36.

Pitts, M., Metzler, S., & Hillyard, S. (2014). Isolating neural correlates of conscious perception from neural correlates of reporting one's perception. *Frontiers in Psychology*, 5, 1078.

Postle, B. (2006). Working memory as an emergent property of the mind and brain. *Neuroscience*, 139, 23–38.

Povinelli, D. (1999). *Folk Physics for Apes*. Oxford University Press.

Preston, A. & Eichenbaum, H. (2013). Interplay of hippocampus and prefrontal cortex in memory. *Current Biology*, 23, R764–73.

Prinz, J. (2012). *The Conscious Brain*. Oxford University Press.

Putnam, H. (1975). The meaning of "meaning". *Minnesota Studies in Philosophy of Science*, 7, 131–93.

Pylyshyn, Z. (2003). *Seeing and Visualizing*. MIT Press.

Ramsoy, T. & Overgaard, M. (2004). Introspection and subliminal perception. *Phenomenology and the Cognitive Sciences*, 3, 1–23.

Rauschecker, J. (2018). Where, when, and how: Are they all sensorimotor? Towards a unified view of the dorsal pathway in vision and audition. *Cortex*, 98, 262–8.

Rauschecker, J. & Tian, B. (2000). Mechanisms and streams for processing of "what" and "where" in auditory cortex. *Proceedings of the National Academy of Sciences*, 97, 11800–11806.

Ravi, S., Garcia, J., Wang, C., & Dyer, A. (2016). The answer is blowing in the wind: Free-flying honeybees can integrate visual and mechano-sensory inputs for making complex foraging decisions. *Journal of Experimental Biology*, 219, 3465–72.

Raymond, J., Shapiro, K., & Arnell, K. (1992). Temporary suppression of visual processing in an RSVP task: An attentional blink? *Journal of Experimental Psychology: Human Perception and Performance*, 18, 849–60.

Redgrave, P., Rodriguez, M., Smith, Y., Rodriguez-Oroz, M., Lehericy, S., Bergman, H., Agid, Y., DeLong, M., & Obeso, J. (2010). Goal-directed and habitual control in the basal ganglia: Implications for Parkinson's disease. *Nature Reviews Neuroscience*, 11, 760–72.

Redick, T., Unsworth, N., Kelly, A., & Engle, R. (2012). Faster, smarter? Working memory capacity and perceptual speed in relation to fluid intelligence. *Journal of Cognitive Psychology*, 24, 844–54.

Regan, T. (1983). *The Case for Animal Rights*. University of California Press.

Rensink, R., O'Regan, J., & Clark, J. (1997). To see or not to see: The need for attention to perceive changes in scenes. *Psychological Science*, 8, 368–73.

Rey, G. (1985). Concepts and conceptions: A reply to Smith, Medin and Rips. *Cognition*, 19, 297–303.

Riekki, T., Lindeman, M., & Lipsanen, J. (2013). Conceptions about the mind–body problem and their relations to afterlife beliefs, paranormal beliefs, religiosity, and ontological confusions. *Advances in Cognitive Psychology*, 9, 112–20.

Roazzi, M., Nyhof, M., & Johnson, C. (2013). Mind, soul and spirit: Conceptions of immaterial identity in different cultures. *International Journal for the Psychology of Religion*, 23, 75–86.

Roberts, W., Feeney, M., MacPherson, K., Petter, M., McMillan, N., & Musolino, E. (2008). Episodic-like memory in rats: Is it based on when or how long ago? *Science*, 320, 113–15.

Rosati, A. & Santos, L. (2016). Spontaneous metacognition in Rhesus monkeys. *Psychological Science*, 27, 1181–91.

Rosenthal, D. (2005). *Consciousness and Mind*. Oxford University Press.

Rosenthal, D. (2011). Exaggerated reports: reply to Block. *Analysis*, 71, 431–437.

Rosenthal, D. (2018). Consciousness and confidence. *Neuropsychologia*. doi.org/10.1016/j.neuropsychologia.2018.01.018.

Roth, G. & Dicke, U. (2005). Evolution of the brain and intelligence. *Trends in Cognitive Sciences*, 9, 250–57.

Rumbaugh, D., Beran, M., & Savage-Rumbaugh, E. S. (2003). Language. In D. Maestripieri (ed.), *Primate Psychology*. Harvard University Press.

Russell, B. (1927). *The Analysis of Matter*. Kegan Paul.

Saint-Cyr, J., Ungerleider, L., & Desimone, R. (1990). Organization of visual cortical inputs to the striatum and subsequent outputs to the pallido-nigral complex in the monkey. *Journal of Comparative Neurology*, 298, 129–56.

Salti, M., Monto, S., Charles, L., King, J-R., Parkkonen, L., & Dehaene, S. (2015). Distinct cortical codes and temporal dynamics for conscious and unconscious percepts. *eLife*, 4, e05652.

Savage-Rumbaugh, E.S. & Lewin, R. (1994). *Kanzi: The Ape on the Brink of the Human Mind*. Wiley.

Schacter, D., Addis, D., & Buckner, R. (2007). Remembering the past to imagine the future: The prospective brain. *Nature Reviews Neuroscience*, 8, 657–61.

Schroer, R. (2010). Where's the beef? Phenomenal concepts as both demonstrative and substantial. *Australasian Journal of Philosophy*, 88, 505–22.

Sebo, J. (2017). Agency and moral status. *Journal of Moral Philosophy*, 14, 1–22.

Seeley, T. (1995). *The Wisdom of the Hive: The Social Physiology of Honey Bee Colonies*. Harvard University Press.

Seligman, M., Railton, P., Baumeister, R., & Sripada, C. (2013). Navigating into the future or driven by the past. *Perspectives on Psychological Science*, 8, 119–41.

Sergent, C., Wyart, V., Babo-Rebelo, M., Cohen, L., Naccache, L., & Tallon-Baudry, C. (2013). Cueing attention after the stimulus is gone can retrospectively trigger conscious perception. *Current Biology*, 23, 150–55.

Seyfarth, R., Cheney, D., & Marler, P. (1980). Monkey responses to three different alarm calls: Evidence of predator classification and semantic communication. *Science*, 210, 801–3.

Shea, N. (2014). Using phenomenal concepts to explain away the intuition of contingency. *Philosophical Psychology*, 27, 553–70.

Shtulman, A. & Valcarcel, J. (2012). Scientific knowledge suppresses but does not supplant earlier intuitions. *Cognition*, 124, 209–15.

Siclari, F., Baird, B., Perogamvros, L., Bernardi, G., LaRocque, J., Riedner, B., Boly, M., Postle, B., & Tononi, G. (2017). The neural correlates of dreaming. *Nature Neuroscience*, 20, 872–8.

Siewert, C. (1998). *The Significance of Consciousness*. Princeton University Press.

Siewert, C. (2011). Phenomenal thought. In T. Bayne & M. Montague (eds), *Cognitive Phenomenology*. Oxford University Press.

Simon, J. (2017). Vagueness and zombies: Why "phenomenally conscious" has no borderline cases. *Philosophical Studies*, 174, 2105–23.

Simons, D. & Levin, D. (1997). Change blindness. *Trends in Cognitive Sciences*, 1, 261–7.

Singer, P. (1981). *The Expanding Circle*. Oxford University Press.

Singer, P. (1993). *Practical Ethics*, 2nd edn. Cambridge University Press.

Sklar, A., Levy, N., Goldstein, A., Mandel, R., Maril, A., & Hassin, R. (2012). Reading and doing arithmetic nonconsciously. *Proceedings of the National Academy of Sciences*, 109, 19614–19.

Sligte, I., Scholte, H.S., & Lamme, V. (2008). Are there multiple visual short-term memory stores? *PLoS ONE*, 3, e1699.

Smith, J. D., Couchman, J., & Beran, M. (2014). Animal metacognition: A tale of two comparative psychologies. *Journal of Comparative Psychology*, 128, 115–31.

Smith, R. & Lane, R. (2016). Unconscious emotion: A cognitive neuroscientific perspective. *Neuroscience & Biobehavioral Reviews*, 69, 216–38.

Souza, A. & Oberauer, K. (2015). Time-based forgetting in visual working memory reflects temporal distinctiveness, not decay. *Psychonomic Bulletin and Review*, 22, 156–62.

Sperling, G. (1960). The information available in brief visual presentations. *Psychological Monographs: General and Applied*, 74, 1–29.

Stanovich, K. (2009). *What Intelligence Tests Miss: The Psychology of Rational Thought*. Yale University Press.

Stevens, J. (2014). Evolutionary pressures on primate intertemporal choice. *Proceedings of the Royal Society B*, 281, 0499.

Stoerig, P. & Cowey, A. (1997). Blindsight in man and monkey. *Brain*, 120, 535–59.

Strawson, G. (1994). *Mental Reality*. MIT Press.

Strawson, G. (2006). Realistic monism: Why physicalism entails panpsychism. *Journal of Consciousness Studies*, 13(10–11), 3–31.

Strawson, G. (2011). Cognitive phenomenology: Real life. In T. Bayne & M. Montague (eds), *Cognitive Phenomenology*. Oxford University Press.

Sutton, J. & Shettleworth, S. (2008). Memory without awareness: Pigeons do not show metamemory in delayed matching-to-sample. *Journal of Experimental Psychology: Animal Behavior Processes*, 34, 266–82.

Tagliabue, C., Mazzi, C., Bagattini, C., & Savazzi, S. (2016). Early local activity in temporal areas reflects graded content of visual perception. *Frontiers in Psychology*, doi: 10.3389/fpsyg.2016.00572

Tamietto, M., Castelli, L., Vighetti, S., Perozzo, P., Geminiani, G., Weiskrantz, L., & de Gelder, B. (2009). Unseen facial and bodily expressions trigger fast emotional reactions. *Proceedings of the National Academy of Sciences*, 106, 17661–6.

Taylor, A., Elliffe, D., Hunt, G., & Gray, R. (2010). Complex cognition and behavioral innovation in New Caledonian crows. *Proceedings of the Royal Society B: Biological Sciences*, 277, 2637–43.

Templer, V. & Hampton, R. (2012). Rhesus monkeys (*Macaca mulatta*) show robust evidence for memory awareness across multiple generalization tests. *Animal Cognition*, 15, 409–19.

Templer, V., Lee, K., & Preston, A. (2017). Rats know when they remember: Transfer of metacognitive responding across odor-based delayed match-to-sample tests. *Animal Cognition*, 20, 891–906.

Terzaghi, M., Sartori, I., Tassi, L., Rustoni, V., Proserpio, P., Lorusso, G., Manni, R., & Nobili, L. (2012). Dissociated local arousal states underlying essential clinical features of non-rapid eye movement arousal parasomnia: An intracerebral stereo-electroencephalographic study. *Journal of Sleep Research*, 21, 502–6.

Thibault, L., van den Berg, R., Cavanagh, P., & Sergent, C. (2016). Retrospective attention gates discrete conscious access to past sensory stimuli. *PLoS One*, 11, e0148504.

Tomasello, M. (2008). *Origins of Human Communication*. MIT Press.

Tong, F., Meng, M., & Blake, R. (2006). Neural bases of binocular rivalry. *Trends in Cognitive Sciences*, 10, 502–510.

Tong, F., Nakayama, K., Vaughan, J.T., & Kanwisher, N. (1998). Binocular rivalry and visual awareness in human extrastriate cortex. *Neuron*, 21, 753–9.

Tononi, G. (2008). Consciousness as integrated information: A provisional manifesto. *Biological Bulletin*, 215, 216–42.

Tononi, G. & Koch, C. (2008). The neural correlates of consciousness: An update. *Annals of the New York Academy of Sciences*, 1124, 239–61.

Tononi, G. & Koch, C. (2015). Consciousness: Here, there, and everywhere? *Philosophical Transactions of the Royal Society B*, 370, 20140167.

Topál, J., Gergely, G., Miklósi, A., Erdöhegyi, A., & Csibra, G. (2008). Infants' perseverative search errors are induced by pragmatic misinterpretation. *Science*, 321, 1831–4.

Trübutschek, D., Marti, S., Ojeda, A., King, J.-R., Mi, Y., Tsodyks, M., & Dehaene, S. (2018). A theory of working memory without consciousness or sustained activity. *eLife*, 6, e23871.

Tsubomi, H., Fukuda, K., Watanabe, K., & Vogel, E. (2013). Neural limits to representing objects still within view. *Journal of Neuroscience*, 33, 8257–63.

Tsuchiya, N. & Koch, C. (2005). Continuous flash suppression reduces negative afterimages. *Nature Neuroscience*, 8, 1096–101.

Tulving, E. (1985). Memory and consciousness. *Canadian Psychology*, 26, 1–12.

Tunçgenç, B. & Cohen, E. (2016). Interpersonal movement synchrony facilitates prosocial behavior in children's peer-play. *Developmental Science*, 21, e12505.

Tversky, A. & Kahneman, D. (1983). Extensional versus intuitive reasoning: The conjunction fallacy in probability judgment. *Psychological Review*, 90, 293–315.

Tye, M. (1995). *Ten Problems of Consciousness*. MIT Press.

Tye, M. (2000). *Consciousness, Color, and Content*. MIT Press.

Tye, M. (2006). In defense of representationalism: Reply to commentaries. In M. Aydede (ed.), *Pain: New Essays on the Nature and Methodology of its Study*, MIT Press.

Tye, M. (2009). *Consciousness Revisited: Materialism without Phenomenal Concepts*. MIT Press.

Tye, M. (2017). *Tense Bees and Shell-Shocked Crabs: Are Animals Conscious?* Oxford University Press.

Tye, M. & Wright, B. (2011). Is there a phenomenology of thought? In T. Bayne & M. Montague (eds), *Cognitive Phenomenology*. Oxford University Press.

Uller, C. & Lewis, J. (2009). Horses select the greater of two quantities in small numerical contrasts. *Animal Cognition*, 12, 733–8.

van der Meer, M., Kurth-Nelson, Z., & Redish, A. (2012). Information processing in decision-making systems. *The Neuroscientist*, 18, 342–59.

van Gaal, S., Naccache, L., Meuwese, J., van Loon, A., Leighton, A., Cohen, L., & Dehaene, S. (2014). Can the meaning of multiple words be integrated unconsciously? *Philosophical Transactions of the Royal Society B*, 369, 20130212.

van Vugt, B., Dagnino, B., Vartak, D., Safaai, H., Panzeri, S., Dehaene, S., & Roelfsema, R. (2018). The threshold for conscious report: Signal loss and response bias in visual and frontal cortex. *Science*, 360(6388), 537–42.

Vandenbroucke, A., Sligte, I., Barrett, A.B., Seth, A., Fahrenfort, J., & Lamme, V. (2014). Accurate metacognition for visual sensory memory representations. *Psychological Science*, 25, 861–73.

Varner, G. (2012). *Personhood, Ethics, and Animal Cognition*. Oxford University Press.

Veillet, B. (2012). In defense of phenomenal concepts. *Philosophical Papers*, 41, 97–127.

Völter, C. & Call, J. (2014). Younger apes and human children plan their moves in a maze task. *Cognition*, 130, 186–203.

von Bayern, A., Danel, S., Auersperg, A., Mioduszewska, B., & Kacelnik, A. (2018). Compound tool construction by New Caledonian crows. *Nature Scientific Reports*, 8, 15676.

Wallis, T., Bethge, M., & Wichmann, F. (2016). Testing models of peripheral encoding using metamerism in an oddity paradigm. *Journal of Vision*, 16, 4.

Ward, E. & Scholl, B. (2015). Inattentional blindness reflects limitations on perception, not memory: Evidence from repeated failures of awareness. *Psychonomic Bulletin and Review*, 22, 722–7.

Watts, T., Duncan, G., & Quan, H. (2018). Revisiting the marshmallow test: A conceptual replication investigating links between early delay of gratification and later outcomes. *Psychological Science*, 29, 1159–77.

Weisberg, J. (2011). Misrepresenting consciousness. *Philosophical Studies*, 154, 409–33.

Weiskrantz, L. (1986). *Blindsight*. Oxford University Press.

Wellman, H., Cross, D., Bartsch, K., & Harris, P. (1986). Infant search and object permanence: A meta-analysis of the A-not-B error. *Monographs of the Society for Research in Child Development*, 51, 1–67.

Wilke, M., Logothetis, N., & Leopold, D. (2003). Generalized flash suppression of salient visual targets. *Neuron*, 39, 1043–52.

Willard, A. & Norenzayan, A. (2013). Cognitive biases explain religious belief, paranormal belief, and belief in life's purpose. *Cognition*, 129, 379–91.

Wilson, T. & Gilbert, D. (2005). Affective forecasting: knowing what to want. *Current Directions in Psychological Science*, 14, 131–4.

Wilson, T. & Schooler, J. (1991). Thinking too much: Introspection can reduce the quality of preferences and decisions. *Journal of Personality and Social Psychology*, 60, 181–92.

Wilson, T., Schooler, J., Hodges, S., Klaaren, K., & LaFleur, S. (1993). Introspecting about reasons can reduce post-choice satisfaction. *Personality and Social Psychology Bulletin*, 19, 331–9.

Winkielman, P. & Berridge, K. (2004). Unconscious emotion. *Current Directions in Psychological Science*, 13, 120–3.

Winkowski, D. & Knudsen, E. (2007). Top-down control of multimodal sensitivity in the Barn Owl optic tectum. *Journal of Neuroscience*, 27, 13279–91.

Winkowski, D. & Knudsen, E. (2008). Distinct mechanisms for the top-down control of neural gain and sensitivity in the Owl optic tectum. *Neuron*, 60, 698–708.

Wittgenstein, L. (1922). *Tractatus Logico-Philosophicus*. Trans. C. Ogden. Routledge.

Wolpert, D. & Ghahramani, Z. (2000). Computational principles of movement neuroscience. *Nature Neuroscience*, 3, 1212–17.

Wolpert, D. & Kawato, M. (1998). Multiple paired forward and inverse models for motor control. *Neural Networks*, 11, 1317–29.

Wood, W. & Rünger, D. (2015). Psychology of habit. *Annual Review of Psychology*, 67, 289–314.

Wu, C.-C. & Wolfe, J. (2018). A new multiple object awareness paradigm shows that imperfect knowledge of object location is still knowledge. *Current Biology*, 28, 3430–34.

Wu, W. (2014). *Attention*. Routledge.

Xia, Y., Morimoto, Y., & Noguchi, Y. (2016). Retrospective triggering of conscious perception by an interstimulus interaction. *Journal of Vision*, 16, 3.

Zhang, S., Bock, F., Si, A., Tautz, J., & Srinivasan, M. (2005). Visual working memory in decision making by honey bees. *Proceedings of the National Academy of Sciences*, 102, 5250–5.

Zhang, W. & Luck, E. (2009). Sudden death and gradual decay in visual working memory. *Psychological Science*, 20, 423–8.

Index of Names

For the benefit of digital users, indexed terms that span two pages (e.g., 52–53) may, on occasion, appear on only one of those pages.

Index of Subjects

For the benefit of digital users, indexed terms that span two pages (e.g., 52–53) may, on occasion, appear on only one of those pages.